THE COMPLETE
CONTAINER GARDEN

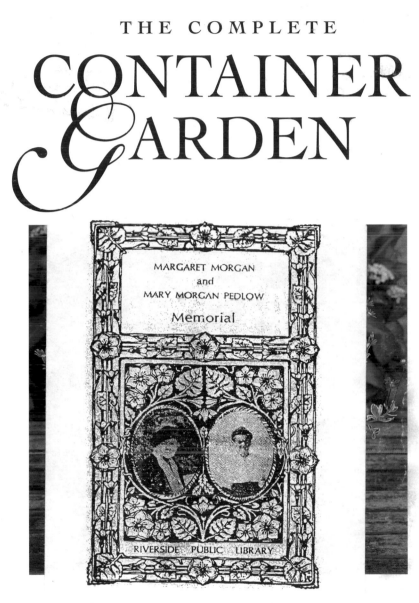

THE COMPLETE
CONTAINER GARDEN

DAVID JOYCE

Reader's Digest

THE READER'S DIGEST ASSOCIATION, INC.
Pleasantville, New York/Montreal

To Anna

A READER'S DIGEST BOOK

Conceived, edited, and designed by Frances Lincoln Limited, London

First printing in paperback 2003
Third US hardback

Copyright © 1996 Frances Lincoln Limited
Text copyright © 1996 David Joyce
Planting plans © 1996 Frances Lincoln Limited

The acknowledgments that appear on page 215 are hereby made a part of this copyright page

Library of Congress Cataloging in Publication Data
Joyce, David
    The Complete Container garden/ David Joyce
        p. cm
    Includes index.
    ISBN 0-89577-848-3 (hardcover)
    ISBN 0-7621-0422-8 (paperback)
    1. Container gardening 1. Title
SB418.J685 1996
635.9'86–dc20   95-49969

Reader's Digest and the Pegasus logo are registered trademarks of The Reader's Digest Association, Inc.

Printed in Hong Kong

13579108642 (hardcover)
13579108642 (paperback)

HALF TITLE PAGE *Blue daisies in a patterned bowl.*

FRONTISPIECE *A collection of pots containing abutilon, agapanthus, petunias, heliotropes, and trailing Scaevola aemula.*

RIGHT *A large pot of hostas provides a focal point in a formal garden.*

JACKET PHOTOGRAPHS: *front jacket:* © Jerry Harpur, *back flap:* © Pots and Pithoi *Back jacket top left:* © Tim Ridley, *top right:* © Andrew Lawson, *bottom left:* © Clive Nichols, *bottom right:* © Anne Hyde

CONTENTS

VERSATILE CONTAINERS

In its long history, reaching back even into antiquity, container gardening has never been as popular as it is today. This is partly because it fits in with so many other aspects of modern life. In city centers and other areas where space is at a premium, for many the garden is a small yard, terrace, balcony, or rooftop, even a simple windowsill. In these settings, plants take on a special value, and often the only way to grow them successfully is in containers. Householders who have more space increasingly enjoy a relaxed lifestyle in which the distinction between indoor and outdoor living is often blurred. Container-grown plants provide an ideal way of softening a hard-surfaced area, bringing the garden right to the very door of the house.

Whether we choose strong or subtle colors, lavish or simple planting plans, container-grown plants provide a versatile way of making the places we live in more beautiful. Container gardening is also rewarding in offering both the proficient gardener and the beginner an enjoyable challenge that leaves ample opportunity for individual creativity.

In a small city garden, planting in containers is often the best way to capture the full richness of the passing seasons. This little garden is full of interesting detail with containers of different materials, shapes, textures, and colors placed at strategic points. Large terracotta pots planted with petunias frame a view to a spectacular raised container brimming with plants. Pots of daturas (Brugmansia) *and regal lilies* (Lilium regale) *add to the interest of the foreground planting.*

STRONG AND BRIGHT COLORS

In the wild, it is mainly tropical plants that have flowers of brilliant and intense color. Thanks to centuries of plant selection and breeding, in temperate regions too we can now choose pelargoniums of vivid pinks or reds, nasturtiums (*Tropaeolum majus*), or African and French marigolds (*Tagetes*) of smoldering and sometimes incandescent oranges, impatiens of polychrome fluorescence, and violets and petunias in vibrant, startling colors. Such exotically colored flowers bring an adventurous glamor to container gardening.

Many of the most colorful flowers are sun-lovers, but there are strong colors, too, for containers in shade. In spring, the gold of daffodils radiates cheerfully from a dark corner. Many camellias have vivid pink or red flowers, while rhododendrons and azaleas cover a broader range of color, from cool blues to burning oranges and reds. For long summer displays, among the most useful of brightly colored, shade-tolerant plants are tuberous begonias, fuchsias, impatiens, lilies, monkey flowers (*Mimulus*), and pansies (*Viola*). Plants that need strong light to thrive but put up with short periods of shade are also available. Capitalize on this by regularly rotating your displays,

ABOVE *The thickly clustered flowers of the fuchsia 'Thalia' are orange-red and their color is intensified by the velvety maroon depths of the foliage. Here, the pairing with a bright Ivy-leaved pelargonium is calmed by the feathery gray leaves of* Senecio viravira.

LEFT *Of all spring bulbs, tulips provide the widest range of bright colors. They are exceptionally strong in glowing, satiny reds, like those used here with tall Lily-flowered white tulips, rusty wallflowers, and blue winter-flowering pansies.*

returning plants such as verbenas and petunias for a rejuvenating spell in full sun after they have served a few days in a shady position.

Dense clusters of clashing bright colors can be jarring. But it is possible to combine clashing colors artfully so that an arrangement makes an impact without overpowering. Modify the effect of clashing colors by using smaller flowers. Introduce a calming influence in the form of a gray-leaved *Helichrysum petiolare* or another foliage plant.

Avoid random mixes of strong colors. Harmonies based on colors close to one another are generally more pleasing. Try orange or brick-red with shades of yellow and lemon, purple-red and bright pink with mauve, purple and violet with blue. Designs based on contrasting colors can also be successful. Associating red with complementary green or pairing yellow and violet will almost always create a pleasant effect.

In the end, whether strong colors appeal is a matter of personal taste, but they will transform a dull setting into a cheerful and eye-catching one. Always use them with discrimination. Vibrant colors that work well in a single pot may seem overwhelming when repeated in several containers. Brilliant colors that sizzle agreeably under a tropical sky can shock where the sunlight is less intense. In soft, moisture-filtered light, the quieter colors, pallid under a blazing sun, reveal their full subtlety.

ABOVE *Many of the summer-flowering Ivy-leaved pelargoniums have flame-red flowers, but the lustrous rich green of their leaves is cooling.* Bidens ferulifolia *produces airy sprays of golden stars.*

RIGHT *The* Arctotis *hybrids are happiest when basking in full sun to give a long succession of daisy flowers, often in hot, strong colors. Other warm colors can be used with them, but cooling green foliage will provide a welcome contrast.*

SOFT AND COOL COLORS

Soft flower colors range through pastel shades of pink, mauve, yellow, and blue to pale tints of blush, cream, and lavender. White and pale blue are the coolest of these colors. Pale flower colors can successfully ally with the many shades of foliage green, which, with their contrasts of texture, provide some of the loveliest and most restful components of the container garden.

These subtle colors show well in diffused and subdued light. They are also the easiest to live with on intimate terms, making them especially valuable in the confined space of a small patio. Soft colors blend readily with many building materials and look pleasing against stonework or weathered brick. Pale colors and white inspire a buoyant mood in large and small gardens and can give a sense of space where buildings, trees, and shrubs seem to crowd in. Their luminosity in the failing light of evening lends a ghostly beauty to a garden or yard that continues long after the sun has set.

The dramatic confrontations that make vibrant colors difficult to combine do not occur with the softer range in the gardener's palette. Random mixtures of soft colors can be very appealing, although more sophisticated designs are best based on harmonious associations of closely related colors or on subtle contrasts. Among the most

successful contrasts are those using pale yellows and soft blues. Pinks, mauves, and pale blues also work well together and complement pots of weathered gray stone.

Another design option is a single-color scheme, a device which can be used as a unifying theme in a garden. The repetition of a single color in a collection of planted containers strikes a formal note. White, especially, gives a clean and precise finish, and there are innumerable white flowers to fill containers. Window boxes and pots of white spring bulbs – snowdrops, crocuses, daffodils, and tulips – can be replaced in summer with lavish plantings of white Paris daisies (*Argyranthemum*), petunias, flowering tobacco plants (*Nicotiana*), and verbenas, as well as foliage plants with cool variegation.

ABOVE *Pastel shades of pink, blue, and yellow mingle easily, but another component is needed to give drama. In this country garden, a dramatic effect has been created by planting the creamy yellow Anthemis tinctoria 'E. C. Buxton' in a dark ceramic pot placed at the intersection of two paths.*

Alternatively, consider a sequence of color schemes, starting with a mixed theme in spring, moving on to white and then perhaps to yellow for late summer and fall. Or add light touches of another color to a predominantly monochrome scheme. For example, hints of cream, blue, or blushing pink will relieve the starkness of a white scheme without detracting from the overall impression of white, and silver foliage will set off a predominantly pink scheme.

THEATRICAL EXTRAVAGANCE

Any planting that makes a strong and immediate visual impact will heighten the drama of a garden. Use such a planting to provide an eye-catching individual feature within a large garden, or to turn a city plot or a small courtyard into an extravagant outdoor room set. Placing a theatrical planting in a container allows it to be positioned exactly where it will attract the most attention.

Often, the most dramatic effect is created by a single plant of shapely form, such as a Japanese aralia (*Fatsia japonica*), or one that is exotic in character, like the slightly tender daturas (*Brugmansia*), positioned to make a strong and immediate impression. Alternatively, groups of pots, tubs, and planters can be brought together in a collection in which the role of individual pots is subordinated to the overall plan. Yet another way to create theatrical extravagance is by mixing plants in a layered arrangement in a single container so that they combine the lax charm of a sumptuous border with the artful flourish of a lavish flower arrangement. Although mixed plantings on a grand scale offer the stiffest challenges – and the most satisfying rewards – of container gardening, they are within the competence of even novice gardeners. The most important ingredient is a dash of creative flair.

Any large or medium-sized container can be used for an extravagant planting, provided that it is stable and holds sufficient potting mix to anchor and sustain the plants. Avoid light or narrow-based containers, which, when densely planted, are vulnerable in high winds. Wooden half-barrels, Versailles tubs, large terracotta pots, and stone jars or urns all lend themselves to extravagant planting.

To maximize the dramatic effect of a lavishly planted container, position it carefully. In a formal layout, choose a prime location such as the endpoint of a major vista. In a courtyard, make it the focus of an informal cluster of pots. Use a plinth or improvised base to raise a handsomely planted container to the commanding position it deserves.

LEFT *The converging bars of a metal arbor focus attention on a magnificent display of plants imaginatively assembled in a huge terracotta pot. Off-center but dominating is* Melianthus major, *with jagged gray-green leaves. Beneath it are New Zealand flaxes* (Phormium), Paris daisies (Argyranthemum), *and pelargoniums, all woven together by the trailing stems of a gray-leaved helichrysum.*

RIGHT *Layered arrangements feature prominently in this garden, where formal elements contrast with loose planting. In the center background, a topiary sweet bay with a twisted stem is underplanted with gold-laced polyanthus and black violets. In the foreground, mophead boxwoods are ringed by dwarf butterfly flowers* (Schizanthus), *matching a nearby candy-pink ranunculus.*

EFFECTIVE SIMPLICITY

There are often practical reasons for restricting the range of plants grown in a container. Cultivation is simplified, and it is easier to maintain displays that change with the seasons. However, the prime reason for growing plants or groups of the same kind of plants in individual containers is aesthetic. Seen in isolation, the character of a plant's flowers, the architecture of its branches, and the subtlety or boldness of its foliage are fully appreciated.

Many plants of distinctive character need to be displayed alone to be seen to best advantage. This is true for certain shrubs as well as for good foliage perennials – including grasses, hostas, and ferns – and some bulbs. The beautifully irregular Japanese maples (*Acer palmatum*) make magnificent solitary container shrubs for sheltered gardens. The swordlike leaves of the evergreen New Zealand flaxes (*Phormium*) make bold clumps for sunny positions and are equally effective when used as focal points or as components of a container grouping.

Plants, such as boxwood (*Buxus sempervirens*), that are trimmed into topiary shapes, usually look best without the clutter of additional plants. Boxwood can be pruned into fanciful shapes, but for a smart, tailored look just trim it into simple cones, pyramids, and balls. Specimens of topiary can be distributed at regular intervals along a path or clustered into groups, but the plants themselves need to be grown in individual pots.

The dwarf bulbs of late winter or early spring have a season that is quite brief but so special that they are worth growing on their own in shallow pots. The refined detail of snowdrops (*Galanthus*) and of the various cultivars of *Crocus chrysanthus*, as well as the exquisite beauty of fall-flowering *Cyclamen hederifolium,* stand up well in isolation.

Lilies are some of the loveliest of all summer flowers, and they always look best grown alone. To maximize their visual impact, grow them in a nursery area and move them into position in the garden only as they come into flower.

ABOVE *In the eighteenth and nineteenth centuries, when auriculas and other old-fashioned flowers were shown competitively, they were displayed growing individually in plain pots, which allowed a plant to speak for itself. Repetition enhances the charm of these small-flowered violets in hand-thrown terracotta pots.*

LEFT *The pale pink buds of the lily 'Mont Blanc' open to radiant white blooms lightly speckled with maroon. This display, standing in isolation, makes a bold, sumptuous effect in the magnificent old copper vat with a rich, sea-green patina.*

RIGHT *Few perennials can match the magnificence of large hostas such as* H. sieboldiana *var.* elegans. *The restrained dignity of a bold clump planted in a handsome container makes an effective contrast to a border mixture.*

EYE-CATCHING CONTAINERS

Many containers fulfill their practical role satisfactorily while remaining inconspicuous. A successful hanging basket will obscure the frame in a miraculously suspended cloud of flowers and foliage. Plastic pots often remain virtually unnoticed when placed among a cluster of other containers, hidden by leaves, flowers, and more glamorous pots.

In contrast are ornamental containers. Pots and troughs made of traditional materials such as terracotta, plain wood, and stone are perennial favorites, because of their color and texture. While being quietly decorative, they make an appealing setting for plants. Terracotta containers are often ribbed, fluted, criss-crossed with a basketweave pattern, or decorated with bas reliefs in the form of swags, masks, or figures. Surface decoration such as this can relieve the severity of a formal planting.

Oversized containers and urns and jars of distinctive shapes and proportions are often best left unplanted, playing a sculptural role in the garden. But if you are filling them with plants, choose those that show off the shape of the container. A cascading clematis creates a flattering

BELOW LEFT *Fanciful coloring and shape give a container an eccentric charm. Although nestling deeply among plants, this pot signals for attention with the muted glow of its mosaic pattern. It is planted with* Lavandula stoechas *subsp.* pedunculata, *which has curious earlike bracts.*

BELOW RIGHT *A high-shouldered, dark ceramic pot retains its somber dignity beneath the jagged leaves and airy flower sprays of* Heuchera micrantha *var.* diversifolia *'Palace Purple'.*

off-the-shoulder effect in a tall vase, while a mixture of bushy and spreading plants such as diascias, pelargoniums, and fuchsias gives a satisfying fullness to a wide urn. Place shapely containers carefully so that their form is seen to best advantage, or isolate a large pot or urn, giving it additional height and importance by setting it on a plinth or an upturned pot.

Strongly colored containers can be used deliberately to give a planting layout more depth or dash. Capitalize on the green patina of an old copper pot by planting it with amber and gold tulips and wallflowers (*Erysimum*). Containers can be painted to match a specific color scheme. This is often done with wooden window boxes, so they echo the colors of the exterior paintwork. Large tubs painted white and black make impressive bases for formally shaped trees such as the Portugal laurel (*Prunus lusitanica*). Abstract or representational decoration is usually most successful when the shape of the pot is stronger than the color or the decoration – for example, in large jars ornamented with oriental motifs. Boldly colored and decorated containers can be used as structural components in the garden. Place a single, vividly colored pot, perhaps filled with a plain foliage plant such as the bamboo *Fargesia murieliae*, at a focal point.

BELOW LEFT *The basketweave pattern and minimal planting of dwarf boxwood (Buxus sempervirens 'Suffruticosa') relieves the severe form of this impressive weathered stone container on its matching plinth and pavings.*

BELOW RIGHT *A lively pattern of arches makes a buoyant motif around the wide basin of a terracotta vase planted with the ground elder Aegopodium podagraria 'Variegatum' and framed by a hop (Humulus lupulus 'Aureus').*

CONTAINERS IN FORMAL GARDENS

Formal gardens are generally based on a symmetrical geometric ground plan, often with a generous use of hard surfaces. Planted containers may be positioned to emphasize the geometry and at the same time to relieve the severity of the layout. In small formal gardens they are especially useful, since they overcome the difficulty of planting where there is no soil. Position containers wherever they are most effective, keeping in mind the amount of light available. Placed at focal points they draw the eye, paired they form a frame, repeated at regular intervals they establish a rhythm.

Using matched containers is a simple device that works in gardens of any period. Flanking a garden feature with matching containers gives it importance in the overall design. Position matched containers as sentries at gateways and doorways, adding to their significance, or give visual weight to a simple garden bench by placing planted pots on either side of it.

Matched containers can also be used to frame a view, provided they and their plants are large enough to draw the eye. Place a pair of urns outside a window to create a channeled vista along a chosen axis. The scale must be in keeping with the feature that terminates the view. Use matched containers to mark a change of level, setting them on either side at the bottom and top of a flight of steps. In a garden that is almost entirely flat, they will add drama to even a single step.

LEFT *You can focus attention on a garden feature by positioning matched planted containers on either side of it. Here, a pair of pots planted with tall* Lilium regale *is reinforced with* Hosta sieboldiana *var.* elegans. *While the hostas are out of scale with the arbor they flank, the piles of overlapping blue-green leaves make a strong formal statement.*

RIGHT *These planted containers are arranged with fastidious symmetry. The components are centered on a wall fountain that is almost concealed by the vigorous growth of a large golden hop.*

RIGHT *This formal walkway shows how, even on a small scale, a rhythm can be created by repeating plantings in pairs at regular intervals. Running alongside a brick path are miniature beds planted with evergreen boxwood. Placed between them and echoing their rhythm are terracotta pots filled with white petunias. The petunia flowers and the loose shapes of the boxwood—more often seen tightly clipped—introduce an unruly element, but the restricted color scheme underscores the formality.*

19

LEFT *Large terracotta pots are ideal for the classic formula of matched containers flanking a doorway. In a sunny courtyard Paris daisies (*Argyranthemum*) will flower nonstop from early summer into fall.*

BELOW *The geometric shapes of boxwood topiary, with domes and balls arranged symmetrically around a standard mophead, create a miniature formal garden in a small trough. The mild disorder introduced by the snowdrops is not enough to disturb the equilibrium.*

A formal garden's geometric plan generally dictates where decorative elements should be placed. To complete their role, vistas and paths require an end site that is visually satisfying. A single planted container of suitable scale makes an ideal eye-catcher. An old lead cistern or a modern replica set against a wall might work well in a small garden. Where a more dramatic effect is desired, place a large urn on a plinth (which can be as simple as a stack of unmortared bricks). This platform will help to show off the shape of the urn and the planting, making a strong focal point. Such a planted urn needs the uniform background of a hedge or wall to block out the distracting detail of the landscape beyond.

Single containers, especially when mounted on a base, make impressive centerpieces for the round, square, or rectangular beds that are the main components of formal gardens, and for the intersection of paths. The repetition of matching containers reinforces the geometry of a formal garden. For a really formal, tailored effect, plant them with topiary boxwood, clipped into neat cones or pyramids.

A single line of evenly spaced containers can make an emphatic statement. An ideal position for a matched collection of beautiful urns or latticework terracotta pots is a low wall or balustrade that creates an internal division. To make a stately procession along one side of a walkway, set large pots with restrained planting at regular intervals.

Even spacing is the key to other groupings of containers in formal gardens. Instead of placing an urn or a large pot as a centerpiece in an open space where paths meet, arrange matching containers at points of the compass

around the periphery of the area. Embellish a formal or-namental pool with containers at its four corners. As move-able ornaments, containers also offer the best solution for relieving the blank rectangle of a swimming pool.

A variety of containers can be used successfully in for-mal gardens. Traditional shapes and materials are most appropriate when trying to reflect a particular historical style. The clean-cut wooden planters known as Versailles tubs suggest classical French formality. In an Italianate garden, it is better to use large terracotta pots of simple form. Where an opulent effect is required, stemmed urns with broad basins allow lavish planting.

To complete the pleasing proportions of a formal gar-den, choose containers of an appropriate size and also keep the planting in scale. Plants of regular shape are often the

ABOVE *Large containers, planted on a grand scale, are needed to match grand architecture. The plantings in these evenly spaced terracotta pots have a grass palm making a jagged crown, exotic purple-leaved and red-flowered cannas, and a full skirt of Pelargonium 'Paul Crampel' and flowering tobacco (Nicotiana).*

first choice for containers in formal gardens. The most regimented of all are topiary specimens clipped geometri-cally, the simple evergreen forms giving the garden a parade-ground precision year-round. For more colorful flowering uprights in summer, use standards of familiar plants such as fuchsias, and less common plants such as the yellow-flowered *Lantana camara*, which lend themselves to layered arrangements. On a smaller scale, spring bulbs, especially hyacinths and tulips, have a decidedly military air.

INFORMAL EFFECTS

In informal gardens, straight lines are replaced by curves, and symmetry gives way to a more fluid, but still balanced, distribution of space. Not all informally arranged spaces are large, rambling gardens with meandering paths. Decked and paved areas also often have asymmetrical and informal layouts, when containers can be moved around to suit changing needs.

To create an informal effect, the plants are more important than the pots and tubs containing them. Draw on all the variations available among the wealth of good container plants to make lively and informal planting combinations. Contrast plants that differ in scale and character, for example, tall bamboos such as *Fargesia nitida* with the much laxer low-growing grass *Hakonechloa macra* 'Aureola'.

Put upright plants together with those of bushy or spreading growth: lilies, say, with petunias and verbenas. Mix good foliage plants, such as the glossy-leaved and evergreen *Choisya ternata*, with tireless flowerers such as Paris daisies (*Argyranthemum*).

Introduce variety in the shape and size of containers. A large container surrounded by a flock of small ones creates a pleasing hen-and-chickens effect. Differences in height can be emphasized by the way containers are staged. Use plant stands with an overspill of pots clustered around their base. A similar effect can be created with containers arranged on a flight of steps, but position them carefully to avoid a hazardous walkway. Where several hanging baskets are suspended from a pergola or porch, vary their

LEFT *Interlocking shapes and blending colors give this informal cluster of containers coherence. The mauve Swan River daisy* (Brachyscome iberidifolia), *the blue salvia, and the shades of pink in diascias and verbenas make a pleasing harmony.*

ABOVE RIGHT *Tulips, so often regimented for spring displays, can also help to create a relaxed and casual mood in the garden, especially when they come in this soft shade of apricot. Here, late tulips and a hosta are tucked in at the base of an arching bamboo.*

RIGHT *The best informal arrangements look as though they have happened quite by chance. This calm assembly of simple pots is based on an uncomplicated color theme of white, in cosmos, gray, in the elegantly cut leaves of* Senecio viravira, *and violet, in lobelia.*

height to prevent monotony. At ground level, grouping containers of different color and texture can add to the charm of a cluster of containers. Set a glazed ceramic jar among plain terracotta pots, or mix wickerwork baskets with wooden tubs.

While it is appealing to have potted plants distributed throughout a large garden, in a yard, patio, or decked area, where space is relatively restricted, containers cannot be distributed with such abandon. Room must be left for people to move about and for garden furniture. Stray containers are likely to get in the way. For practical reasons, it is a good idea to place pots together; aesthetically, there is much to be said for an almost random collection of pots and tubs. Use such a grouping to form a narrow border of fluctuating depth along one side of a courtyard, or to create an eddy in a corner of a terrace.

CONTAINERS TO DRESS BUILDINGS

The embellishment of unusual architectural details with container-grown plants offers many exciting possibilities. Well-planted containers can also relieve the dullness of blank walls and mask commonplace or unsightly domestic buildings such as sheds.

Place container-grown plants at ground level, by windows, and on balconies, or hung from fixtures on walls or from porticoes, or suspended above doorways. Simple forms of dressing might use only one kind of container – a window box or a set of window boxes, for example. More ambitious schemes might coordinate plantings in a range of containers – including troughs, pots, window boxes, and hanging baskets – at every level of a façade.

At ground level, a simple but effective way of enhancing the front of a building is to position containers in pairs with matched plantings on either side of a door or window. The geometric shapes of topiary specimens can reflect and emphasize a symmetrical façade. Softer planting, using trained standards, shrubs such as the mophead hydrangeas, and tubs of spring bulbs or summer annuals, will spruce up a rambling or characterless building.

Soften the rigid lines of a building surrounded by hard surfaces with a narrow border of container-grown plants. At its simplest, the border might be a row of potted pelargoniums along a street front, but it can be made more elaborate using containers of varying sizes arranged two or three deep and stacked at different levels.

The classic way of dressing buildings is with window boxes and balconies filled with containers. The most suitable plants are those that are wind tolerant, such as short-stemmed daffodils, dwarf tulips, and compact cultivars of popular bedding plants. A window box filled with exquisite beauties such as dwarf bulbs will give intense pleasure when viewed from inside. Balconies, which provide the setting for intimate gardens seen at their best from inside, really come into their own as impressive hanging gardens using classic trailing plants such as the gray-leaved foliage plant *Helichrysum petiolare* and nasturtiums (*Tropaeolum majus*). Grow the plants in troughs or in pots attached to the surround of a balcony.

ABOVE *In this hanging basket, a welcoming touch at a doorway, soft yellow trailing begonias and* Cuphea ignea *spill over speckled leaves of* Tolmiea menziesii *'Taff's Gold' and pale lobelia.*

LEFT *Mophead topiary, and white to cream flowers – roses, lilies, pansies, and hippeastrums – are grouped around shuttered windows to make a pleasing display from inside and out.*

ABOVE *In some settings the simpler the touch the better. Here, a tiny shutter is fastened back to leave a perfect rustic frame for a single potted pelargonium.*

SUCCESSFUL GARDENING IN CONTAINERS

Foliage and flowering plants, from ground-hugging miniatures to large shrubs and even trees, can be grown easily in the vast range of containers available. Even novice gardeners will be rewarded with success if they follow the few simple guidelines that ensure the right conditions for vigorous and healthy plant growth, especially in terms of good drainage, and adequate supplies of water and food.

The following chapter brings together all the practical information essential to satisfy the demands of plants grown in confined containers. It includes advice on the containers themselves, with suggestions for improvisations as well as decorative finishes. It gives illustrated guides to all the main techniques for planting a wide range of containers with different types of plants. Gardeners will also find guidance on general maintenance, including pruning and training, and how best to deal with problems caused by pests and diseases. For those who take pleasure in raising their own plants and increasing stocks, it explains the main methods of propagation. In short, this chapter provides all the background information needed to make a successful container garden.

This garden path is lined with a wonderful collection of terracotta containers, some planted, some waiting to be filled. Apart from skill in marrying plant shapes with the right pot or planter, what distinguishes container gardening is the critical role of the gardener in satisfying the needs of plants at every stage of the growing season.

CONTAINER CHOICE

Garden containers are manufactured from various materials – at one extreme of the price range are cheap plastic ones and at the other end are marble and bronze – and all are available in a wide range of shapes and sizes. The essential requirements of containers are simple: they must hold enough potting mix for plants to root securely and to supply sufficient moisture and nutrients to sustain growth; they must have drainage holes to allow excess moisture to escape so that the mix does not become stagnant; and they must be reasonably stable. Cost, appearance, and a few additional practical considerations will therefore influence your choice.

All planted containers must be watered by hand or linked to an irrigation system. Plastic and fiber glass are light and impermeable materials and planters made of them require less frequent watering than those made of porous terracotta. However, sheet plastic liners help conserve moisture in terracotta planters.

Heavy containers are more stable than those made from lightweight materials such as plastic and fiber-glass. In many cases their extra weight is an advantage, unless the planter needs to be moved about. Choose lightweight containers for rooftops and balconies, where the load-bearing capacity is limited.

Durability matters when containers are expensive. Frost can damage earthenware containers, cracking and lifting glazes and shattering terracotta that has been fired at low temperatures. In frost-prone areas, such pots should always be brought under cover in winter. Any corrosion on metal containers can to some extent be halted by chemical treatment, and wooden containers can be treated with preservatives. Synthetic materials, especially plastics, are easily scrubbed and cleaned to reduce the risk of diseases and pests being carried from one season to the next.

TERRACOTTA AND GLAZED CONTAINERS

The use of terracotta (literally "baked earth") to make pots stretches back into antiquity. The material is porous so plants need frequent watering, the surface is difficult to clean, and containers, which shatter easily, are only frost-proof if fired at high temperatures. However, the material is visually so appropriate to plants that its shortcomings are easily overlooked. Variations in color result from different clays or firing temperatures. Pots of glazed earthenware, which are nonporous and easier to clean, rarely tolerate frosts, so their planting and siting require especially careful consideration.

WOOD

Versatile wood is an ideal choice when containers have to be made to measure, and is durable if treated with a preservative. It can be used for formal containers such as classic window boxes and Versailles tubs as well as for rustic troughs and rugged half-barrels (right).

TERRACOTTA WALL CONTAINERS

Small wall-mounted terracotta containers (below) are suitable for displaying a range of trailing plants. They need to be securely fixed to a support.

STONE AND SUBSTITUTES

Containers made from composition stone and concrete (right) are both more moderately priced and readily available than marble and sandstone ones. They quickly assume a weathered appearance that suggests the patina of natural stone. All these materials are heavy and durable.

PLASTIC AND WIRE-FRAMED CONTAINERS

Various wire and plastic frames (above) that hold pots can be attached to walls, railings, and downspouts. Traditional hanging baskets have a galvanized or plastic-coated wire frame, and are used with a liner — as are many wall-mounted metal containers.

PLASTIC

Plastic (left) is now the most widely used material for containers, although there is a strong aesthetic prejudice against it when displaying plants. As well as being cheap, plastic is lightweight and easily cleaned, and the heavy-duty kinds are strong and long-lasting. Rigid plastic containers come in many shapes and sizes; sheet plastic can be used as a liner for other containers.

FIBER GLASS

This light, man-made material can be molded into a wide variety of shapes (below). It is often used to imitate traditional but expensive materials such as lead and bronze and is very effective when formed in plain, clean-lined shapes. Although somewhat brittle, it is quite durable.

LEAD

Containers of beaten or cast metal — lead, copper, bronze, and iron — were extensively used in the past and now help to give a period flavor to a garden. Old lead cisterns and urns have proved remarkably durable but they are expensive and hard to find. Modern pieces (above) usually have a traditional design. Even when new, the subdued silver-gray of the metal tones subtly with foliage and flowers.

MAKING A WOODEN WINDOW BOX

Wood is the most versatile material for made-to-measure containers, and a simple window box or trough can be assembled even by a gardener who has only basic skills in handling tools. The simple method of construction demonstrated here could easily be adapted to window boxes of different dimensions, although it is unlikely that it would be necessary to alter height and width. The front and back each consist of two lengths, since narrow widths are easier to obtain than broader ones. The base also consists of two lengths, with a narrow gap in between to allow for drainage. If you make a window box longer or shorter than the one illustrated, remember that the base is the same length as the front and back, minus the thickness of the end pieces.

The softwood lumber used here provides a practical alternative to expensive seasoned hardwood, such as oak. It is easy to work and its life can be extended if it is treated with a preservative. Have it cut to these dimensions by the lumber yard :

Front and back: four lengths of $20 \times 3\frac{3}{4} \times \frac{5}{8}$ inches
  $(50 \times 9.5 \times 1.5\text{cm})$
Ends: 2 lengths of $7 \times 7\frac{1}{2} \times 1$ inches $(17 \times 19 \times 2.5\text{cm})$
Base: 1 length of $18 \times 3\frac{3}{4} \times \frac{5}{8}$ inches $(45 \times 9.5 \times 1.5\text{cm})$
  and 1 length of $18 \times 3 \times \frac{5}{8}$ inches $(45 \times 8 \times 1.5\text{cm})$
Feet: 3 lengths of $8\frac{3}{8} \times 2 \times 1$ inches $(21 \times 5 \times 2.5\text{cm})$

ASSEMBLING AND DECORATING A WOODEN WINDOW BOX

1 *On a suitable work surface, assemble the precut lengths of lumber, together with a hammer and three dozen 1½in (4cm) oval nails.*

2 *Without nailing the lumber together, place the base pieces over the feet, allowing a ¼in (5mm) gap between the two lengths for drainage, and mark their positions. Check the fit of the end pieces.*

3 *Set front, back, and end pieces aside, then nail the base to the feet, driving in two nails at converging angles where each base piece lies over a foot.*

4 *Put together the main framework, hammering two nails at converging angles through both ends of the front and back to join them to the end pieces.*

5 *When the main framework has been assembled, turn the box upside down and tap the base, which you have already put together, in place (step 3).*

6 *Place the container on its back and at three points nail through the front into the base. Then repeat the same operation for the back of the window box.*

7 *After priming or treating the container with a wood preservative that is nontoxic to plants, apply an exterior latex undercoat. Allow to dry according to manufacturer's instructions.*

8 *Apply an exterior emulsion paint that matches with any adjacent architectural features of the house. A stencil or freehand-painted decoration could be added if desired.*

9 *The finished wooden container is suitable either as a window box or as a trough at ground level. Here, it is planted with a combination of French marigolds, zinnias, and rudbeckias to create a warm, bright focus on a patio.*

DECORATING POTS

One way to give the container garden an individual stamp is to apply your own decoration to pots, window boxes, and tubs. The simplest way of personalizing containers is to paint them, and a painted finish is suitable for a wide range of materials, including wood, terracotta, concrete, plastic, and metal. Paint is often applied to make the container fit into an overall architectural color scheme, but the use of color and decoration can be much more ambitious than this. A light color wash can be introduced to make a container fit in with a subtle color scheme. More assertive decoration can be painted on either as a single color, or in a mixture of colors, as stripes or borders for example. It is easier to paint stripes if the parts of the pot to be left unpainted are protected with masking tape, as in the three-color terracotta container shown on these pages. Paint can easily be reapplied to rectify mistakes.

Using stencils – whether commercially produced or homemade and cut out of sturdy stencil card – is another way to apply a bold and simple design motif with one or several different colors. A wide range of other effects can be achieved with spongeware techniques, stippling, gilding, or freehand decoration. The various methods of decoration can be applied on their own or they may be used in combination with one another to produce a more intricate result.

Paint finishes can also be used to imitate the effects of different metals, in particular the wonderful patina that weathering produces on old copper or bronze containers, such as the copper vat shown on page 109. The rich complexity of the patina is suggested by applying several layers of paint of different colors and distressing them while the paint is still wet (*see pages 36-37*).

*A simple planting is often the most successful choice for a boldly patterned or colored pot. This compact, purple-flowered lavender (*Lavandula angustifolia *'Hidcote') fits well with the striped decoration of its container.*

STRIPED DECORATION FOR A TERRACOTTA POT

1   *Clean and dry the pot, then apply an even coat of blue latex paint on the outside and continue over the top 1–2in (2.5–5cm) of the inside of the container.*

2   *When the paint is dry, fix masking tape around the rim, then radiate strips of tape from the base, starting with strips about ¼in (5mm) apart at the bottom of the pot.*

3   *Apply a coat of reddish-brown mat latex paint on the exposed surface of the pot. Leave the masking tape in place until the paint is completely dry.*

4   *If you want to add narrow bands beside the blue stripes, place further strips of masking tape parallel and just to the right of the strips of tape already in position.*

5   *Apply a coat of cream mat latex paint over the narrow bands of reddish-brown paint that are exposed between the strips of masking tape. Remove the tape gently when the paint is dry.*

6   *The simple pattern on this striped pot is only one of many decorative effects that can be achieved with a variety of techniques using either mat or glossy paints.*

BRONZE FINISH FOR A TERRACOTTA POT

1 *Clean and dry the pot before applying dark green mat exterior latex paint on the outside. On the inside, paint to just below the expected potting mix level.*

2 *When the first coat is dry, use a short-haired, dense stippling brush, lightly loaded with paint, to apply blue-green mat exterior latex paint. Define the relief decoration first.*

3 *Continue dabbing on the blue-green paint with the stippling brush, leaving some areas with little or no paint applied, so that the shadows are accentuated. Allow to dry.*

4 *Apply a thin coat of white mat exterior latex paint. Work quickly and preferably paint a section at a time, so that the next step can be carried out while the paint is wet.*

5 *Using a damp, clean rag, wipe off excess white paint, leaving only enough to subdue the blue-green coloring and to soften the underlying dark green.*

6 *When assessing the painted pot, keep in mind that you are aiming for an impressionistic effect, and remember that you can always reapply paint if you find the results disappointing.*

It is easier to imitate the rich patina of old copper or bronze on a molded surface, such as that of this handsome terracotta planter, than on one that is smooth. Layers of paint are applied in a way that accentuates highlights and shadows. The stems of a lacecap hydrangea have been individually staked to keep them erect and to ensure a balanced display of the flower heads.

37

UNUSUAL AND RECYCLED CONTAINERS

Decorating garden pots, planters, and window boxes in a personal style is one way to give the container garden an individual character. Another is to plant in containers that are themselves highly distinctive or original. This generally means looking outside the vast range of garden containers, although even here items of unusual shape and coloring can be found. Old ceramic bowls and jars, metal colanders, pots, and buckets, and baskets of various shapes and sizes are among the many domestic items that can be recycled at negligible expense. Some antique pieces make impressive containers but these items inevitably fetch high prices and are vulnerable to theft in a garden that is not secure. Examples include wellheads, fonts, sarcophagi, tubs, and sinks in marble or lesser stone, as well as copper vats and lead water cisterns. Chimney pots are more modest architectural features that make useful focal points in small gardens.

The essential requirement of all containers is that they hold enough potting mix to sustain plants and also have sufficient drainage holes so that the mix never becomes waterlogged. Even when containers already have holes, these often need enlarging so that excess moisture can drain away quickly without the potting mix becoming soggy. Some materials, including glazed ceramic, are difficult to drill. When drilling might risk damaging a piece, use the vessel simply as a holder; plant up a close-fitting, lightweight pot of a suitable depth and place it inside the more decorative container.

Containers with an open structure, including baskets, are best lined with sheet plastic before planting. Slit holes in the base to provide drainage. Lining will also help to extend the life of some materials, but it is a good idea to treat basketweave with a preservative or to varnish it with a coat of clear polyurethane as an extra precaution.

The imaginative gardener can give many old household items — including discarded cooking pots, galvanized pails, milk crates, and wicker vegetable baskets — a new lease on life by recycling them as plant containers. Salvaged architectural fragments such as chimney pots can also make distinctive planters. Most recycled containers will need to have drainage holes drilled in the base.

RIGHT *A wooden wheelbarrow is ideal for displaying a movable display of summer flowers.*

BELOW LEFT *Trailing plants, such as the* Helichrysum petiolare *'Limelight' used here, are ideal for a tall chimney pot. Line chimney pots with sheet plastic, or drop a close-fitting lightweight container into the top.*

BELOW RIGHT *The texture of basketweave, often imitated in terracotta pots, makes a good contrast to foliage and flowers. Petunias and ivies spill out of this basket.*

LEFT *Zonal pelargoniums play the leading role in an attractive mixture of foliage and flowers planted in an old metal container. Its mat slate-blue band, toning with the silver-gray of an old tree stump, makes an inconspicuous but pleasing base for the plants.*

RIGHT *An old copper vat plays a key position in the garden, adding distinction by virtue of its size and shape, its regular riveting, and the richness of its patina.*

BELOW *Old stone sinks are frequently used as containers for small collections of alpine-garden plants. Their beauty is more easily appreciated when sinks are raised well above ground level. This old sink, set high against a wall, contains a less conventional planting of bright gazanias.*

ABOVE *A lead water cistern bearing an eighteenth-century date makes a splendid container for a planting of pelargoniums, argyranthemums, and a mixture of foliage plants. Authentic examples of these cisterns — as well as nineteenth- and twentieth-century imitations, which often carry bogus dates — are among the most handsome of large containers. They need to be set in position before being filled with potting mix and planted.*

LEFT *Double daisies* (Bellis perennis) *and blue* Scilla siberica *jostle together in a wire basket designed to hold fruit.*

MOVING CONTAINERS

Large containers filled with potting mix and plants are heavy and unwieldy, so window boxes and planters should be planted in their final positions. If they do need to be moved after planting, allow water to drain from them first.

When containers, potting mix, and plants have to be transported around the garden, mechanical aids will greatly reduce the effort involved. A wheelbarrow is useful for transporting all but very heavy objects, which have to be lifted over the sides. A hand truck is more appropriate for such items, and is a piece of equipment that can be rented. A simple trolley mounted on castors is extremely useful for moving planted containers on a flat surface. Some models are intended to provide a permanent base for pots. Rollers, consisting of lengths of pipe or pole about 1½–2 in (4–5cm) in diameter, with planks laid on top, provide another way of moving large pots.

A simpler method of moving a heavy item is to drag it, for example on a sheet of heavy-duty plastic sheeting. To negotiate steps, make a short ramp with planks. Move pots with a circular base by rolling, rather than lifting. Enlist the help of a strong person when lifting heavy items; keep your back straight and bend your legs to take the strain.

MOVING PLANTS AND POTS BY WHEELBARROW

LEFT *A wheelbarrow is very useful in a medium-sized or large garden for moving empty containers, bags of potting mix, and large numbers of plants. The disadvantage when moving heavy objects is that they need to be lifted over the sides.*

ROLLING A CONTAINER

A PURPOSE-MADE TROLLEY

FAR LEFT *Rolling is the easiest way to move a large pot with a circular base.*

LEFT *A trolley mounted on castors is convenient for moving containers on flat surfaces.*

SECURING CONTAINERS

Containers that are not stable and securely positioned risk being blown or knocked over. Particular care must be taken with hanging baskets, window boxes, and containers on roof gardens and balconies.

A freshly watered hanging basket is a heavy item that needs a stout support, strong chains, or rope to suspend it and a securely fitted attachment, preferably incorporating a swivel. Wall brackets should have an arm that is long enough for the basket to hang well clear of the wall. A pulley system allows you to lower hanging baskets, making the task of watering them much easier.

The weight of full window boxes makes them quite stable, but safety provisions must be made for those above groundfloor level. A tailor-made safety rail can be inconspicuous. If window boxes need to be set below the window, support them on metal brackets with the ends turned up at right angles. This kind of support, firmly fixed to the wall, can be combined with safety chains.

Load-bearing limitations on roof gardens and balconies often dictate the use of light containers and mixes. Choose broad-based pots and group them together near walls or screens for maximum shelter.

WINDOW BOX SAFETY

RAISING POTS ON SUPPORTS

SUPPORTING A HANGING BASKET

ABOVE LEFT *Safety must be a priority with a window box such as this one, unusually positioned above a door. Brackets hold it firmly in position.*

ABOVE RIGHT *All containers that do not have built-in feet or ridged bottoms should be set on low supports, either purchased or improvised from bricks, stones, or wood, so that water can drain away freely.*

LEFT *A sturdy bracket is needed to take the weight of a freshly watered hanging basket. The bracket used to support this basket is a substantial ornamental feature in its own right. The arm is long enough to hold the hanging basket well clear of the wall.*

PLANTING EQUIPMENT

Very little equipment is needed for container gardening. It is worth buying tools of good quality, selecting well-made containers and using a planting medium formulated for containers and for the range of plants you want to grow.

GARDEN TOOLS

Although it may be handy to have a range of tools, only a few are essential. The two most useful items are a trowel and a hand fork. Pruners are needed for shearing woody plants; both those with a scissor-like action and anvil models are suitable. The blades must be kept sharp. Hedge shears are only necessary if you have to clip topiary. Kitchen scissors are ideal for clipping the stems of most annuals and perennials.

Many gardeners feel lost without a folding knife, either straight-bladed or with a curved blade for shearing, but a small kitchen knife is a useful substitute. The gardener also needs a watering can and a simple trigger-pump sprayer. Additional useful items include labels, a selection of bamboo and split stakes, garden twine, and ties. Old kitchen spoons and forks make handy supplementary tools. When large, heavy containers are planted, some equipment to facilitate moving is desirable (*see page 42*).

POTTING MIXES

One of the main reasons why even novice gardeners often have great success when growing plants in containers is that they are using ready-made potting mixes that are well aerated and also water-retentive, contain a balanced supply of nutrients, and are free of weed seeds and soil-borne pests and diseases. It is unlikely that soil from the garden would be so trouble-free or that its structure would stand up to heavy watering in the confined space of a container. Gardeners can prepare their own mixes, sterilizing soil and adding other ingredients to get a balance between free drainage, water-retention, and a good nutrient level. However, mixing requires space, and significant savings can be made only when the materials are bought in bulk.

There are two main categories of ready-made potting mix: soil-based and soil-less. The principal component of soil-based mixes is sterilized loam, which is usually mixed with peat and coarse sand. However, the vast majority of mixes commercially available in North America are soil-less. Until recently, most of these potting mixes were based on peat, but concern at the environmental impact of large-scale exploitation of peat reserves has led to experimentation with other materials, including bark and coconut fiber. Soil-less mixes are available in a range that includes seed, cuttings, standard, all-purpose (sold as suitable for seeds and cuttings as well as for general use), and acidic-soil mixes. They are light, clean to use, and usually cheaper than soil-based ones. Their nutrient levels fall relatively quickly, however, so that in a normal growing season plants require additional fertilizer (*see page 67*), and they tend to dry out quickly and are then difficult to rewet, yet become waterlogged if overwatered.

A trowel is indispensable for the container gardener. A narrow-bladed one is an advantage when working on a small scale but a standard model suits most purposes. A hand fork, pruners, kitchen scissors, and a folding knife complete the list of essential container garden tools.

ABOVE *Soil-less mixes are lightweight, so they are ideal for hanging baskets.*

RIGHT *Several important groups of plants, including rhododendrons (here* Rhododendron *'Bow Bells') and heaths, generally require an acidic-soil mix.*

ABOVE *Alpine-garden plants need free drainage and retain their compact growth on a lean diet. Add grit to a soil-based mix low in nutrients.*

LEFT *Soil-based mixes maintain their nutrient levels well. Use them for long-term planting and to give stability. This standard* Hydrangea paniculata *needs weight to counterbalance its top growth.*

PLANTING A TREE OR LARGE SHRUB

The enduring beauty of shrubs and small trees gives the container garden an air of maturity. Many of these impressive, larger plants are easily grown and, once they have been satisfactorily planted, their main requirement is a regular supply of water.

Container-grown specimens can be planted at almost any time of year, although fall or spring planting generally gives the best results. The dormant season, however, is best for planting bare-root trees (almost invariably deciduous) and root-balled specimens (often evergreens), which have the roots and surrounding soil wrapped in a material such as burlap. Both these types should be planted in the same way as container-grown specimens, except that in the case of root-balled plants the wrapping must be removed from the roots while planting.

For trees and large shrubs, the stability of the planter is important, as is its size. A tub or pot about twice the width and depth of the root ball will allow room for roots to develop and will hold sufficient reserves of nutrients and moisture to sustain healthy growth. Avoid using lightweight containers and those with a narrow base.

Use a soil-based potting mix (acidic for trees and shrubs that need it), to which a slow-release fertilizer has been added. Standard trees may need staking, in which case insert the stake before planting and secure it to the tree with a tree tie.

A tall jar, distinguished by its texture and pale green glaze, makes a handsome container for a purple-leaved Japanese maple (Acer palmatum f. atropurpureum). Since the narrow base of the container is potentially unstable, it must be positioned in a sheltered spot where it is not exposed to strong winds.

PLANTING A JAPANESE MAPLE

1 *Scrub the terracotta pot and soak it thoroughly in clean water. If possible, position it in its final site before filling with potting mix because it will be difficult to move once planted. Put pottery shards over the drainage holes.*

2 *Fill the pot about one-third full with a soil-based potting mix to which a slow-release fertilizer has been added. Japanese maples thrive in an acidic-soil mix such as those that are formulated specially for rhododendrons.*

3 *Holding the young tree on its side, ease it out of the planter, taking care to keep the root ball intact. It is important to check a tree before purchase to see that it is not potbound, for such a specimen will not establish well.*

4 *Set the tree carefully in the new container, gently loosening the root ball. Add potting mix until, when firmed, the tree is at the same depth that it was growing at previously, as indicated by the soil mark on its stem.*

5 *Ensure that the tree remains upright while adding more mix, working it around the roots and firming in the tree. When finished, the level of the potting mix should be 1–2in (2.5–5cm) below the rim of the container.*

6 *Water the planted tree. If it is not already in its final position, do not attempt to move the planter until it has drained fully. In subsequent springs, remove the top 1–2in (2.5–5cm) of potting mix and replace with fresh mix.*

PLANTING BULBS

Bulbs are neatly packaged stores of plant energy that are easy to handle. Whether they are true bulbs (such as daffodils) or plants with corms (crocus) or tubers (cyclamen), most are planted when they are dormant, in fall. In most cases, they produce a gladdening display several months later without having made any serious demands on the gardener. Snowdrops can be planted as dry bulbs in fall, but they are among a small group of bulbs that do better when planted immediately after flowering, while still in leaf.

Since most bulbs require good drainage, the container must have adequate drainage holes. It also needs to be of sufficient depth: crocuses and other small bulbs should be set 2–3in (5–8cm) deep while, at the other extreme, stem-rooting lilies, such as *Lilium regale*, require 6–8in (15–20cm) of potting mix above the bulb. Where winters are very severe, give pots of bulbs protection until there are signs of growth.

Plant only healthy and undamaged bulbs, preferably in a soil-based mix. For bulbs needing really good drainage, add grit or coarse sand. Provided they are watered regularly, well-nourished, and allowed to die down naturally, many bulbs will flower satisfactorily in subsequent years. But the deterioration in flower quality in most tulips, daffodils, and hyacinths makes it worth planting fresh bulbs each year.

The sweetly scented, bunch-flowered Tazetta narcissi are much used for forcing, succeeding outdoors only in very mild areas. Some hybrids, including the frilly-centered 'Cragford', are hardier and a dense planting makes a full, wonderfully fragrant display.

PLANTING DAFFODILS IN LAYERS

1 *Plant in early fall, covering the base of the container with a layer of drainage material 1–2in (2.5–5cm) deep.*

2 *Put in potting mix to a depth of 2–3in (5–8cm) and plant the first layer of bulbs about 2in (5cm) apart.*

3 *Cover the bulbs with more mix until their tips only just show, then plant a second bulb layer above the gaps between the first layer.*

4 *Add more potting mix to a level about 1in (2.5cm) below the container's rim. Gently firm the mix and water.*

PLANTING TULIPS IN A POT

Plant tulip bulbs in late fall, 1–2in (2.5–5cm) apart, in one or two layers according to the depth of the pot. This pot (above) holds a single layer of eight bulbs.

Tulips add a touch of spring glamor to boxwood topiary set in an old copper container (right).

PLANTING LILIES

1 *All lilies require good drainage. Place a generous layer of drainage material in the base of the container before planting lilies singly or in small groups.*

2a *Plant stem-rooting lilies on a 1–2in (2.5–5cm) layer of potting mix. They should be 6–8in (15–20cm) deep to allow for the development of roots above the bulb.*

2b *Plant basal-rooting lilies, which produce no roots above the bulbs, about 4–6in (10–15cm) deep, on a layer of potting mix about 2–3in (5–8cm) deep.*

The stem-rooting regal lily (Lilium regale) *is an easy bulb to grow and its magnificent trumpets are richly scented.*

PLANTING A BASKET OF IVY AND CROCUSES

1 *Plant dwarf bulbs in early fall. Line a wickerwork basket about 8in (20cm) across with plastic sheeting, slitting the plastic for drainage.*

2 *Fill the basket halfway with potting mix, then plant three small-leaved ivies evenly spaced around the perimeter of the basket.*

3 *Insert 10 crocus corms, about 2in (5cm) deep, between the ivy plants. Add potting mix until it reaches a level about 1in (2.5cm) below the rim of the container when gently firmed.*

4 *The ivy foliage will look attractive kept outside all winter, and in late winter or early spring the crocuses will push through its variegated leaves, opening their goblet-shaped flowers in warm sunlight.*

PLANTING SMALL BULBS

Plant spring-flowering small bulbs such as puschkinias or scillas in early fall (above). For a dense display set the bulbs close, but not touching, at a depth of about 2in (5cm) from the top of the container.

PLANTING A PLASTIC-LINED WOODEN WINDOW BOX

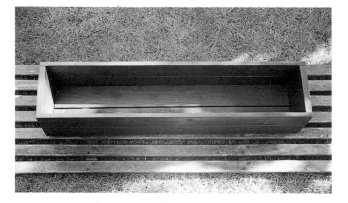

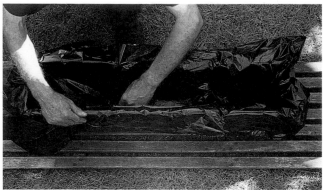

1 *Wooden window boxes are constructed in a variety of ways. The drainage is sometimes provided by a central slit instead of by a series of small holes.*

2 *Lining the box with sheet plastic may prolong the life of a wooden container. Place the plastic in position, allowing a generous overlap, and make slits in its base.*

3 *Cover the bottom of the container with pottery shards and a layer of washed gravel, about 1in (2.5cm) deep. Fill the box halfway with a soil-less potting mix.*

4 *Without removing the plants from their pots, position them so that they are displayed to best effect. Begin the planting with the key plant of the arrangement – here, a tellima.*

5 *Position the other plants – monkey flowers, creeping jenny, and pansies – around the tellima. Firm gently, adding mix to a level about 1in (2.5cm) below the rim of the window box.*

6 *When the planting has been completed, trim the sheet plastic to just above the rim and neatly tuck the remainder down inside the window box.*

Yellow flowers, dominated by dark-centered rudbeckias, with ivies and maidenhair ferns make up the planting in this simple wooden window box (above). It is the contrasts in flower sizes that give this cheerful single-color theme its special charm. The window box itself is supported on brackets below the sill so that plants do not keep too much light from the room.

PREPARING A PLASTIC WINDOW BOX FOR PLANTING

1 Plastic window boxes are often sold with the drainage holes marked but not pierced. Use a sharp implement such as a screwdriver to make holes where indicated.

2 Some plastic window boxes have sides that bow slightly inward when empty, but these will expand when they are filled with potting mix and plants.

PLANTING HANGING BASKETS

Hanging baskets are generally most effective when planted with bushy and trailing plants that overwhelm and obscure the container. Planting through the sides and top of a hanging basket – easy to do with wire-framed baskets – makes the plant cover even more complete. If you are using the traditional lining material, sphagnum moss, increasingly replaced by substitutes, simply make a hole in it and work young plants through to the potting mix underneath. When using rigid, pre-formed liners, cut holes for trailers. Most of the other liners, made from materials such as matted fibers, foam plastic, and wadding, come in the form of circular sheets cut radially almost to their center. The segments formed by these cuts overlap when the liner is laid in the basket. Planting through the sides of the hanging basket is best done where sections overlap.

Be practical in choosing a site for your hanging basket. Do not hang it where it will be in the way, and bear in mind how it is to be watered. Avoid exposed positions. There will always be rapid loss of moisture in a breezy location, and high winds could bring a basket down.

The considerable weight of a planted basket needs a secure fixture. While the basket is still empty, try it in the position where it is to hang, make sure that the support for it is secure, and, if necessary, adjust the lengths of the chains or cords that attach it to its support. Make sure you can reach the basket for watering.

RIGID LINER

Pre-formed shapes of various materials come in standard sizes. Positions for holes are usually scored in the sides.

LINER OF MATTED FIBERS

Liners made of matted natural fibers such as coconut are usually cut so that the segments overlap when laid in a basket.

WADDING LINER

Thick liners of natural and synthetic materials are also often cut so that the segments overlap.

LINING A BASKET WITH LOOSE FIBER

1 Dyed coconut fiber is a natural lining material with a loose texture similar to that of sphagnum moss, for which it is a substitute.

2 Lay the loosened fiber inside the basket at a uniform thickness. The fiber can be used in conjunction with a plastic sheet pierced for drainage.

3 Fill the basket halfway with a soil-based or soil-less potting mix. Push plants through the sides and gently firm them in before adding more mix.

PLANTING A SHEET-LINED BASKET WITH TRAILING PLANTS

1 *Support the hanging basket during planting by resting it on an empty pail or pot. Place a liner (a synthetic capillary matting liner is used here) in the basket and arrange it so the segments just overlap.*

2 *Mix granules of slow-release fertilizer with a soil-less potting mix. This will be lighter than a soil-based mix and so better for a hanging basket. Fill the basket halfway with mix. Do not compact by pressing.*

3 *Plant trailers in the side of the basket where the liner segments overlap. Use a pair of scissors or a sharp knife to make a small lateral cut in the edge of the liner so that plants can be inserted easily.*

4 *Using both hands, work the root system of trailing plants such as lobelias through the liner where the cuts have been made. Add potting mix around the roots and firm lightly. Repeat this operation at intervals around the basket.*

5 *Add about 2in (5cm) of potting mix before planting the top of the basket. Any large, bushy plant such as this New Guinea hybrid impatiens makes a good centerpiece. Begin with this plant, working potting mix around its roots and firming gently before adding other plants.*

6 *Complete planting from the top, making sure that plants such as the fuchsia, trailing begonia, and variegated ivies are positioned to give a balanced display. Work mix around the roots and firm gently. Add mix so that the final level is just below the basket's rim.*

7 *When planting is finished, remove any damaged leaves and stems, and then water the basket thoroughly. Leave standing for about 10 minutes while excess water drains away, and then move the basket to the position where it will hang.*

PLANTING ALPINE-GARDEN PLANTS

Many of the exquisite dwarf plants that thrive in mountainous areas and other rocky places can be cultivated successfully in containers as well as in raised beds and alpine gardens. Whether they are grown in stone troughs or tubs, concrete or composition-stone planters, terracotta pots, or even window boxes, most require only full sun and free drainage. The low terracotta planter, 14in (35cm) across and 7in (17cm) deep, shown being filled on the opposite page, is a good size for a small collection of these lovely miniatures.

Fall and early spring are the best times to plant, although spring is preferable in areas that experience cold winters. Heavy containers should always be positioned before planting; they need a spot where they are exposed to maximum sun. To ensure free drainage, put a layer of gravel in the base of the container. Use a soil-based potting mix and add one-fourth to one-third of its volume in grit or gravel. Cover the surface with a layer of gravel, to keep the necks of plants clear of moist potting compost. Plants will not need additional fertilizing if a little slow-release fertilizer has been added to the mix. In subsequent years, top-dress the plants in early spring: remove the layer of gravel and set aside, replace the top 1in (2.5cm) of potting mix with fresh mix containing slow-release fertilizer, then cover again with gravel.

Stone is a sympathetic material for a container planted with alpine-garden plants. This roughly hewn planter, its weathered surface encrusted with lichens, holds a small collection including phlox, sedums, and thrift, arranged around a mossy stone.

CREATING A MINIATURE ALPINE-GARDEN IN A PLANTER

1 *Scrub the planter and let it soak in clean water in order to rehydrate the stone. If possible, put it in position – which should be a sunny spot – and put pottery shards over the drainage hole.*

2 *Cover the shards and the bottom of the planter with a layer of well-washed small stones or gravel about 2in (5cm) deep. If the container is very deep, increase the amount of drainage material.*

3 *Fill the planter halfway with slightly moist, soil-based potting mix containing a slow-release fertilizer to which grit or gravel (up to one-third by volume) has been added.*

4 *Experiment with arrangements for plants – including here sisyrinchium, dianthus, sempervivum, and a dwarf juniper – by moving them, still in their pots, around the container.*

5 *Embed some large stones in the potting mix, then begin planting, starting with the shrubby plants. Loosen the root ball slightly before inserting into a prepared hole. Add mix, if necessary, and firm.*

6 *Add the remaining plants, working potting mix around them and firming them. When this stage is completed, the surface of the potting mix should be about 2in (5cm) below the planter's rim.*

7 *Top-dress with well-washed small stones or gravel to just below the planter's rim, working these around the necks of plants to ensure good drainage and so reduce the risk of rot.*

8 *Water the alpine garden gently with a hose or watering can until excess water runs out of the drainage hole. If the container is to be repositioned, move it only when it has drained completely.*

9 *Although most alpine-garden plants need free drainage, they also require plenty of moisture, especially during the growing season, so water regularly. Trim excessive or untidy growth.*

PLANTING HERB AND STRAWBERRY JARS

A traditional planter commonly used for herbs consists of a terracotta pot with planting holes at two or three levels in the sides. A similar container of larger size is used for strawberries. Planters that accommodate plants arranged vertically are also available in other materials. Among these are wooden tubs with a series of holes bored in the sides large enough to hold plants, usually strawberries. A gardener with only moderate practical skills can create a strawberry jar from a half-barrel.

The method of planting is essentially the same for all these containers. They require drainage material in the base, over which potting mix is added to just below the lowest holes. From the outside, push the root ball of a plant through each hole and firm it in the mix. When the holes at one level are filled, add potting mix to just below the next level of holes. Follow the same procedure until the holes at every level are planted.

Herbs must have even exposure to light, so rotate the jar regularly; light is not as critical for strawberries. Less conventional plantings can be made of ornamental plants. In a large, heavy pot that is not easily rotated, plant one side with sun-lovers, the other with shade-tolerant plants.

PLANTING A TERRACOTTA HERB JAR

1 *Scrub and soak the jar in clean water, then put pottery shards over the drainage holes and add a layer of drainage material.*

2 *Fill the jar to just below the lower holes with a soil-based mix containing one-fourth added grit for drainage and stability.*

3 *Push the root balls of plants through the lower holes and firm in the mix. Then add more mix to just below the upper holes.*

4 *Repeat for the upper holes. To prevent the mix falling out, pack small stones around plants. Add 2in (5cm) more mix.*

5 *Add a final plant in the top of the jar. Work more mix around it and firm so the final level is 1in (2.5cm) below the jar's rim.*

6 *Put the jar in position and water thoroughly. Rotate every five to seven days to ensure that all plants get plenty of light.*

Alpine strawberries bear small fruit of distinctive flavor throughout the summer. The fruit is not readily available in stores so it is well worth growing plants, and in a pot pierced with holes you can easily supply the conditions they need. The more familiar large-fruited strawberries, which bear prolific crops in summer, can be grown in the same way.

61

PLANTING A WATER GARDEN

An attractive miniature water garden can be created in a watertight container no more than 18in (45cm) in height and diameter. Glazed ceramic pots are ideal containers except in frost-prone areas, where they may be shattered when the water freezes. Even where the winters are cold they can be used outdoors in summer and moved under cover from fall to spring, although you may need to empty the container in order to move it.

Metal and wood are the most suitable materials for year-round exposure. Metal is best treated with a rubber-based paint, because if left uncovered it may be harmful to plants and fish. Wooden half-barrels and tubs will usually remain fairly watertight once the wood is thoroughly soaked

and has had a chance to swell. Plastic and fiber glass make good watertight containers, but since they are less visually pleasing you may wish to mask them with plants, or disguise them in some other way.

When planting, aim to strike a balance between the different groups of plants. Those that cover the surface, such as water lilies (*Nymphaea*), block out the light that encourages discoloring algae. Several water lilies are happy in as little as 18in (45cm) of water. Waterside plants, such as the dwarf cattail (*Typha minima*), with only their feet in water, soften the edge, while submerged plants help to clean and oxygenate the water – especially important if fish are to be introduced.

Even a water garden in a small tub can be enlivened by the sound and movement of flowing water. Here an old water pump has been converted into an ornamental feature, brightened by a variegated moisture-loving grass. An electric-powered submersible pump is used to circulate the water.

POTTING AQUATICS

1 *Plant aquatics in spring, using open-sided plastic baskets (lined with burlap if the holes are large) and a specially formulated aquatic mix.*

2 *Use a sharp knife to trim roots – here of a dwarf iris – if necessary. Insert the plant deep in the container, working the mix around it, and firm it in gently.*

3 *Top-dress the mix with a layer of washed gravel about 1in (2.5cm) deep. Water newly planted baskets before introducing them to a pool.*

PLANTING A WATER GARDEN IN A TUB

1 *Position the tub in its final sunny spot, checking that it is level on the ground. Then cover the base of the tub with a 2in (5cm) layer of washed gravel.*

2 *Add the aquatics – including here a dwarf water lily (Nymphaea), Juncus effusus, Caltha palustris, and Typha minima – in baskets. Raise the waterside plants on bricks around the edge and place the water lily on the base of the tub.*

3 *Slowly fill the tub with water, directing the flow from the hose at the wall of the tub. If water is added too quickly, it will disturb the potting mix in the baskets.*

4 *Rapid growth by the water lily and the waterside plants should soon mask the containers and the inside of the tub. Add water from time to time, always doing this slowly and gently.*

WATERING

Plants in containers depend on the gardener for their water supplies. Even in rainy weather watering may be necessary, either because the canopy of foliage sheds rainwater outside the container or because the pot sits in an area of rain shadow. Failing to water can quickly prove fatal to plants but overwatering can also make plants sicken. Drip trays and saucers left unemptied will cause waterlogging.

Check moisture levels frequently by pushing a finger below the surface of the potting mix. Do this at least once a day in summer, when plants are making vigorous growth. Even in cloudy weather, strong winds speed up water loss. When the potting mix is nearly dry, water thoroughly but gently until water runs out of the bottom of the container.

In hot, sunny weather avoid splashing water on the leaves, which otherwise may scorch. Tap water is usually satisfactory but, if it is hard, use rainwater or distilled water for rhododendrons, camellias, and other lime-haters. For hanging baskets it may be necessary to use alternatives to the standard hose or watering can (*see below*). Automatic drip-feed irrigation systems are a boon when large numbers of containers need watering.

Lining terracotta pots with sheet plastic, adding water-retaining granules to the potting mix, covering the surface of the mix with a gravel mulch, and spraying plants such as conifers with an anti-desiccant will slow down water loss. Self-watering containers are available.

OVERHEAD WATERING

AUTOMATIC IRRIGATION

FAR LEFT *Rigid hose extensions with a curved nozzle simplify the watering of hanging baskets and window boxes (or you can improvise using a bamboo cane tied to the end of a hose). Pump-action compression units are useful if there are only a few pots to water.*

LEFT *Drip-feed, sometimes known as trickle, systems of automatic irrigation incorporate a unit to reduce the pressure. They also include a filter but the tubes feeding water into individual containers still need regular cleaning. For efficient operation use these systems in conjunction with a timer to regulate the water supply.*

REVIVING WILTING PLANTS

LEFT *Act promptly if container-grown plants begin to wilt because watering has been neglected. Stand the container in a vessel of water in a position out of strong sunlight. Leave for about 30 minutes. When the mix is thoroughly wet, take out the pot and stand to drain. Some plants are remarkably resilient and revive quickly but others soon reach the point of no return once the mix is allowed to dry out.*

FEEDING

Standard potting mixes contain a balanced supply of nutrients but the reserves in the small amount of mix in a pot or planter can be used up quickly by plants. They are also leached out by watering. The application of fertilizers, simply referred to as feeding, is a way of maintaining the level of nutrients.

The fertilizers used are either organic, that is, derived from plant or animal material, or inorganic, usually man-made from various minerals. Proprietary formulations of inorganic fertilizers are particularly useful in the container garden. They have a balanced supply of the major minerals required for plant growth – nitrogen (N), phosphorus (P), and potassium (K) – together with minute quantities of trace elements. The label should state the constituents and their relative proportions. These fertilizers fall into two main categories. Quick-acting formulations are sold in liquid or soluble powder form and applied at regular intervals throughout the growing season. Slow release fertilizers, usually in granular form, are incorporated in the potting mix at the beginning of the growing season. Their nutrient value lasts over a long period.

In applying fertilizers, always follow the manufacturer's instructions closely. Do not be misled into thinking that exceeding the recommended rates and frequencies of application will result in bigger and better plants. Over-application may be harmful and is certainly wasteful.

SLOW-RELEASE FERTILIZERS

ABOVE *Slow release inorganic fertilizers, generally manufactured in granular form, are particularly useful when preparing a topdressing for trees or shrubs.*

FOLIAR FEEDING

ABOVE *Plants respond quickly to applications of a liquid foliar feed. Use a pump-action spraygun to apply and avoid spraying in hot, sunny conditions, which might result in leaf scorch.*

APPLYING A LIQUID FERTILIZER

LEFT *Water quick-acting soluble fertilizers into containers at the rate and the frequency recommended by the manufacturer. Avoid wetting the leaves of the plant.*

PRUNING

Many container-grown shrubs, vines, and trees require little if any pruning. When you do need to prune, use sharp, clean pruners and, for larger branches, loppers or a pruning saw. Make clean cuts so that pruning wounds heal rapidly. If you are not pruning back to a main stem, make the cut above a vigorous side-shoot or growth bud. If plants have opposite shoots, make a straight cut immediately above a pair of buds or shoots (one bud or shoot can be removed if growth is needed in one direction only). If plants have alternate buds or shoots, make an angled cut just above a selected bud or shoot.

Formative pruning may be necessary to shape a young plant, but is often already done on nursery-raised stock. In the dormant season remove weak shoots and badly placed stems, especially if these clutter the center, and aim to build a balanced framework of main branches or shoots. Heavy corrective pruning at a later stage is rarely needed and should be avoided because it stimulates strong growth.

To maintain a plant's vigor and health, remove any dead, diseased, or damaged wood promptly. Cutting back to healthy wood will reduce the risk of diseases gaining entry or of infections spreading. Annual pruning of some popular and mainly deciduous flowering shrubs and vines improves their display. Those that flower in spring or early summer usually do so on wood produced in the previous growing season. Cut out the old wood as soon as the flowers fade to encourage vigorous new growth that will flower the following year. If flowers are produced on the current season's growth, prune in winter or early spring.

A number of shrubs, including lavender, that become bare at the base if allowed to grow unchecked can be kept compact by annual pruning. Plants that are pruned heavily benefit from feeding early in the growing season.

Most fruit trees and vines also require annual pruning to encourage the formation of fruit-bearing wood. After the initial training of apples, build up fruiting spurs by shortening the side-shoots. In fall or winter cut these back to two buds. All methods of pruning grapevines are based on establishing a permanent framework and pruning annually to encourage the production of new wood that will carry fruit the following year. A convenient way of growing a grapevine in a container is to train a standard and to prune shoots at the head, cutting back to one bud annually during the dormant season.

Variegated shrubs sometimes produce non-variegated shoots. Cut out these reverted shoots as soon as they develop. If they are left, it is likely that they will eventually dominate the plant.

BASIC CUTS

Make angled pruning cuts using sharp, clean pruners on plants such as roses that have alternate growth buds or leaves. Cut just above a bud or shoot that will make growth in the desired direction, starting the cut opposite the base of the bud and sloping it so that it finishes about ¼in (5mm) above the bud.

Use pruners to make a straight pruning cut on plants that have opposite buds or leaves, such as hydrangeas. Make the cut just above strong buds or shoots, without damaging them. If growth is wanted in one direction only, remove the unwanted bud or shoot after making the cut.

HARD PRUNING TO KEEP PLANTS COMPACT

1 *Several shrubs, including lavender and lavender cotton, become straggly and deteriorate if not cut hard back regularly. Prune lavender in mid-spring, just as new shoots are forming, or, in areas with a mild climate, in fall.*

2 *Use sharp pruners or hand shears to cut off flower heads and most of the growth made in the previous season. Spring-pruned plants can have flower heads removed in fall. Avoid cutting into old wood since this rarely produces new growth.*

3 *When making cuts, follow the natural domed outline of the plant. When pruning is finished, remove all trimmings, brushing over the bush to shake off any loose shoots remaining. Repeat this pruning annually.*

PRUNING TO MAINTAIN VIGOROUS GROWTH

1 *Begin pruning shrubs, for example a mophead hydrangea, by removing all dead, diseased, weak, and damaged wood. Take out a stem or stems if branches are crossing, which would otherwise result in congestion, and wounds that could be entry points for diseases.*

2 *Many shrubs benefit from additional pruning to encourage new growth. Some shrubs flower on new wood, and the aim of pruning is to take out wood once it has flowered. A number of shrubs, including mophead hydrangeas, flower on old wood, but they still need some pruning to ensure a succession of vigorous growths.*

3 *Cut a proportion of old stems back to base or to strong shoots low down on the bush and lightly trim other stems to healthy buds. Prune more drastically shrubs that flower on the current season's growth, including roses.*

FALSE TOPIARY

A simple and relatively quick method of forming both geometric and representational shapes with plants is to train small-leaved vines over frames. Once the frame is densely covered with leaves, these shapes look very much like traditional topiary, which is why the technique is referred to as false topiary. In a more elaborate form of training, the frame is used not only to define the shape but also to hold a material, such as sphagnum moss, into which small plants are densely planted.

Commercially produced frames that provide a skeleton for climbing plants are usually made of sturdy galvanized or enameled wire. Bold, stylized shapes are not difficult to fashion out of chicken wire over a simple framework

of heavy-gauge galvanized wire. All frames need feet that can be inserted firmly in the container, and a soil-based potting mix is required to provide a solid foundation.

In temperate gardens the most versatile plants to use for training over shapes are the small-leaved common English ivies (*Hedera helix*), which have flexible stems and neat foliage, and form dense growth when pinched back. In one growing season, a single plant will usually give good cover to a simple frame 12–18in (30–45cm) high. To achieve even cover on a large frame with a broad base, use two or three plants spaced out around the frame. The climbing fig (*Ficus pumila*) is also a good plant for training, but it needs warmer conditions.

The small-leaved cultivars of the common English ivy have flexible stems that are easily trained over frames and make a dense evergreen cover if bare lengths of stem are trimmed back. A bird shape in wire, with a small head, plump body, and *angled tail, can easily be recognized without the need for fine detail. A single ivy plant will be sufficient to clothe the smaller frame in green, while two or three plants will be required to achieve quick results on each of the larger frames.*

TRAINING IVY ON A WIRE FRAME

1 *In the spring plant a well-branched small-leaved ivy in a pot containing soil-based potting mix. After watering, allow the pot to drain, then insert the frame over the ivy. Make sure the foot of the frame is firmly embedded in the mix.*

2 *Gently pull the stems of the ivy through the base of the frame so that they hang outside it. Before training them upward, tease out the stems, then drape the longest stems over the frame, distributing them evenly over the wires.*

3 *Twist the ivy stems around the wires of the frame to keep them in position. In the early stages it may be necessary to hold the stems in place with a few inconspicuous ties of plastic-coated wire or garden string.*

4 *Train the shorter stems up the outside of the frame, spacing them evenly and twisting them around the wires. Continue to train these stems as they grow, tucking them around the frame.*

5 *Water regularly and apply liquid fertilizer every two weeks during the growing season. Tuck in new growth and trim any excess. A small frame such as this will be covered in two or three months.*

TRAINING VINES

Growing vines in flat-sided containers is a good solution to clothing walls where a paved surface means that there is no bare earth for planting. Container-grown vines can be grown independently of walls, either trailing freely or else trained over a support system fitted into the pot or planter. Vines grown in this way need heavy, deep containers and should be placed in a sheltered position. Use a soil-based potting mix for all vines.

The kind of support a vine needs depends on its manner of growth. Those that cling by means of adhesive pads or aerial roots, ivies among them, do best on a solid surface such as a house or garden wall. Although vigorous and tenacious once established, these self-clingers are often slow to get started. Secure young stems against the surface they are to climb until the aerial roots begin to grip. Many vines, like the common jasmine (*Jasminum officinale*), are twiners, while others, such as the sweet pea, hold onto supports by tendrils. Both these categories of vines need supports they can work around, such as wires, netting, trellis, or a wigwam of stakes. Secure wall supports firmly, allowing a gap of about 2in (5cm) so that air can circulate. Some ready-made supports are available that can be fitted into planters and you can make your own with trellis or bamboo stakes. Put them in before planting. Twiners and tendril vines need to be guided and lightly tied in until they start to surge upward.

Roses need to have their lax stems regularly tied into netting or trellis supports. Train in the main stems as near the horizontal as possible, to encourage free flowering. Check ties often to see that they are secure but not too tight.

MAKING A CLIMBING FRAME FOR SWEET PEAS

1 *A wigwam of bamboo stakes inserted in a tub or half-barrel makes an effective support for annual vines such as sweet peas and beans. In a tub 18–24in (45–60cm) across, evenly space six stakes that are 6–8ft (1.8–2.5m) long.*

2 *Between the tall stakes, insert other stakes that are approximately half their length. Tie the tall stakes together at the top and then tie twine around all stakes at a height of about 9in (23cm) and 2ft (60cm).*

ABOVE *Sweet peas can easily hoist themselves up a columnar support consisting of bare twiggy branches that are lightly trimmed and tied together. Before planting, insert the support in a heavy container filled with a soil-based potting mix.*

ABOVE *Transplanted sweet peas tend to flop about unless they are tied to a support, and are easily attached using twist ties. Any vine that twines or attaches itself by tendrils will benefit from initial training.*

ABOVE *Fix climbing roses to trelliswork, netting or other supports, using twine tied in a figure-eight or plastic ties. Check ties frequently and loosen them if they become too tight.*

BELOW *A golden-leaved hop (*Humulus lupulus *'Aureus') is trained to grow over a homemade wicker frame. This vigorous vine will have completely hidden its support by mid-summer.*

ABOVE *Where paving runs to the walls, containers offer the only practical way of growing climbers. Large pots planted with jasmines and clematis have softened the architecture of this paved courtyard.*

BELOW *Many moderately vigorous clematis, including the spring-flowering C.* macropetala, *are superb grown without supports.*

TRAINING STANDARDS

Standards give height in the container garden, and a well-shaped head on a clear stem makes a pleasing contrast to low-growing rounded or more spreading shapes. One method of forming standards, used for roses and some other woody plants, is to train vertically a stem of a suitable rootstock and to bud or graft a selected cultivar at the desired height. This specialized technique is usually carried out by the nursery, and the plants you buy have the head partly or fully formed.

The method that is more relevant to the amateur gardener involves training the plant stem vertically, cutting back the tip at a given height, encouraging the development of a bushy head by pruning, and removing shoots and leaves from the stem below the head. This technique can be used on many woody plants and on subshrubs such as fuchsias. The soft young growth of subshrubs can usually be pinched out between finger and thumb, a method of shortening stems often known as "pinch pruning." In frost-prone areas, you must keep standard fuchsias and other plants that are not hardy – including Paris daisies (*Argyranthemum*), heliotrope (*Heliotropium*), and pelargoniums – indoors or under glass through winter.

Fuchsias are among the easiest plants for the amateur gardener to train as standards. The combination of standard and bush fuchsias in one container is often highly successful, the two kinds providing a display of dangling flowers that continues through much of summer and into the fall.

TRAINING A STANDARD FUCHSIA

1 *In fall, select a healthy rooted cutting taken in late summer to train as a standard and pot it individually. In winter keep in a well-lit position at a minimum temperature of 50°F (10°C).*

2 *When the young fuchsia reaches a height of 8–10in (20–25cm), insert a stake in the pot and, using simple twist ties, secure the stem of the plant so that it continues to make strong vertical growth.*

3 *Continue to tie in the stem, using a longer stake if necessary. Remove leaves from the lower part of the stem only when the plant has almost reached the desired height.*

4 *When the plant has reached the desired height, pinch back the tip of the terminal shoot. This stimulates branching that will form the framework of the head. Once a strong stem has been formed, strip off all leaves below the head.*

5 *To support a well-branched head, standard fuchsias need to be tied to a permanent stake. Build up the head by pinching back the growing tips of stems three or four times, removing completely any stems that are weak or badly placed.*

PROPAGATING FROM SEED

Amateur gardeners can easily raise many of their own plants. Propagating from seed is a simple and cheap way of raising large numbers of hardy and half-hardy annuals, the mainstays of the summer garden. Except in areas with very mild winters that are not affected by frosts, the normal pattern is to start seeds of annuals in warmth during late winter or early spring for planting outdoors in late spring or early summer. Good germination results can be achieved on a windowsill using plastic flower pots filled with seed starter mix. Cover the pot with a clear plastic bag until the seed has germinated. A more sophisticated version of this is the unheated plant incubator.

To give plants the best chance of success sow thinly, scattering very fine seed on the surface and just covering larger seeds with a layer of seed starter mix as thick as the seeds. Germination of most annuals takes two to three weeks. As soon as they are large enough to handle, thin the seedlings or move them to a larger container.

Once the transplanted or thinned seedlings are making good growth, harden them off by gradually exposing them to conditions outdoors over a period of two or three weeks in readiness for planting them out. A cold frame makes an ideal halfway house in which the increase in ventilation can be controlled.

SOWING SEED IN A PLANT INCUBATOR

1 *Fill the seed flat of a plant incubator with a layer of seed starter mix. Level the surface of the mix and lightly firm it with the hand or with a piece of wood.*

2 *Sow all seed thinly. To ensure an even distribution, use a finger on one hand to tap the seed out of the other, or sprinkle seed carefully from a folded piece of paper.*

3 *Cover seeds with a layer of fine mix equal in depth to the size of the seed. Place the flat gently in a pail or sink filled with shallow water until the starter mix is thoroughly moistened.*

4 *Allow the flat to drain, then cover it with the plant incubator lid. Keep in a position that is warm but not exposed to direct sunlight until the seeds germinate.*

TRANSPLANTING

1 *Transplant or thin seedlings when they are large enough to handle. If transplanting, use a knife blade or plant label to ease them out of the flat, holding them by the leaves.*

2 *Plant the seedlings individually in compartmented packs or evenly spaced about 1½in (4cm) apart in larger pots filled with gently firmed soil-based or soil-less potting mix.*

PLANTING LARGE SEEDS

1 *Sow large seeds such as nasturtiums two to a small pot filled with seed starter mix. Water gently from above or below.*

2 *Nasturtiums can be moved into their final container once they are large enough to handle. Harden them off before placing outdoors.*

Alternatvely, nasturtiums can be sown directly outdoors in mid- to late spring, two seeds per station (number of stations depending on container size). Thin seedlings, removing the weakest. Here, the scarlet nasturtium 'Empress of India' has a purplish-blue tinge to the foliage that is brought out by the unusual color of the pot.

PROPAGATING BY DIVISION

The easiest way to increase stocks of many herbaceous perennials is by division. This method of vegetative propagation can also be applied to shrubs that produce suckers on their own roots and to bulbs and corms, most of which naturally produce offsets. When bulbous plants are lifted, the offsets can be detached and grown until they reach flowering size. This may take several years, so for the container garden, where space is usually at a premium, it is only worth growing offsets of bulbous plants that are unusual and therefore difficult to obtain.

Over several years, perennials tend to become either woody, and then they produce little growth at the center, or else congested, with the result that they make poor growth and produce fewer flowers. Division is an important way of rejuvenating plants as well as of propagating them. Because they are growing in cramped conditions, perennials in containers should be lifted and divided every one or two years. Fibrous-rooted perennials such as heucheras are the easiest to deal with. To divide large crowns of hostas and other perennials with tough rootstocks, it is generally best to lift or tip the plant out of its container and divide by cutting with a spade.

DIVIDING FIBROUS-ROOTED PERENNIALS

1 *Lift the perennials to be divided in fall or in early spring. Discard the old, unproductive center but retain growth from the outer part of the plant.*

2 *Divide by hand into as many viable sections as you need, if necessary cutting thick roots with a sharp knife. Make sure that each piece has vigorous shoots as well as healthy roots.*

3 *Remove any damaged leaves or stems and either pot up individually to grow or replant directly with other ornamentals, using fresh soil-based potting mix.*

4 *Water thoroughly. If the plant was large enough to break up into several portions, repeat the process of division followed by replanting.*

WINTER PROTECTION

In frost-prone areas, many plants in containers need protection in winter. One solution is to move container-grown tender plants indoors or under glass in the fall. Even unheated greenhouses, sunrooms, and glassed-in porches will give some protection, but with heating, a wider range of plants can be overwintered successfully.

The most convenient way of overwintering many tender perennials and shrubs is in the form of rooted cuttings. If plants of marginal hardiness are being left outdoors, it is always worth overwintering a few cuttings indoors in case the parent plant is lost. Pelargoniums can be lifted and stored through the winter (*see below*) and planted the following spring or used to provide material for cuttings. Keep all plants overwintered indoors or under glass nearly dry and at the lowest temperature they will tolerate, since moisture and warmth stimulate premature growth.

Even reasonably hardy plants may need protection when left outdoors, since container-grown specimens are more vulnerable to frost than those in the open ground. Wrap a shrub and its container in some form of insulation, such as straw inside a burlap cover, to minimize the risk of damage caused by alternating freeze and thaw.

OVERWINTERING PELARGONIUMS

1 *Lift pelargoniums before there is a risk of frost, shaking potting mix off the roots. Cut back the stems just above a joint about 3–6in (8–15cm) from the base.*

2 *Trim the roots back so that they are not more than 2–3in (5–8cm) long. At the same time, check that all the remaining growth is healthy and free of pests.*

3 *Prepare a container such as a wooden box with drainage holes, line it with plastic (slit at the base) and fill halfway with a soilless potting mix.*

4 *Put in the plants, close but not touching, and top with more mix. Water the mix and let it drain thoroughly before storing the box in a frost-free but light position.*

MODEL PLANTINGS

Beautiful and interesting container plantings are achieved by combining sound garden practice with a feel for putting plants together creatively. The practical skills are easily acquired, and a flair for planting comes from experience and inspiration from successful models.

The following section provides instructions for 35 different container plantings. Each double page begins with an introduction describing the theme of the planting or plantings. This is followed by advice on when best to plant and how to maintain each design. There is a list of the ingredients used, and a step-by-step guide clearly shows how each container is put together. Some gardeners may want to reproduce the plantings more or less exactly as they are illustrated. Others may wish to use the ideas and information as the inspiration for planting plans of their own creation. Using a container of a different material or coloring, or even a slightly different size or shape, changes the character of a planting. Daffodils, fuchsias, petunias, and tulips are among the many plants with numerous cultivars that can be chosen according to taste and availability. Substituting plants with characteristics similar to those illustrated is another interesting way to give your container garden a personal stamp. A selection of plants listed by characteristics is given on pages 204–5.

Fuchsias produce masses of flowers over a long season from mid-summer into fall. Here, the bushy fuchsia 'Tom Woods' and the trailing cultivar 'Jack Shahan' complement one another perfectly in a traditional terracotta pot decorated with a basketweave pattern. The trailing foliage of Salvia discolor, *which thrives in hot conditions, adds a silvery note in the foreground. Details of this planting are given on page 114.*

DEEP PINKS FOR SPRING

For colorful variety and reliability in spring, bulbs are the best. After planting in fall, they require little attention until their brilliant explosions transform the container garden. They can, of course, be planted alone, but for extra interest try combining them with other spring-flowering plants.

Plants that go well with bulbs include some long-lived herbaceous perennials, among them Lenten roses. Those that are hardy can be planted at the same time as the bulbs. Others can be added in early spring, but make sure you mark the position of the bulbs planted in the fall.

A POT WITH LENTEN ROSES

Plant in early to mid-fall, in sun or shade, leaving space for the dwarf primroses. Apply liquid fertilizer when the hyacinths and primroses come into flower, then again two weeks later. It is possible to maintain Lenten roses and ivy permanently in pots, but the hyacinth bulbs and the primroses should be replanted in the open garden after flowering.

Terracotta pot, diameter 8in (20cm), depth 5in (13cm)

Pottery shards

Soil-based potting mix incorporating a slow-release fertilizer

3 pink hyacinths (*Hyacinthus orientalis* 'Pink Pearl'), page 156, **A**

2 Lenten roses (*Helleborus orientalis*), page 156, **B**

3 pink dwarf primroses (*Primula*), page 139, **C**

1 small-leaved ivy (*Hedera helix* 'Donerailensis'), page 181, **D**

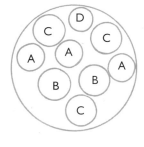

1 Scrub the pot and soak it in clean water.
2 Put pottery shards over the drainage hole and fill with potting mix to a depth of 2in (5cm).
3 Plant the hyacinth bulbs (**A**), then add more mix so that the bulbs are nearly covered.
4 Position a Lenten rose (**B**) on either side of the central hyacinth, and insert at their previous growing depth.
5 Plant the primroses (**C**) and the ivy (**D**), then add potting mix to a level about 1in (2.5cm) below the pot's rim. Firm in the plants.
6 Water well.

TULIPS IN A MIXED PLANTING

Plant the bulbs in late fall, and add the other plants in spring. Place in full sun. Apply liquid fertilizer when the tulip leaves emerge and again as the buds open. Replant in the open garden after flowering.

Terracotta pot, diameter 18in (45cm), depth 14in (35cm)

Pottery shards

Soil-based potting mix incorporating a slow-release fertilizer

12 pink tulips (*Tulipa* 'Garden Party'), page 157, **A**

2 variegated daylilies (*Hemerocallis fulva* 'Kwanzo Variegata'), page 141, **B**

2 pink double ranunculus (*R. asiaticus*), pages 163–4, **C**

1 white double ranunculus (*R. asiaticus*), pages 163–4, **D**

2 large-flowered, deep pink, double English daisies (*Bellis perennis*), page 156, **E**

2 small-flowered, deep pink, double English daisies (*Bellis perennis* 'Pomponette'), page 156, **F**

3 deep pink, double English primroses (*Primula vulgaris*), page 139, **G**

1 pink dicentra (*D.* 'Stuart Boothman'), page 160, **H**

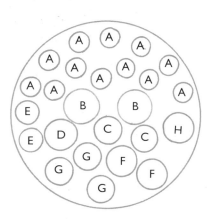

1 Scrub the pot and soak it in clean water.
2 Put pottery shards over the drainage holes, and fill the pot with potting mix to a depth of 2–3in (5–8cm).
3 Plant the tulip bulbs (A) in a dense group at two depths at the back of the pot. Add the daylilies (B) in the center.
4 Completely fill the back half of the pot with potting mix, marking the position of the tulips. Fill the front half two-thirds full with mix.

5 When the tulips begin to appear the following spring, remove 3–4in (8–10cm) of the potting mix in the front of the pot. Plant the ranunculus (C, D), then the English daisies (E, F), primroses (G), and dicentra (H). Work potting mix around the roots and add more mix to a level about 1in (2.5cm) below the pot's rim. Firm in all the plants.
6 Water well.

SPRING FRESHNESS

There is a refreshing charm about plants which retain the simplicity of their wild ancestors. One of the most beautiful recent introductions from China falls in this category. *Corydalis flexuosa* (*below*) has fernlike foliage, sometimes gray-green or purple-green with red markings, and showers of curiously tilted blue flowers that succeed one another throughout most of the spring. The cowslip (*opposite*) is more familiar, and is one of the classic wild flowers of spring. Small-flowered pansies have an unaffected beauty that makes them perfect companions for both cowslips and corydalis. All these plants thrive in partial shade.

Elaborate containers can overwhelm simple plants. Here, the corydalis and violets are planted in a plain terracotta pot. In the case of the terracotta trough, a pale blue wash tones down the relief decoration and makes it part of the overall color scheme.

CORYDALIS AND VIOLETS

Plant in late winter or early spring, positioning in partial shade. Apply liquid fertilizer three weeks after planting and again two weeks later. Deadhead the violets to promote a succession of flowers. When the perennial corydalis has stopped flowering, move it to the open garden. If the violets are still in flower, add them to a summer planting; otherwise discard them.

Terracotta pot, diameter 10in
   (25cm), depth 7in (17cm)
Pottery shards
Soil-based potting mix
1 corydalis (*C. flexuosa*),
   page 172, **A**
3 violets (*Viola* 'Johnny Jump
   Up'), page 143, **B**

1 Scrub the pot and soak it in clean water.
2 Put pottery shards over the drainage holes, and fill the planter with potting mix to a depth of 3–4in (8–10cm).
3 Plant the corydalis (A) in the center of the pot, ensuring that it is at its previous planting depth.
4 Space the violets (B) evenly around the edge of the pot, then add mix to a level 1–2in (2.5–5cm) below the pot's rim. Firm in the plants.
5 Water well.

COWSLIPS AND VIOLETS

Plant in late winter or early spring and position in partial shade. The cowslips flower for weeks in mid-spring; the violets, provided they are deadheaded, have a longer season. Apply liquid fertilizer three weeks after planting and every two weeks throughout the violets' flowering season. When the cowslips have finished flowering, plant them in the open garden. The violets can be retained as an edging for a replacement planting.

Terracotta trough, length 18in (45cm), depth and width 6in (15cm)

Pottery shards

Soil-based potting mix

3 cowslips (*Primula veris*), page 139, **A**

6 violets (*Viola* hybrids), page 143, **B**

1 Scrub the trough and soak it thoroughly in clean water.

2 Put pottery shards over the drainage holes, and fill the trough with potting mix to a depth of 3–4in (8–10cm).

3 Plant the three cowslips (**A**), evenly spaced, along the length of the trough.

4 Plant a violet (**B**) at each front corner and on the same front line plant two more between the cowslips. Plant the last two violets in the back on either side of the center cowslip.

5 Add potting mix to a level 1–2in (2.5–5cm) below the rim of the trough. Firm in the plants.

6 Water well.

TULIP TIME

Tulips are among the most versatile of spring bulbs and invaluable in the container garden. The numerous hybrids offer a color range that is matched by few flowers of any description. Their season extends for about three months, reaching its peak in mid- to late spring. Tulips are also easy to grow, requiring little attention between planting in late fall and flowering in spring. Choosing among them according to when they bloom, flower color and shape, even foliage markings, is a matter of personal taste although for window boxes and other containers in exposed positions it is best to use the shorter-growing kinds.

Provided the container is deep enough, it is worth planting the bulbs at two levels, to make a dense display. The effect of the tulips can also be enhanced by a skirt of companion plants. In the plantings here, dwarf yellow wallflowers and yellow and purple violets are combined with scarlet single tulips to make a bold arrangement (*below*), while the centers of double white English daisies echo the rich color of double yellow tulips (*opposite*). Tulips tend to deteriorate in flower size and quality after their first season. Use fresh bulbs in containers and, once they have flowered, move them to the open garden.

TULIPS AND DWARF WALLFLOWERS

Plant tulip bulbs and biennial wallflowers in late fall for this mid-spring display, which needs a sunny spot. Violets can be tucked in when available in early spring. Apply liquid fertilizer as the tulip leaves emerge and again as their buds open. Discard the wallflowers and violets after flowering. Save the tulips for planting in the open garden.

Terracotta pot, diameter 10in (25cm), depth 7in (17cm)

Pottery shards

Soil-based or soil-less potting mix

6 red single tulips (*Tulipa* 'Red Riding Hood'), page 151, **A**

6 dwarf yellow wallflowers page 138, **B**

2 violets (*Viola* 'Johnny Jump Up'), page 143, **C**

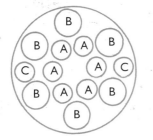

1 Scrub the pot and soak it thoroughly in clean water, to rehydrate it.
2 Put pottery shards over the drainage holes, and add potting mix to a depth of 3–4in (8–10cm).
3 Arrange the tulip bulbs (**A**) so that they are evenly spaced and separate, and cover them with potting mix.
4 Plant the wallflowers (**B**) and violets (**C**) around the edge. Add potting mix to 1–2in (2.5–5cm) below the rim. Firm in the plants.
5 Water well.

DOUBLE TULIPS AND DAISIES

For this mid- to late spring display, which requires a sunny spot, plant the tulip bulbs in mid-fall. In mild climates, the daisies can be planted at the same time. Where winters are more severe, add the daisies in early spring: remove 2in (5cm) of the potting mix, insert the plants, and replace the mix, working it around the roots. Apply liquid fertilizer as the tulip leaves emerge and again as the buds open. Discard the daisies after flowering, but replant the tulip bulbs in the open garden.

Terracotta pot, diameter and
   depth 12in (30cm)
Pottery shards
Soil-based or soil-less
   potting mix
15 double yellow tulips (*Tulipa*
   'Gold Medal'), page 140, **A**
4 white double English daisies
   (*Bellis perennis*),
   page 156, **B**

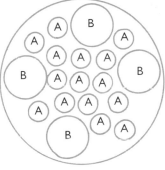

1 Scrub the pot and soak it in clean water.
2 Place a layer of pottery shards in the base of the pot, covering the drainage holes, and add potting mix to a depth of 4in (10cm).
3 Evenly space eight tulip bulbs (**A**) to form the first layer, and cover with potting mix so that the tips are just showing.

4 Arrange the remaining seven bulbs between the tips of those already planted. Add potting mix until it is 3–4in (8–10cm) below the planter's rim.
5 Evenly space the four daisies (**B**) around the edge of the pot, adding potting mix until it is 1–2in (2.5–5cm) below the rim. Firm in the plants.
6 Water well.

ORNAMENTAL VEGETABLES

Ornamental vegetables are among the many plants with decorative foliage. These can be used imaginatively with flowers or other foliage plants to create unusual designs. Red-leaved chard, often listed as ruby chard, has crimson stems and dark foliage which make a good match for red and purple flowers, such as many of the petunias (*below*). The flowerlike rosettes of ornamental cabbages will remain attractive for weeks and are especially useful in fall or winter as a replacement for summer ornamentals. Here, they have been used as an underplanting for a mopheaded standard boxwood (*opposite*). Chard is edible, but ornamental brassicas (cabbages and kale) are not good to eat. They are raised for the decorative appearance of their variegated leaves, in various combinations of green, red, pink, white, and cream, and often beautifully cut, crinkled, and waved.

RUBY CHARD WITH PETUNIAS

Ruby chard makes an ideal centerpiece for a late spring planting of purple petunias, which will bloom all through the summer until fall. Position in full sun. Water regularly and apply a liquid fertilizer every two weeks, starting two to three weeks after planting. Discard after flowering.

Glazed terracotta pot, diameter 12in (30cm), height 12in (30cm)

Pottery shards

Soil-based or soil-less potting mix

1 ruby chard (*Beta vulgaris* Cicla Group), page 200, **A**

5 purplish-red petunias, page 170, **B**

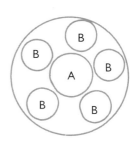

1 Scrub the pot and soak thoroughly in clean water.
2 Put pottery shards over the drainage holes, and fill the container with potting mix to a level 3in (8cm) below the rim.
3 Plant the ruby chard (**A**) in the middle, and work mix around the roots. Space five petunias (**B**) evenly around it.
4 Add potting mix until it is about 1in (2.5cm) below the planter's rim. Firm in the plants.
5 Water well.

BOXWOOD MOPHEAD WITH CABBAGES

In this scheme, boxwood balls are planted in smaller pots to repeat the rounded shape of the mopheaded standard. Lifting the head of a topiary specimen, by growing it on a short stem, leaves room for generous underplanting. Discard the cabbages once they are past their prime.

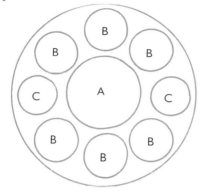

Terracotta pot, diameter 20in (50cm), height 20in (50cm)

Pottery shards

Soil-based potting mix incorporating slow-release fertilizer

1 standard boxwood (*Buxus sempervirens*), page 179, **A**

6 red and 2 white ornamental cabbages (*Brassica oleracea* Capitata Group), pages 186 and 189, **B** and **C**

1 Scrub the pot and soak it thoroughly in clean water.

2 Put pottery shards over the drainage holes, and fill the container with potting mix to a depth of about 14in (35cm).

3 Plant the boxwood (**A**) in the middle, at its previous planting depth.

4 Add potting mix to 3in (8cm) below the pot's rim. Plant the red and white cabbages (**B**, **C**) around the edge.

5 Work more mix around the cabbages until it is 1–2in (2.5–5cm) below the pot's rim. Firm in the plants.

6 Water well.

YELLOW FOR SUN AND SHADE

Trailing plants that flower well are invaluable in containers. Some, such as nasturtiums and creeping jenny, spill decorously over the pot's sides, their foliage and flowers masking the hard edge of the pot. Others, including bidens, are free-branching and create a swirl of color that floats around a container without appearing to be confined by it.

In a partially shaded trough (*below*), the golden-leaved creeping jenny works harmoniously with an attractive range of bedding plants and herbaceous perennials that all prefer moist conditions. A vivid scarlet double nasturtium and airy sprays of yellow *Bidens ferulifolia* (*opposite*) escape the confines of a narrow container in a sunny niche.

A WOODEN TROUGH FOR PARTIAL SHADE

Plant this moisture-loving mixture in late spring or early summer. Regular deadheading of the pansies and monkey flowers will help to sustain the display well into summer. Water regularly and apply a liquid fertilizer every two weeks, starting three weeks after planting. At the end of the season, save the tellima and the creeping jenny by replanting in another pot or in the open garden.

Wooden trough, length 3ft (90cm), width and depth 8in (20cm)
Black plastic sheet for liner
Soil-based potting mix
1 fringecup (*Tellima grandiflora*), page 182, **A**
6 red-faced yellow pansies, page 143, **B**
12 monkey flowers (*Mimulus* Malibu Mixed), page 147, **C**
6 golden creeping jenny (*Lysimachia nummularia* 'Aurea'),
    page 185, **D**

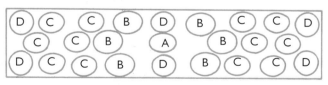

1 Insert the plastic sheet to line the trough completely. Cut drainage holes in the base. Fill the container with potting mix until it is 4in (10cm) below the rim.
2 Plant the fringecup (A) in the center, and place three pansies (B) in an arc on each side of it. Plant a group of six monkey flowers (C) toward each end of the trough.
3 Tuck in the creeping jenny (D), one at each corner and the remaining two on either side of the fringecup.
4 Add potting mix to 1in (2.5cm) below the trough's rim. Firm in the plants.
5 Water well.

A POT OF SUN-LOVING TRAILERS

If planted in late spring or early summer, this bright mixture will flower freely until fall. Water regularly through the summer and apply a liquid fertilizer every two weeks, starting three weeks after planting. Tie up the fuchsia stems as necessary. Discard plants after flowering, but overwinter cuttings of the fuchsia (see pages 82–83, 85).

Terracotta pot diameter 12in (30cm), height 16in (40cm)

Pottery shards

Soil-based potting mix with slow-release fertilizer

1 red fuchsia (*F.* 'Thalia'), page 153, **A**

1 double scarlet nasturtium (*Tropaeolum majus* 'Hermine Grashoff'), page 149, **B**

1 bidens (*B. ferulifolia*), page 140, **C**

1 coral gem (*Lotus berthelotti x maculatus*), page 147, **D**

2 dark blue salvias (*S. discolor*), page 176, **E**

2 gray-leaved helichrysums (*H. petiolare*), page 193, **F**

4 30in (75cm) bamboo stakes

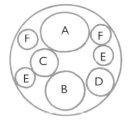

1 Scrub the pot and soak it thoroughly in clean water.
2 Put pottery shards over the drainage hole, and add potting mix to within 4in (10cm) of the pot's rim.
3 Plant the fuchsia (**A**) at the back of the pot, at its previous planting depth. Center a well-grown nasturtium (**B**) in the front of the pot, with the bidens (**C**) to its left and the coral gem (**D**) to its right. Tuck in the salvias and helichrysums at the sides.

4 Add potting mix to a level 1–2in (2.5–5cm) below the rim of the pot.
5 Firm in the plants and water well, then allow to drain.
6 Before placing the pot in a sunny place, insert stakes around the fuchsia to serve as supports for the plant as it develops.

Note: such a tall pot may need to be wedged in position to prevent it from being blown over.

A WHITE-BASED PLANTING

Of all the single-color planting themes, white is the most consistently successful. White makes flowery containers dazzling in full sun, and gives them a light freshness that stands out in gloomy shade, and retains a ghostly beauty as darkness falls. Skillfully applied touches of color make a planting distinctive, without detracting from the overall impression of whiteness. Here, single and double white Paris daisies establish the white theme but shades of pink – soft in another double daisy and deeper in the trailing plants that form the skirt – give the planting an individual character.

WHITE WITH SHADES OF PINK

Plant this scheme during late spring. Place the pot in full sun and it will flower all through the summer and fall, until it is stopped by frost. Deadhead all the plants regularly, and cut back Paris daisy stems with yellowing foliage to vigorous new shoots. Apply weak liquid fertilizer every two weeks, starting three to four weeks after planting. It is worth overwintering cuttings of all these plants (see pages 82–83, 85).

Terracotta pot, diameter 20in (50cm),
    depth 2ft (60cm)
Pottery shards
Soil-based potting mix
I white single Paris daisy (*Argyranthemum foeniculaceum*), page 131, **A**
I pink double Paris daisy (*Argyranthemum* 'Mary Wootton'), page 158, **B**
I white double Paris daisy (*Argyranthemum* 'Mrs F. Sander'), page 131, **C**
I reddish-pink verbena (*V.* 'Sissinghurst'), page 165, **D**
I malvastrum (*M. lateritium*), page 148, **E**

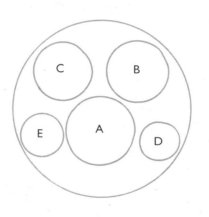

I Scrub the pot and soak it thoroughly in clean water.
2 Put pottery shards over the drainage holes, and fill the container with potting mix to a level 5in (13cm) below the rim.
3 Plant the single white Paris daisy (A) slightly forward of the center, working potting mix around the roots. Behind it, plant the double pink Paris daisy (B) to its left and the double white (C) to its right, adding sufficient mix to hold these in place.
4 At the front edge, plant the verbena (D) left of the center and the malvastrum (E) right of the center.
5 Add potting mix until it is about 1–2in (2.5–5cm) below the pot's rim, working it around the plants. Firm in the plants.
6 Water well.

SUBTLE GRAYS

Gray foliage, despite its apparent reticence, is often the making of successful container plantings. It is particularly useful as a moderator, calming mixtures of vibrant and even clashing colors and showing off to advantage more subdued plantings, especially in shades of pink, mauve, purple, and blue. When intensified to silver, as it is in some of the most finely cut gray foliage plants, it makes a lovely eye-catching accent among flowers.

The richly felted and splendidly hoary senecio *S. cineraria* is a popular gray-leaved plant for summer. The bleached filigree beauty of the cultivar 'Silver Dust' shows up well in a densely planted pot that also contains a curry plant, which has fine pewter-gray leaves (*below*). One of the most widely used plants with gray foliage is *Helichrysum petiolare*, which is a major component in a delightfully interwoven mixture featuring shades of pink (*opposite*). It sometimes produces cream flowers, which tone in well with this planting.

1 Scrub the pot and soak it thoroughly in clean water.

2 Put pottery shards over the drainage holes and fill with mix to within 4in (10cm) of the rim.

3 Position the two salvias (**A**).
Add potting mix to keep them in place.

4 Place the flossflower (**B**) at the front with the curry plant (**C**) and senecio (**D**) on either side.

5 Add the two verbenas (**E**), one beside each of the sage plants.

6 Add potting mix until it is 1in (2.5cm) below the rim of the pot. Firm in the plants.

7 Water well.

SHADES OF GRAY

Plant in late spring or early summer for a display that will last through to the fall. Keep the pot in an open, sunny position. The dense planting of annuals and perennials will make frequent watering necessary. Apply a liquid fertilizer every two weeks, starting two to three weeks after planting. Deadhead regularly. After flowering, remove the curry plant to the open garden and discard the rest.

Terracotta pot, diameter 10in (25cm), depth 7in (17cm)
Pottery shards
Soil-based potting mix
2 dark blue salvias (*S. farinacea* 'Victoria'), page 176, **A**
1 compact flossflower (*Ageratum houstonianum*), page 173, **B**
1 curry plant (*Helichrysum italicum*), page 193, **C**
1 silver senecio (*S. cineraria* 'Silver Dust'), page 195, **D**
2 purple verbenas (*V. tenuisecta*) , page 171, **E**

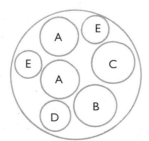

PINK WITH GRAY

Plant in early summer. Place in a sunny position, water well and apply a liquid fertilizer every two weeks, starting two to three weeks after planting. After flowering, discard the petunias and verbenas and move the diascias to the open garden. Overwinter the plectranthus and nemesias and take cuttings of the Paris daisy and helichrysum (see pages 82–83, 85).

Wooden planter, 20in (50cm) long and wide, 18in (45cm) deep
Rigid, fitted plastic liner
Pottery shards
Soil-based potting mix
3 white osteospermums (*O.* 'Blue Streak' and 'Silver Sparkler'), page 135, **A**
1 white double Paris daisy (*Argyranthemum* 'Qinta White'), page 131, **B**
1 white petunia, page 136, **C**
1 pink osteospermum (*O.* 'Pink Whirls'), page 135, **D**
2 pink verbenas (*V.* 'Silver Anne'), page 165, **E**
2 pink diascias (*D. vigilis*), page 160, **F**
1 gray-leaved helichrysum (*H. petiolare*), page 193, **G**
3 nemesias, 2 mauve and 1 purple (*N. caerulea*), page 169, **H**
2 plectranthus (*P. madagascariensis* 'Variegated Mintleaf'), page 187, **I**

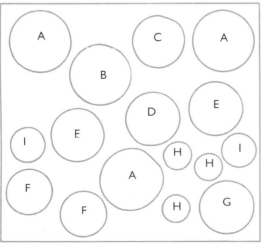

1 Scrub out the plastic liner and position it inside the planter.
2 Place pottery shards over the drainage holes. Fill the liner with potting mix to within 5in (13cm) of the rim.
3 Plant the white osteospermums (**A**), one in each of the back corners and one in the center near the front. Add mix around them.
4 Place the Paris daisy (**B**) and the petunia (**C**) between the two osteospermums in the back. In front of this row plant the pink osteospermum (**D**) with a verbena (**E**) on either side of it.
5 Put the two diascias (**F**) in the front left corner and the helichrysum (**G**) with nemesias (**H**) in an arc around it on the right.
6 Add the two plectranthus (**I**), one on either side of the planter.
7 Add potting mix to 2in (5cm) below the rim. Firm in the plants.
8 Water well.

101

PURPLE FOLIAGE

Deep purple foliage is uncommon among the plants most often used in container mixtures, but it is well worth including, because it seems to intensify the color of flowers that are placed close to it. Here, in a simple terracotta pot, a magnificently rich magenta petunia meets its match in a purple-leaved sweet basil (*below*). A wooden trough that is planted with a conventional mixture of scarlet nasturtiums and dwarf French marigolds is transformed by the addition of sultry purple-leaved cabbages (*opposite*). The daring mix of scarlet and orange flowers with the large, plum-purple leaves of the interlopers from the vegetable garden creates a stunning effect.

A POT OF BASIL AND PETUNIAS

Plant in late spring and place in a sunny, sheltered spot. Water regularly, but allow the potting mix to become almost dry between waterings. Apply a liquid fertilizer every two weeks, starting three to four weeks after planting. Pinch back the basil flowers as they develop and deadhead the petunias regularly. Discard all the plants in the fall.

Terracotta pot, diameter 8in (20cm), height 7in (17cm)
Pottery shards
Soil-based potting mix
1 purple-leaved sweet basil (*Ocimum basilicum* 'Purple
    Ruffles'), page 196, **A**
2 magenta petunias, page 170, **B**

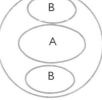

1 Scrub the pot and soak it thoroughly in clean water.
2 Put pottery shards over the drainage holes.
3 Fill the planter halfway with potting mix. Position the basil (A) in the center of the pot and a petunia (B) in front of and behind it.
4 Add mix to 1–2in (2.5–5cm) below the rim. Firm the plants.
5 Water well.

A TROUGH OF ANNUALS WITH CABBAGES

Put the trough in position, in full sun, before filling it. Planted in late spring, this combination will be attractive through most of the summer and into the fall. Water regularly and apply a weak liquid fertilizer every two weeks, starting two to three weeks after planting. Deadhead the marigolds and nasturtiums and tidy the leaves of both these plants and the cabbages frequently. Discard all the plants in the fall.

Wooden trough, length 54in (1.35m),
    width 12in (30cm), depth 10in
    (25cm)
Pottery shards
Soil-based or soil-less potting mix
9 purple-leaved cabbages (*Brassica
    oleracea* Capitata Group),
    page 189, **A**
18 dwarf French marigolds (*Tagetes*
    'Paprika'), page 148, **B**
5 scarlet-flowered nasturtiums
    (*Tropaeolum majus* 'Empress of
    India'), page 155, **C**

1 Scrub the trough thoroughly.
2 Place a layer of pottery shards over the bottom of the trough, making sure that the drainage holes are covered.
3 Fill with potting mix to within 4in (10cm) of the rim.
4 Plant the cabbages (A), placing one at each corner and one in the center at the back; distribute the other four in the remaining space.
5 Add a group of five French marigolds (B) in the front left of

the trough and another group of five at the back, to the right of the center cabbage. Then add two groups of three marigolds, one in front of the center cabbage and one in the front right. Finally, position another two marigolds at the back left.

6 Plant the nasturtiums (**C**), two at the back beside the corner cabbages and one in the middle of each end between the cabbages. Add another one off-center, to the front and left of the center cabbage.

7 Add potting mix to about 1–2in (2.5–5cm) below the rim of the trough. Firm in the plants.

8 Water well.

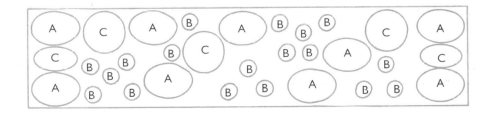

FOLIAGE CONTRASTS

Though flowers usually steal the limelight, it is often the skillful use of foliage that ensures the success of a container planting. The warm shades of the verbena 'Peaches and Cream' add their chameleon charm to this hanging basket. But the underlying strength of the planting is based on contrasts of foliage texture, leaf shape, and color, summed up in the rich mixture of the coleus.

BASKET OF BRIGHT FOLIAGE

Plant this hanging basket in late spring for a display that will last throughout the summer. Hang in a sunny, sheltered corner. Water the plants regularly and apply a liquid fertilizer every two weeks, starting two to three weeks after planting. Pinch back the coleus flowers as soon as they start to form; and deadhead the verbenas. Dismantle the planting in the fall, saving the heuchera for planting in the open garden. Rooted cuttings of the helichrysum can be overwintered (see pages 82–83, 85).

Wire-framed hanging basket,
    diameter 18in (45cm)

Wadding (or other) liner, page 56

Soil-based or soil-less potting mix

1 clump of purple-leaved heuchera
    (*H. micrantha* var. *diversifolia*
    'Palace Purple'), page 189, **A**

3 dark-leaved coleus (*Solenostemon*),
    page 191, **B**

3 warm-colored verbenas (*V.*'Peaches
    and Cream'), page 149, **C**

3 helichrysum with yellow-green
    leaves (*H. petiolare* 'Limelight'),
    page 184, **D**

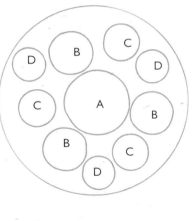

1 Position the hanging basket on an empty pail or large pot to give a stable base. Detach one chain. Position the liner in the hanging basket.

2 Fill the lined basket three-fourths full with potting mix.

3 Place the heuchera (**A**) in the center and and space the coleus (**B**) evenly around it. Add the verbenas (**C**) between the coleus and tuck the helichrysums (**D**) between the coleus and the verbenas.

4 Add more potting mix, to about 1in (2.5cm) below the rim of the basket. Firm in the plants.

5 Water well. Allow to drain before arranging the chains and hanging the basket in a sheltered but open and sunny position.

PLANTINGS IN IMPROVISED CONTAINERS

The blemishes of recycled containers sometimes need to be masked by planting, but when improvised pieces are of the quality of this oval terracotta vessel (*below*), originally intended for salting pork, or the fine copper tub (*opposite*), used for washing clothes, the planting should complement and not obscure the container. Both of these containers have drainage holes drilled in their bases.

A limited palette of pinks and purples has been used in the oval container. The copper tub is outstanding for its simple full shape, the regular pattern of its riveting, and above all for its magnificent patina. Trailing magenta petunias and deep purple heliotropes seem to intensify its blue-green hue, making a richly colored base to which white and pink Paris daisies provide a light topping.

AN OVAL CONTAINER

Planted in late spring and placed in an open, sunny position, this design will continue through summer into fall. Water well and apply a liquid fertilizer every two weeks, starting three weeks after planting. Deadhead regularly. Overwinter cuttings of the pelargoniums, helichrysum and verbenas (see pages 82–83, 85).

Terracotta container, length 20in (50cm),
   maximum width and depth 10in (25cm)
Pottery shards
Soil-based potting mix
1 white Paris daisy (*Argyranthemum*),
   page 130, **A**
2 white pelargoniums, page 135, **B**
2 trailing convolvulus (*C. sabatius*),
   page 174, **C**
1 gray-leaved helichrysum (*H. petiolare*),
   page 193, **D**
4 white verbenas (*V. tenuisecta* f. *alba*),
   page 136, **E**

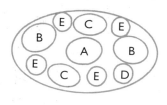

1 Scrub the container thoroughly and soak it in clean water.
2 Place pottery shards over the drainage holes, and fill with mix to within 4in (10cm) of the rim.
3 Position the Paris daisy (**A**) in the center and two pelargoniums (**B**) at either end. Draw potting mix around them.
4 Put in the convolvulus (**C**), one on either side of the Paris daisy. Place the helichrysum (**D**) at one end of the trough. Add the verbenas (**E**).
5 Add mix to 1–2in (2.5–5cm) below the rim. Firm in all plants.
6 Water well.

A BLUE-GREEN COPPER TUB

Set the copper tub in a sunny position before planting in late spring to provide a display that will continue through summer and into the fall. Water regularly but allow the mix to become nearly dry between waterings. Feed with liquid fertilizer every two weeks, starting two to three weeks after planting. Deadhead regularly. Overwinter cuttings of the hibiscus, Paris daisies and heliotropes (see pages 82–83, 85).

Copper tub, diameter 22in (55cm),
   depth 18in (45cm)
Pottery shards
Soil-based potting mix
3 white Paris daisies (*Argyranthemum foeniculaceum*), page 131, **A**
1 blue hibiscus (*Alyogyne huegelii*),
   page 158, **B**
2 pink double Paris daisies
   (*Argyranthemum* 'Vancouver'),
   page 158, **C**
2 dark purple heliotropes
   (*Heliotropium* 'Princess Marina'),
   page 169, **D**
2 magenta-flowered trailing petunias,
   page 170, **E**

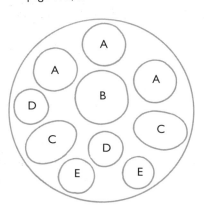

1 Scrub the copper tub and wash it thoroughly in clean water.

2 Place a layer of pottery shards in the base, covering the drainage holes, and fill to within 5in (13cm) of the rim with potting mix.

3 Set one white Paris daisy (A) at the back of the tub and the other two on either side and in front of it, adding potting mix around them to keep them firmly in position.

4 Plant the blue hibiscus (B) in the center and the two pink Paris daisies (C) on either side and in front of it.

5 Add potting mix to about 2in (5cm) below the rim and firm in the plants.

6 Plant one heliotrope (D) in front of the lilac hibiscus and the other at one edge behind a pink Paris daisy. Add the two petunias (E) to trail over the front of the copper tub. Firm in the plants.

7 Water well.

EYE-CATCHING REDS

These two plantings, very different in scale, both have prominent foliage centerpieces with brightly colored flowers assembled around them. In the window box planting (*below*) a hart's-tongue fern is surrounded by red New Guinea hybrid impatiens, extremely useful plants that provide bright colors over a long season and do best in partial shade. Their foliage can also be an attractive feature:

sometimes it is variegated and sometimes a dark purplish red. The imposing design in the large pot (*opposite*) features red pelargoniums and a spiky-leaved grass palm, in a spectacular display suitable for a sunny terrace or patio. Pelargoniums come in a good range of vibrant reds and also flower prolifically over a long season, but they need a position in full sun.

A WINDOW BOX FOR PARTIAL SHADE

Because the window box is light, it can be filled before being positioned. Place in partial shade in early summer. Water well and apply liquid fertilizer every two weeks, starting three to four weeks after planting. Deadhead the impatiens and pinch back plectranthus shoots (cuttings can be overwintered, see pages 82–83, 85). Discard the impatiens at the end of the season. The fern can be used in another planting.

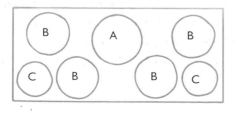

Terracotta window box, length 2ft (60cm), width and depth 10in (25cm)

Pottery shards

Soil-based potting mix

1 hart's-tongue fern (*Asplenium scolopendrium*), page 179, **A**

4 red impatiens (*I.* New Guinea hybrids), pages 161–62, **B**

2 variegated plectranthus (*P. madagascariensis* 'Variegated Mintleaf'), page 187, **C**

1 Scrub the window box and soak it thoroughly in clean water. Put pottery shards over the drainage holes, and fill the container three-fourths full with potting mix.

2 Plant the fern (**A**) as a centerpiece, slightly to the back, then surround it with the impatiens (**B**), two in the front and one on either side. Position the plectranthus (**C**) at the front corners of the window box.

3 Add potting mix to about 1in (2.5cm) below the rim of the window box. Firm in the plants.

4 Water well.

A SPECTACULAR POT OF VIBRANT COLOR

Plant in late spring or early summer and place the pot in full sun. Water regularly. If a slow-release fertilizer is incorporated into the potting mix, further applications of fertilizer should be unnecessary. The pelargoniums and the canna rhizomes can be overwintered (see page 85) and the grass palm reused in a subsequent planting.

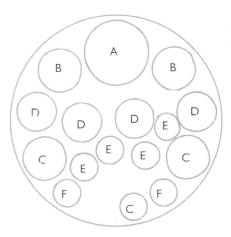

Terracotta pot, diameter 2ft (60cm), height 26in (65cm)

Pottery shards

Soil-based potting mix with slow-release fertilizer added

1 mature purple-leaved grass palm (*Cordyline australis* Purpurea Group), page 189, **A**

2 red cannas (*C.* 'Roi Humbert'), page 189, **B**

3 red Ivy-leaved pelargoniums (*P.* 'Yale'), page 154, **C**

4 red Zonal pelargoniums (*P.* 'Paul Crampel'), page 154, **D**

4 lime-green flowering tobacco plants (*Nicotiana* 'Lime Green'), page 142, **E**

2 red salvias (*S. fulgens*), page 155, **F**

1 Scrub the pot and soak it thoroughly in clean water. Place pottery shards over the drainage holes, and fill the pot halfway with potting mix.

2 Arrange the plants so they get maximum light on the side that provides the main view. Plant the grass palm (A) in the center but toward the back of the container. Position the cannas (B) on either side of it. Add potting mix around them to firm them in.

3 Position the Ivy-leaved pelargoniums (C), evenly spaced and tilted outward, around the edge of the pot. Plant the Zonal pelargoniums (D) along the centerline. Position the flowering tobacco plants (E) and the salvias (F) in front of the Zonal pelargoniums.

4 Add potting mix to about 2in (5cm) below the pot's rim. Firm in the plants.

5 Water well.

PLANTING FOR THE SETTING

These two plantings are appropriate for their setting, yet could be adapted to fit happily into other contexts. Both benefit from being raised on tree-stump pedestals. The plain terracotta pot (*below*) is planted with gray foliage, a magenta petunia and sprawling fan flowers. It is mounted at the boundary between the ordered garden and a wilder area. The color harmony extends the theme of the garden, but the asymmetry of the plants is in keeping with the gentle wildness beyond. Helichrysum and an upright grass (*opposite*) add height to the container planting in a yellow, cream, and mauve color theme that is radiant against a blue and yellow backdrop.

GRAY FOLIAGE WITH FAN FLOWERS AND PETUNIAS

Plant in late spring for an open sunny position. Water regularly and apply a weak liquid fertilizer every two weeks, starting three to four weeks after planting. Deadhead frequently. It is worth over-wintering cuttings of the plecostachys and the fan flower (see pages 82–83, 85).

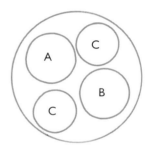

Terracotta pot, diameter 14in (35cm), height 12in (30cm)

Pottery shards

Soil-based potting mix

1 magenta petunia, page 170, **A**

1 plecostachys (*P. serpyllifolia*), pages 194–95, **B**

2 fan flowers (*Scaevola aemula* 'Blue Fan'), page 176, **C**

1 Scrub the pot and soak it thoroughly in clean water.
2 Cover the drainage holes with pottery shards. Fill with potting mix to within 4in (10cm) of the rim.
3 Set the petunia (**A**) and the plecostachys (**B**) on either side of the center of the pot. Place the two fan flowers (**C**) nearer to the edges.
4 Add potting mix to 2in (5cm) below the rim. Firm in the plants.
5 Water well.

A YELLOW, CREAM, AND MAUVE PLANTING

Plant in late spring for a summer-long display suitable for an open, sunny position. This dense planting will need frequent watering and should have a liquid fertilizer applied every two weeks, starting two to three weeks after planting. Mix water-retaining granules with the potting mix to even out fluctuations in moisture content. Deadhead petunias and trim back untidy or excessive growth. When the planting is dismantled in the fall, discard the petunias and flowering tobacco plants. It is worth overwintering the gardener's garters and cuttings of the other plants (see pages 82–83, 85).

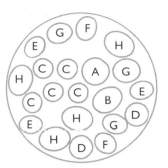

Ceramic container, diameter 20in (50cm),
    depth 16in (40cm)

Pottery shards

Soil-based or soil-less potting mix, with
    water-retaining granules incorporated

1 yellow petunia, page 142, **A**

1 white petunia, page 136, **B**

6 dwarf white flowering tobacco plants
    (*Nicotiana* 'White Bedder'), page 135, **C**

2 golden fleece (*Thymophylla tenuiloba*),
    page 143, **D**

3 gray-leaved helichrysum (*H. petiolare*),
    page 193, **E**

2 variegated helichrysum (*H. petiolare*
    'Variegatum'), page 193, **F**

2 gardener's garters (*Phalaris arundinacea*
    var. *picta*), page 187, **G**

4 brachyscomes (*B. multifida*),
    page 173, **H**

1 Scrub the container and wash it thoroughly.

2 Cover the drainage holes with pottery shards and fill to within 4in (10cm) of the rim with potting mix.

3 Position the petunias (A and B) and the flowering tobacco plants (C) in slightly off-center groups.

4 Space the golden fleece (D) and both the gray-leaved (E) and the variegated (F) helichrysum around the rim.

5 Add the two gardener's garters (G) at the right and toward the front of the pot. Tuck in the brachyscomes (H), two at the back and two toward the front.

6 Add potting mix to 2in (5cm) below the rim. Firm in the plants.

7 Water well.

CASCADING FUCHSIAS

With their elegant, pendulous flowers carried over a long season, the hybrid fuchsias make an invaluable group of shrubs for containers. Fuchsias with lax stems are particularly good as trailers for pots and hanging baskets, but even on more upright fuchsias the prettily shaped flowers dangle gracefully. Upright and trailing fuchsias can be combined together successfully, as they are in the handsome lattice-pattern terracotta pot (*see page 87*), with a trailing fuchsia forming a broad skirt. Bushy fuchsias help to complete the crown of a hanging basket (*opposite*) which includes several trailing plants, other fuchsias among them. Some especially beautiful fuchsias bear long tubular flowers with small, pointed petals. In another lattice-pattern pot (*pages 116–17*), *Fuchsia* 'Gartenmeister Bonstedt' glows among cool swirls of gray helichrysums and blue lobelias.

A POT OF FUCHSIAS

See illustration page 87

Plant in full sun in late spring. Water regularly and apply a liquid fertilizer every two weeks, starting two weeks after planting. Overwinter cuttings of the fuchsias and the salvia (see pages 82–83, 85).

Terracotta pot, diameter 17in (43cm),
   height 20in (50cm)
Pottery shards
Soil-based potting mix
1 bush fuchsia (*F.* 'Tom Woods'),
   page 168, **A**
1 trailing fuchsia (*F.* 'Jack Shahan'),
   page 161, **B**
1 dark-flowered salvia (*S. discolor*),
   page 176, **C**
2–3 bamboo stakes

1 Scrub and soak the pot.
2 Cover the drainage holes with pottery shards. Fill with potting mix to 5in (13cm) below the rim.
3 Plant the bush fuchsia (**A**) at the back, the trailing fuchsia (**B**) in the center, and the salvia (**C**) in front.
4 Add potting mix to 2in (5cm) below the rim. Firm in the plants.
5 Insert the stakes around the bush fuchsia.
6 Water well.

FUCHSIAS IN A HANGING BASKET

Plant in mid-spring. Fix a strong support in a sunny, sheltered spot (see page 43). Add water-retentive granules to the potting mix and water frequently, applying a liquid fertilizer every two weeks. Deadhead and trim regularly. Cuttings of the fuchsias, Paris daisies, and pelargoniums can be overwintered (see pages 82–83, 85).

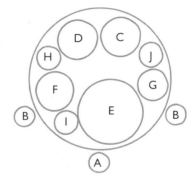

Wire-framed hanging basket, diameter 18in (45cm)
Synthetic liner
Soil-less potting mix with water-retentive granules
1 variegated ground ivy (*Glechoma hederacea* 'Variegata'), page 186, **A**
2 mauve-pink variegated Ivy-leaved pelargoniums, page 170, **B**
1 white bush fuchsia, page 132, **C**
1 pink Paris daisy (*Argyranthemum* 'Pink Australian'), page 158, **D**
1 red trailing fuchsia (*F.* 'Marinka'), page 153, **E**
1 white-and-pink trailing fuchsia, page 133, **F**
1 red Ivy-leaved pelargonium (*P.* 'Rote Mini-Cascade'), page 154, **G**
1 pink Ivy-leaved pelargonium (*P.* 'Madame Crousse'), page 163, **H**
1 gray-leaved helichrysum (*H. petiolare*), page 193, **I**
1 lime-green-leaved helichrysum (*H. petiolare* 'Limelight'), page 184, **J**

1 Detach one of the chains from the basket.

2 Place the basket on an upturned pot. Put a liner inside the basket and halfway fill it with potting mix.

3 Just above the mix level, cut the liner horizontally for 2in (5cm) at the center front of the basket. Make similar cuts on either side.

4 From outside the basket, push the root ball of the ground ivy (A) through the center slit. Push the two variegated pelargoniums (B) through the side slits. Add potting mix to 4in (10cm) below the basket's rim.

5 Plant the bush fuchsia (C) against the back of the basket and the Paris daisy (D) to its left. Place the red trailing fuchsia (E) in the center toward the front, the white-and-pink trailing fuchsia (F) to its left, and the red pelargonium (G) to its right.

6 Tuck in the pink pelargonium (H) and the helichrysums (I, J). Firm in the plants and add potting mix to 1in (2.5cm) below the rim of the basket.

7 Water well and allow to drain.

8 Reattach the chain and hang the basket.

A RED FUCHSIA WITH GRAYS AND BLUES

This planting is well suited to a prominent position. Symmetrical planting ensures that, through the free-flowing lines of the helichrysum veiling the other plants, the pot will look balanced from any angle. If planted in late spring, this design will provide an attractive display through summer into the fall. All the plants need full sun. Water regularly and apply a liquid fertilizer every two weeks, starting three weeks after planting. Rooted cuttings of the helichrysum and the fuchsia can be overwintered (see pages 82–83, 85). Discard the lobelias after flowering.

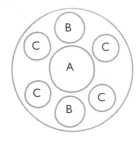

Terracotta pot, diameter 17in (43cm),
    height 20in (50cm)
Pottery shards
Soil-based potting mix
1 red bush fuchsia (F. 'Gartenmeister
    Bonstedt'), page 153, **A**
2 gray-leaved helichrysums (*H. petiolare*),
    page 193, **B**
4 blue-flowered lobelias, pages 175–76, **C**

1 Scrub the pot and soak it
thoroughly in clean water.
2 Cover the drainage holes with
pottery shards and fill the container
with potting mix to 5in (13cm)
below the rim.
3 Plant the fuchsia (**A**) in the center
of the pot. Set the two helichrysums
(**B**) on either side and space the four
lobelias (**C**) evenly around it.
4 Add potting mix to 1–2in
(2.5–5cm) below the pot's rim. Firm
in the plants.
5 Water well.

SOFT ORANGES AND YELLOWS

Intense orange can be magnificent when seen in brilliant sunlight but where the sun shines less fiercely, paler shades of peach and apricot are easier to manage. These colors are well represented in a large number of summer-flowering tender perennials and shrubby plants that thrive in sunny positions. They combine nicely with many other colors, including soft shades of yellow or cream, as shown here in a subtly restrained planting (*below*).

The appeal of the grand planting in the large container (*opposite*) lies partly in its fullness and in the wide range of plants included, but it could easily be simplified to take account of available plants and to suit a smaller pot.

A POT OF PEACHES AND CREAM

In this planting the verbena is placed against a background of the taller Sphaeralcea ambigua. *Plant in late spring, in a sunny position, for a display that will last through summer and into fall.. Water regularly and apply a liquid fertilizer every two weeks, starting three weeks after planting. Deadhead the verbena throughout the summer. It is worth overwintering cuttings of the sphaeralcea (see pages 82–83, 85).*

Terracotta pot,
    diameter 9in (23cm),
    depth 7in (17cm)
Pottery shards
Soil-based potting mix
I sphaeralcea *S. ambigua*,
    page 148, **A**
2 warm-colored verbenas
    ('Peaches and Cream'),
    page 149, **B**

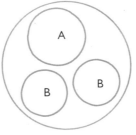

1 Scrub the pot and soak it in clean water.
2 Put pottery shards over the drainage holes and fill the pot halfway with potting mix.
3 Set the sphaeralcea (A) to form the background to the planting, and add mix around it. Place the verbenas (B) at the front.
4 Add mix to about 2in (5cm) below the pot's rim. Firm in the plants.
5 Water well.

TENDER PERENNIALS IN A TUB

Plant this mixture after the risk of frost is past and it will give a display that lasts through summer and into fall. Place this heavy tub in its final position, which should be open and sunny, before planting. The density of the planting makes frequent watering essential. Apply a liquid fertilizer every two weeks, starting two to three weeks after planting. Deadhead the flowers regularly through summer and fall. When dismantling the planting, keep the artemisia to plant in the open garden, or use in a subsequent container planting. Cuttings of the Paris daisies, osteospermum, and pelargoniums can be overwintered (see pages 82–83, 85).

Terracotta pot or tub, diameter 22in
    (55cm), depth 24in (60cm)
Pottery shards
Soil-based potting mix
I creamy yellow osteospermum
    (*O.* 'Buttermilk'), page 135, **A**
I white Paris daisy (*Argyranthemum
    gracile* 'Chelsea Girl'), page 131, **B**
2 yellow Paris daisies (*Argyranthemum
    callichrysum* 'Prado'), page 140, **C**
3 peach-pink pelargoniums, page 147, **D**
I cigar plant (*Cuphea ignea*),
    page 146, **E**
3 African daisies (*Arctotis* x *hybrida*
    'Apricot'), page 145, **F**
2 bidens (*B. ferulifolia*), page 140, **G**
I gray-leaved artemisia
    (*A. stelleriana*), page 192, **H**
I Swan River daisy (*Brachyscome
    iberidifolia*), pages 173–74, **I**

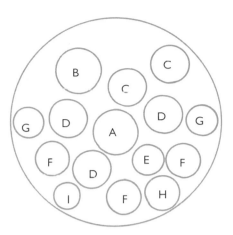

1 Scrub the pot and soak it in clean water.

2 Put pottery shards over the drainage holes, and add potting mix to about 5in (13cm) below the rim.

3 Position the osteospermum (**A**) in the center of the pot, adding mix around it to hold it in position. Place the white and yellow Paris daisies (**B** and **C**) behind the osteospermum.

4 Position the pelargoniums (**D**) and the cigar plant (**E**) to the front and sides of the osteospermum, forming two-thirds of a circle. Set the three African daisies (**F**) to make an arc in the foreground.

5 Position the bidens (**G**) on the center line at the rim and tuck in the artemisia (**H**) and Swan River daisy (**I**) at the edge in the foreground.

6 Add more mix, working it around the plants, to about 2in (5cm) below the rim of the pot. Firm in the plants.

7 Water well.

VIBRANT COLORS

Flamboyant reds and yellows tend to dominate the garden during the second half of summer. A few annuals or perennials gathered together, as in these terracotta pots, can create an incandescent display.

Sunflowers tower over a red and yellow mixture, the fiery tone set by one of the most strongly colored of the strawflowers combined with dwarf rudbeckias and coreopsis (*below*). All the components of this planting could be raised from seed sown in warmth in mid-spring.

A more subdued planting of perennials skillfully links foliage color with plants in the open garden (*opposite*). Bronze-purples in the garden are picked up in the arching leaves of the phormium and in the heuchera with its irregularly cut, heart-shaped leaves, which have a metallic sheen. A dwarf form of the short-lived blanket flower provides a radiant mix of red and yellow.

A FIERY MIXTURE

Whether you raise these bright annuals from seed or buy them as young stock, plant the pot in late spring. The container is positioned to show it off from one angle and to expose all plants to maximum sunlight. Water regularly and apply liquid fertilizer every two weeks, starting two to three weeks after planting. Discard plants at the end of their flowering season.

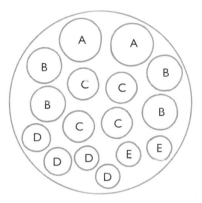

Terracotta pot, diameter 18in
   (45cm), height 20in (50cm)

Pottery shards

Soil-based potting mix

2 sunflowers (*Helianthus annuus* 'Valentine'), page 141, **A**

4 tickseeds (*Coreopsis tinctoria*), page 141, **B**

4 dwarf rudbeckias (*R. hirta* Rustic Dwarfs), page 148, **C**

4 strawflowers (*Helichrysum bracteatum* 'Hot Bikini'), page 146, **D**

2 oncosiphons (*O. grandiflorum*), page 142, **E**

1 Scrub the pot and soak it in clean water. Put pottery shards over the drainage holes and fill with potting mix to 4in (10cm) below the rim.
2 Plant the sunflowers (A) at the back of the pot with the coreopsis (B) on either side. Add rudbeckias (C) in the center, strawflowers (D) in front of them, and the oncosiphons (E) to the left.
3 Add mix to about 2in (5cm) below the pot's rim. Firm in the plants.
4 Water well.

A POT OF PURPLE, YELLOW, AND RED

Plant in mid-spring for a summer display in full sun. Water regularly and apply a liquid fertilizer every two weeks, starting two to three weeks after planting. At the end of their flowering season, dig up the plants and move them to the open garden.

Terracotta pot, diameter 20in (50cm), height 16in (40cm)

Pottery shards

Soil-based potting mix

1 bronze-leaved phormium (*P.* 'Bronze Baby'), page 190, **A**

1 purple-leaved heuchera (*H. micrantha* var. *diversifolia* 'Palace Purple'), page 189–90, **B**

3 dwarf blanket flowers (*Gaillardia* 'Kobold'), page 146, **C**

1 variegated aquilegia, page 167, **D**

1 Scrub the pot and soak it in clean water. Put pottery shards over the drainage holes and fill with potting mix to 4in (10cm) below the rim.
2 Plant the phormium (A) off-center, at the back, and the heuchera (B) in front of it, at their previous planting depths. Space the blanket flowers (C) evenly, and place the aquilegia (D) at the front.
3 Add potting mix to 1–2in (2.5–5cm) below the rim. Firm in the plants.
4 Water well.

A PLANTING FOR WINTER AND SPRING

Where the climate is sufficiently mild, dwarf evergreen shrubs, especially those that bear berries or flower in the coldest part of the year, make outstanding container plants for winter displays. Skimmias are compact, slow-growing, shade-tolerant evergreens that bear male and female flowers on different plants. With oval, leathery, pale or darker green leaves, they are good foliage plants throughout the year; but their glory lies in the brilliant globular red berries, borne in tight clusters, that make the female plants so ornamental from winter through to spring.

To produce good crops of berries the female skimmias need a male plant close by. The ideal arrangement is to use two or three female plants, spangled with polished red berries set among glossy foliage, as a skirt to a taller male skimmia. In the planting here, the low-growing *Skimmia japonica* subsp. *reevesiana* is matched with the more vigorous male plant *S. j.* 'Rubella'. The latter has sweetly scented white flowers that open from pink buds in spring, and is also eye-catching from early to mid-winter, when the beautiful buds, reddish-brown in the early stages, are clustered on red stalks (*below*). The addition of a spring-flowering bulb, such as a white hyacinth, gives the planting a boost in spring (*opposite*). Skimmias need repotting only when their roots become congested.

EVERGREEN FOLIAGE WITH FLOWERS AND BERRIES

Plant this arrangement in early to mid-fall. In winter and spring it can be in a sunny site, but in summer it must have shade. Move the hyacinths to the open garden when they fade.

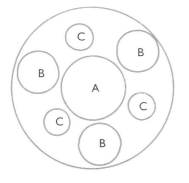

Terracotta pot, diameter 12in (30cm), depth 10in (25cm)

Pottery shards

Acidic-soil mix incorporating slow-release fertilizer

1 male skimmia (*S. japonica* 'Rubella'), page 203, **A**

3 female skimmias (*S. j.* subsp. *reevesiana*), page 203, **B**

3 white hyacinths (*H. orientalis* 'Carnegie'), page 129, **C**

1 Scrub the pot and soak it thoroughly in clean water.

2 Put pottery shards over the drainage holes. Fill the container halfway with potting mix.

3 Position the male skimmia (**A**) in the center with the female plants (**B**) around it. Insert the hyacinths (**C**) between the female skimmias at a depth of 4in (10cm).

4 Add mix until it is 1–2in (2.5–5cm) below the pot's rim. Firm in the plants.

5 Water well.

COLOR FOR LATE WINTER

Numerous dwarf bulbs shorten the long winter months by flowering well before the main burst of spring daffodils and tulips. Their effect is sometimes lost in the open garden but in containers they create a concentrated, vivid display. Irises, crocuses, and dwarf daffodils, star performers in late winter, have flowers that appear fragile yet stand up well to cold, rough weather. Some evergreen foliage with yellow or cream variegation makes a sunny addition to winter containers, and relieves the starkness of bulbs.

Place containers planted with these delightful forerunners of spring in prominent positions where they can be seen in comfort from indoors, or beside paths and doors that are used regularly. The displays put on by the late-winter bulbs may not be long-lived, but they are very heartening while they last. Where there is room, a succession of plantings can be held in reserve. Bring pots out as plants begin to bloom and replace them when the flowering is over.

DECORATED POT WITH DWARF DAFFODILS AND IRIS

The yellow variegation of the osmanthus and ivy is seen at its best in an open, sunny position. Plant these perennial foliage plants in fall, at the same time as the bulbs. Where winters are severe, plant them in spring, adding the bulbs in the early fall. Replace the bulbs annually. Repot the foliage plants every two years, top-dressing with fresh mix in the year between.

Glazed and decorated pot, diameter 8in (20cm),
   depth 6in (15cm)

Pottery shards

Soil-based potting mix

1 yellow-variegated osmanthus (*O. heterophyllus* 'Goshiki'), page 185, **A**

2 green ivies, pages 180–81, **B**

1 yellow-variegated ivy (*Hedera helix* 'Golden Ingot'), page 184, **C**

2 dwarf daffodils (*Narcissus* 'Tête-à-Tête'), pages 138–39, **D**

4 yellow dwarf iris (*I. danfordiae*), page 144, **E**

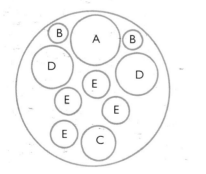

1 Scrub the pot and soak it thoroughly in clean water.

2 Put pottery shards over the drainage holes, and fill to within 2in (5cm) of the rim with potting mix.

3 Position the osmanthus (**A**) and the green ivies (**B**) at the back of the pot and the variegated ivy (**C**) in front.

4 Add potting mix to about 1in (2.5cm) below the rim of the pot, firming in the plants.

5 Plant the daffodil bulbs (**D**) on either side of the osmanthus and place the dwarf irises (**E**) in front of them. Use a sharp stick or a pencil to make holes so that they are set 2–3in (5–8cm) deep. Firm the surface.

6 Water well.

IRIS AND CROCUS WITH THYME

The thyme and bulbs in this planting do best in an open, sunny position, and need a free-draining potting mix. Where the climate allows, plant the thyme in fall, at the same time as the bulbs. Trim the thyme after flowering to keep it neat, but discard when plants become straggly, after three or four years. Use new bulbs each year. Top-dress with fresh potting mix in spring.

Black plastic pot, diameter 8in
    (20cm), depth 6in (15cm)
Pottery shards
Soil-based potting mix with
    added grit
1 yellow-variegated thyme
    (*Thymus serpyllum*
    'Goldstream'), page 185, **A**
15 blue Reticulata irises
    (*I.* 'Harmony'), page 177, **B**
10 deep yellow crocuses
    (*C. chrysanthus* var.
    fuscotinctus), page 144, **C**

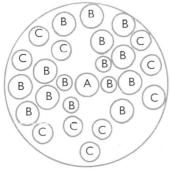

1 Scrub the pot and soak it thoroughly in clean water.
2 Place pottery shards in the base of the pot, covering the drainage holes, and fill to within 2in (5cm) of the rim with potting mix.
3 Plant the thyme (**A**) in the center of the pot, adding potting mix so that when firmed the surface is about 1in (2.5cm) below the rim of the container.
4 Plant the iris (**B**) and crocus bulbs (**C**) all around the thyme. Lift the foliage of the thyme and use a sharp stick or a pencil to make holes so that the bulbs are set 2–3in (5–8cm) deep.
5 Water well.

PLANTS FOR CONTAINERS

This directory lists more than a thousand plants, all of which can be grown by the amateur gardener. It groups entries into four sections. The first section covers the plants, ranging from low-growing trailers to large shrubs, which are grown primarily for their flowers. To help you design attractive schemes, the plants in this section are grouped according to flower color. The second section covers many other ornamental plants with attractive foliage, which are grouped according to the color of their leaves. The third section includes three categories: herbs, vegetables, and fruit. Finally, there is a small section on berrying plants and grasses. Within all of these sections plants are listed alphabetically according to botanical (Latin) name, but the common name introduces each entry. Where there is more than one entry for plants (tulips, for example, have several entries because of their wide color range) a cross-reference in bold type indicates the entry containing cultivation information.

Plants marked poisonous contain certain compounds that may prove toxic to people or pets. There is still much work to be done in this field as more plants are evaluated for toxicity. Never assume that a plant is nontoxic or nonpoisonous.

Many of the simplest but most effective container gardening schemes rely on a happy combination of flowers and foliage. Starry pelargoniums, their flowers elegantly poised above beautifully cut and marked foliage, are a valuable addition to many container garden combinations. A coral and salmon fuchsia emerges here from a subtly textured and colored base formed from its own foliage, the scented-leaved pelargonium 'Lady Plymouth', and the gray-leaved, trailing Helichrysum petiolare.

WHITE TO CREAM FLOWERS

Whether you are looking for individual specimens of refined beauty, dazzling additions to give a lift to mixtures, or collections for all-white schemes, you will find a wide range of plants among the whites. Extending this range are the many near-whites in which tints or stains provide links with stronger colors. The creams are particularly beautiful, almost as luminous as white in the evening light, but softer and warmer in full sun.

SPRING

ARABIS

Arabis alpina subsp. *caucasica* 'Flore Pleno'
EVERGREEN PERENNIAL ZONES 3–8
This spreading evergreen (*below*), often listed as *A. caucasica* 'Flore Pleno', makes a mat of gray-green leaves about 20in (50cm) wide. The double white flowers, clustered on stems 9in (23cm) high in late spring and early summer, look somewhat like miniature stocks.

Plant arabis so that it trails over the edge of a planter filled with other sun-loving alpines, using a gritty, free-draining, soil-based potting mix. Deadhead and trim back straggling stems after flowering.

Arabis *Arabis alpina* subsp. *caucasica* 'Flore Pleno'

Camellia *Camellia japonica* 'Alba Plena'

CAMELLIA

Camellia japonica
EVERGREEN SHRUB ZONES 7–9
Camellias are outstanding shrubs for containers, treasured for their polished dark green leaves as well as for their elegant flowers. Flower color is predominantly pink or red, but there are several white forms, with flowers ranging from single through semi-double to fully double.

The single 'Alba Simplex' has conspicuous stamens, while the petals of the fully double 'Shiragiku' (syn. *C. j.* 'Purity') are arranged with formal precision. An impressive formal double with overlapping petals is the bushy 'Alba Plena' (*above*). 'Lady Vansittart' is a semi-double, with white petals streaked pink.
See also pages **150**, **156**.

CLEMATIS

Clematis
VINE ZONES 3–9 POISONOUS
Many of the spring-flowering clematis are too vigorous to do well in containers, but those that are less rampant add an appealing dimension to the garden when they are trained up supports, or when allowed to trail.

C. alpina var. *sibirica* has a green-tinged selection, 'White Moth', which produces masses of nodding double flowers in late spring. It rarely exceeds 6ft (1.8m) in height.

C. florida 'Sieboldii' (Z6–9) has double flowers, white with a hint of

green surrounding a purple boss. Cut both back lightly when the flowers have faded.
See also pages **131–32**, *156, 159, 167, 174.*

CROCUS

Crocus vernus 'Jeanne d'Arc'
CORM ZONES 3–8
This large Dutch crocus blooms in early spring, producing sturdy flowers up to 5in (13cm) high. The tongues of orange styles are eye-catching in the white bowls formed by rounded petals.

Plant in fall, using a free-draining soil-based or soil-less potting mix (add coarse sand if necessary). Set corms just over 2in (5cm) deep and close to one another but not touching. Use alone or plant together with other spring flowers in pots or a sunny window box.
See also pages *137,* **138**, *144, 149, 166, 171, 177.*

FRITILLARY

Fritillaria meleagris var. *alba*
BULB ZONES 5–8 POISONOUS
The netting and veining on the drooping bells of the checkered lily give this white variety a lovely, green-tinged pallor (*below*). Plant in fall among mixed spring flowers.
See also page **166**.

Fritillary *Fritillaria meleagris* var. *alba*

HYACINTH

Hyacinthus orientalis
BULB ZONES 4–8
The densely packed, waxy flower heads of all hyacinths are intensely fragrant. Two popular whites, 'Carnegie' and 'L'Innocence', both have spikes about 8in (20cm) high. 'Carnegie' produces tightly packed spikes of pure white in mid-spring. 'L'Innocence' is less congested and has ivory-white flowers.
See also pages 138, 150, 156, 172; illustrations pages 41, 123.

DAFFODIL, NARCISSUS, JONQUIL

Narcissus
BULB ZONES 3–8
The bewitchingly fragrant *N. papyraceus* (*N.* 'Paper White', Z9–10), with bunches of white, starry flowers, though deservedly popular as an indoor pot plant for winter, is too tender to be grown outdoors except in very mild areas. However, there are many white daffodils that are more robust.

Early spring brings 'February Silver', a Cyclamineus daffodil that is usually less than 14in (35cm) tall. The trumpet, surrounded by milky petals, fades from lemon-yellow to cream. 'Ice Follies', only 16in (40cm) in height, is more heavily built and useful for exposed gardens. Creamy petals surround a frilled cup, which fades from primrose to near-white as it ages.

In mid-spring, 'Dove Wings' produces flowers with milky white, swept-back petals and a pale yellow trumpet on a stem rarely more than 12in (30cm) high. 'Petrel', only 10in (25cm) high and ideal for a window box, produces two or three stems per bulb, each carrying as many as five small-cupped flowers of pure white.

'Actaea' (*right*), a hybrid of the poet's narcissus (*N. poeticus*), blooms in late spring and is sweetly scented. Growing to a height of 20in (50cm), it has glistening white petals surrounding a small yellow cup with an orange rim. 'Cheerfulness', also late flowering and sometimes more than 20in (50cm) tall, bears one to three double flowers per stem. They are cream with a yellow center and have a delicious scent. 'Silver Chimes' (Z5–8) is slightly more tender. Stems 14in (35cm) high carry about six flowers each; the small cup is pale yellow and the petals are pure white.
*See also pages **138–39**, 144, 145.*

MOSS PHLOX

Phlox subulata 'White Delight'
EVERGREEN PERENNIAL ZONES 3–9
In mid- to late spring, the moss phlox is a mound of flat, starry flowers, mainly in pinks, mauves, and reds. The mat of small linear leaves obscured at this season is not more than 4in (10cm) high, but can have a spread of over twice this. The vigorous 'White Delight' is a dazzling selection.
Grow in a gritty, soil-based potting mix with the container positioned in full sun. Trim plants after flowering to keep them compact.
See also page 163.

JAPANESE PIERIS

Pieris
EVERGREEN SHRUB ZONES 5–9
The medium-sized and occasionally large shrubs that make up this evergreen genus are often remarkable for the brilliant coloring of their young foliage in spring as well as for their sprays of waxy flowers, which are usually attractive in bud throughout the winter months. As container-grown plants they are reasonably compact but since they spread at the base they are best planted alone. None tolerates alkaline soil, so grow in a pot or tub filled with specially formulated acid soil mix.

P. formosa var. *forrestii*, of which there are several named forms, is relatively

Daffodil *Narcissus* 'Actaea'

tender (Z8) and needs a sheltered position. When container grown, it is unlikely to exceed a height and spread of 6ft (1.8m). In spring, it produces brilliant scarlet young leaves, which then pass through pink and pale yellow before turning dark green. The sprays of white lily-of-the-valley flowers often coincide with the most vivid phase of the foliage.

Of similar size are several selections of the hardier *P. japonica*. Their young foliage is generally either bronze tinted or reddish, and lax sprays of fragrant white flowers, attractive in bud, open to white or pink flowers. A good example is 'Scarlett O'Hara', with reddish young foliage and pure white flowers.

Plant alone in a large pot, using an acidic-soil mix, and place in a lightly shaded, sheltered position. Pruning is rarely needed, but remove the seed pods as soon as they start to develop.

RHODODENDRON, AZALEA

Rhododendron
SHRUB ZONES 3–9
'Palestrina', an evergreen or semi-evergreen azalea (Z6–9), makes a bush about 4ft (1.2m) in height and spread, which in late spring carries masses of funnel-shaped flowers. Faint green stripes give their whiteness a cool distinction.

'Silver Sixpence' is one of the *R. yakushimanum* hybrids (Z4–8). Although it can have a spread of 5ft (1.5m), it is rarely more than 3ft (90cm) high. In late spring and early summer, trusses of creamy flowers prettily marked with lemon spots stud the evergreen foliage.
*See also pages 139, 142, 145, 148, 150, **156–57** 167, 173.*

TULIP

Tulipa
BULB ZONES 3–8
White and cream tulips strike a distinctive note in the container garden. Shapely singles in unadulterated white and cream create a formal effect. Much less restrained are the doubles and also the many forms, both doubles and singles, that are streaked and feathered with other colors.

T. turkestanica is a starry-flowered species that is attractive mixed with alpines. Blooming in early spring, its slender stems, up to 12in (30cm) high, carry as many as six or seven white

Tulip *Tulipa* 'White Triumphator'

flowers, marked cream and green on the outside and with a yellow center.

'Diana', a single with pure white, egg-shaped blooms on sturdy stems 14in (35cm) high, flowers in early to mid-spring. 'Purissima', also known as 'White Emperor', flowers at the same time. Strong , 18in (45cm) high stems carry beautifully shaped, milky, single flowers with yellow centers. 'Carnaval de Nice', a double with a densely packed bowl of white petals streaked with red blooms in the same period. The stems, 16in (40cm) high, carry the flowers over variegated leaves.

In mid-spring, 'Schoonoord', a stocky double 12in (30cm) high, has peonylike flowers of milky whiteness; it is suitable for a window box. 'Mount Tacoma' is a long-lasting double for mid- to late spring with pure white flowers on stems 18in (45cm) high.

White tulips for late spring include 'Maureen', a milky white, tall single up to 2ft (60cm) high, and, at the same height, 'Estella Rijnveld', also a single, but such a confection of twisted and fringed petals streaked red and white that the shape appears to dissolve.

'Shirley' flowers in late spring, its stems 20in (50cm) or more high carrying single ivory-white blooms with delicate purple feathering. 'White Triumphator' (*above*) is one of the elegant Lily-flowered tulips, with gracefully curving, pointed petals. The single flowers are carried on stems 26in (65cm) high in late spring.
*See also pages 140, 145, **150–51**, 157, 167; illustration page 8.*

SUMMER

AFRICAN LILY
Agapanthus
PERENNIAL ZONES 8–11
A. campanulatus var. *albidus* is a white variety of the more familiar blue African lily. Strap-shaped leaves and heads of numerous attractive white funnels are held on erect sturdy stems that are 2ft (60cm) high.
*See also page **173**.*

MOUNT ATLAS DAISY
Anacyclus pyrethrum subsp. *depressus*
PERENNIAL ZONES 6–8
Low shrubs and prostrate perennials with a long flowering season are especially useful in planters and other containers featuring alpine-garden plants. The Mount Atlas daisy, a native of Morocco, may prove short-lived, but makes up for this shortcoming by flowering profusely throughout summer. Ground-hugging stems about 12in (30cm) long, which provide the framework for mats of finely cut leaves, radiate from a central rootstock. The up-turned stem tips carry white daisy flowers, which are rusty red in bud.

Plant in a sunny position in early fall or mid-spring, using a gritty, free-draining, soil-based potting mix.

ANTHEMIS
Anthemis punctata subsp. *cupaniana*
EVERGREEN PERENNIAL ZONES 5–9
This relative of the common chamomile makes aromatic silvery cushions up to 12in (30cm) wide and high, composed of finely dissected leaves. Single daisies 2in (5cm) wide or more are borne profusely in late spring and summer.

Plant in a gritty, soil-based potting mix and position in sun, among other alpine-garden plants. Deadhead the blooms regularly to ensure a long flowering season.

SNAPDRAGON
Antirrhinum majus 'White Wonder'
HALF-HARDY ANNUAL
A. majus 'White Wonder' has flower spikes 18in (45cm) high (*right*). The flowers, white with a yellow throat, are of classic snapdragon form, tubular with five flared petal lobes about the closed mouth.
*See also pages 140, **151**, 158, 167.*

AFRICAN DAISY
Arctotis
HALF-HARDY ANNUAL
The sprawling *A. fastuosa* 'Zulu Prince' (*Venidium fastuosum* 'Zulu Prince'), with a height and spread of 2ft (60cm), has gray woolly leaves and large cream daisies, up to 4in (10cm) wide, with a black ring and center. *A. venusta* (syn. *A. stoechadifolia*) has gray-green leaves and flowers that are blue in bud, opening white to show a blue center surrounded by a yellow ring.
*See also page **145**.*

PARIS DAISY, MARGUERITE
Argyranthemum
EVERGREEN PERENNIAL ZONES 9–10
The Paris daisy (sometimes listed under its former name of *Chrysanthemum frutescens*) is one of the most useful standbys of the container garden, with a nonstop display of white daisy flowers through summer and into fall. In its native Canary Islands and in similarly mild areas, it will flower outdoors throughout most of the year. Elsewhere, it can be overwintered under glass, but is commonly treated as an annual, young plants being bought in late spring or early summer and discarded in fall.

This subshrubby perennial grows 18–36in (45–90cm) high, with a spread of up to 30in (75cm). Specimens can be trained as standards to a height of about 5ft (1.5m). The feathery foliage,

Snapdragon *Antirrhinum majus* 'White Wonder'

either gray-green or dark green, is often nearly hidden by the daisies, which are 2in (5cm) across.

A similar and equally free-flowering marguerite is *A. foeniculaceum* of gardens, which is distinguished by its finely dissected, blue-green leaves. *A. gracile* 'Chelsea Girl' is another pretty white single and 'Blizzard', 'Mrs F. Sander', and 'Qinta White' (also listed as *A.* 'Sark') are all good doubles, with a height of 2ft (60cm) and a spread of 18in (45cm).

Plant singly in containers (this is the best way to grow standards) or combine them with other sun-loving plants, using a soil-based potting mix. Deadhead regularly throughout the flowering season to keep plants blooming. If overwintering large specimens under glass, cut back hard in fall and trim in spring. *See also pages 140, 158; illustrations pages 10, 12, 20, 98, 101, 108, 109, 119.*

BROWALLIA

Browallia
HALF-HARDY ANNUAL/PERENNIAL
ZONES 9–10
The blue forms of browallia are the best known, but 'White Troll' makes a useful variation for mixed plantings in hanging baskets, window boxes, and other containers in sunny, sheltered positions. These compact plants, with a height and spread of 10in (25cm), flower through summer and into fall. *See also page 174.*

LING, SCOTCH HEATHER

Calluna vulgaris
EVERGREEN SHRUB ZONES 5–7
There are many forms of this dwarf shrub, with a wide range of flower and foliage color. Those with white flowers provide an attractive variation on the more familiar purples and mauves.

'White Lawn', only 2in (5cm) high but often with a spread of more than 12in (30cm), is ideal for softening the hard edge of a container. An upright alternative with silver-gray foliage is 'Anthony Davis', 18in (45cm) high. Both flower in late summer and fall. *See also pages 159, 183.*

BELLFLOWER

Campanula
PERENNIAL ZONES 3–8
The lovely bellflower *C. carpatica* subsp. *turbinata* f. *alba* makes a clump of toothed leaves, rarely more than 6in

(15cm) high but 10in (25cm) or so wide, covered in mid- to late summer with exquisite, saucer-shaped flowers, their whiteness tinged by the merest hint of blue.

For the second half of summer, another pretty alpine-garden plant is *C. cochleariifolia* subsp. *alba*, which is usually less than 6in (15cm) in height. However, it spreads so vigorously that it is not a suitable companion for really choice miniatures. Little bells of dazzling white hang down from wiry stems. *See also page 174.*

Madagascar periwinkle *Catharanthus roseus* 'Pretty-in-White'

MADAGASCAR PERIWINKLE, VINCA

Catharanthus roseus
HALF-HARDY ANNUAL POISONOUS
With their phloxlike flowers, the Madagascar periwinkles make a delightful contribution to mixed plantings in window boxes, hanging baskets, and pots. In 'Pretty in-White' (*above*) a yellow eye relieves the purity of the petals. Another cultivar, 'Parasol', has a red eye.

MEXICAN ORANGE BUSH

Choisya ternata
EVERGREEN SHRUB ZONES 7–9
Glossy aromatic leaves, boldly divided into three, make *C. ternata* an impressive shrub year round. The leaves are at their best when showing off the large clusters of pure white fragrant

Mexican orange bush *Choisya ternata*

flowers in spring (*above*) and often again at the end of summer, or even in late fall or a mild winter. The main display is particularly prolific, flowers studding plants that in pots are usually less than 5ft (1.5m) high and 6ft (1.8m) across at the base.

Plant singly, using a soil-based potting mix, in full sun or light shade, sheltered from cold winds. Cut out frost-damaged shoots in early spring, and trim any straggling stems in late spring or early summer, when the flowers have faded.

CLEMATIS

Clematis
VINE ZONES 3–9 POISONOUS
Clematis are among the most versatile and beautiful of vines, and there are single and double varieties in a wide color range for most seasons. In the container garden, those of moderate vigor are more useful than their rampant cousins. Those to be trained upward need supports on which leaf tendrils can grip. They can also be grown trailing from tall containers.

The following white-flowered clematis are fairly restrained in their growth and in containers are unlikely to exceed 12ft (3.7m).

'Marie Boisselot', sometimes listed as 'Madame Le Coultre', is a large-flowered hybrid with beautiful form; its flowers are pure white, although pink tinged when opening, and appear in early summer and sometimes again later. 'Henryi', another large-flowered hybrid, may produce its pure white single flowers in late as well as early summer. In late summer and early fall, 'Alba Luxurians' (*below*), one of the loveliest of the *C. viticella* hybrids, produces its small nodding flowers, green at the tips and with dark stamens.

Plant in fall or spring, using a soil-based potting mix. Provide supports for training. Prune early-flowering clematis lightly in early summer, after flowering. Prune late-flowering clematis hard in early spring. Prune large-flowered hybrids lightly in spring. Top-dress with fresh mix in spring.
See also pages 128, 156, 159, 167, 174.

Clematis *Clematis* 'Alba Luxurians'

CUP-AND-SAUCER VINE, MONASTERY BELLS

Cobaea scandens 'Alba'
ANNUAL/PERENNIAL VINE ZONES 9–10
This vigorous but tender vine attaches itself with tendrils to a support and can reach great heights – up to 15ft (5m) in a single growing season. Specimens grown as perennials in frost-free areas flower from spring through to early winter, while those grown as annuals in

Cup-and-saucer vine *Cobaea scandens* 'Alba'

gardens in temperate climates flower from late summer to fall, when started in early spring under glass. The bell-shaped, nodding flowers bloom one to a stem, 'Alba' (*above*) having greenish-white bells with a green calyx.
See also pages 167–68.

COSMOS

Cosmos
HALF-HARDY ANNUAL
Cosmos are easy and rewarding annuals, providing an airy display of single, dahlialike flowers over finely cut leaves in summer and fall. They are most commonly grown as mixtures, with pinks and reds predominating. 'Sonata', with dazzling gold-centered white flowers, is particularly well suited to growing in containers, since it has sturdy stems and grows to a height of 2ft (60cm).

Raise from seed, sowing in warmth in early spring. Plant in groups, using any soil-based or soil-less potting mix. Avoid excessive fertilizing, which will encourage foliage at the expense of flowers. Deadhead regularly.
See also pages 152, 159–60; illustration page 23.

PINK

Dianthus
PERENNIAL ZONES 4–8
Despite their common name, there are several enchanting white forms of these drought-tolerant, sun-loving perennials with their distinctive gray-green foliage. Many of the old-fashioned pinks that have been in cultivation for many years have a ravishing scent. Among them is 'Musgrave's Pink' (also known as 'Charles Musgrave'), a green-eyed, single white with prettily fringed petals. 'Mrs Sinkins', a rather loose double white, is said to have the most powerful scent of all. In some pinks, the form of the flower is emphasized by dark markings: 'Dad's Favorite', for example, has a white ground with purple lacing.

The faster-growing modern pinks flower mainly in early to mid-summer, but often flower again in the fall. A splendid example is the fully double white 'Haytor'.
See also pages 152–53, 160.

AFRICAN DAISY, STAR OF THE VELDT

Dimorphotheca sinuata
HALF-HARDY ANNUAL
Sometimes listed as *Osteospermum aurantiacum*, this sun-loving daisy is normally grown as a summer-flowering annual. 'Glistening White' is compact, usually less than 10in (25cm) high, with silky petals that contrast with the slate-blue center. The flowers do not open in shade or when the weather is dull. For a bold effect, use on its own in a low container.

To raise from seed, sow under glass in early spring in Z8 and colder areas, in either a soil-based or a soil-less potting mix. Position in full sun and deadhead regularly.

FUCHSIA

Fuchsia
DECIDUOUS SHRUB ZONE 10
The dangling flowers of many fuchsia hybrids are bi-colored, the tube and four waxy sepals being of one color and the skirt of petals another. All those selected here have white petals.

The following three cultivars usually produce plants with a height and spread of no more than 2–3ft (60–90cm) in a season. 'Annabel' is a double in which all parts of the flower are white. 'Hawkshead' (Z8–10), a single, has white petals and the rest of the flower is also white but with a green tinge. 'Madame Cornelissen' (Z8–10)is a semi-double with cerise-veined white petals; the rest of the flower is pale pink. These last two are often listed as hardy fuchsias.

Among the trailing hybrids, ideal for hanging baskets and window boxes, is 'Sophisticated Lady', a double in white and pale pink. 'Swingtime' (Z9–10), another double, has creamy white petals; the rest of the flower is red. *See also pages 153, 160–61, 168; illustration page 115.*

SUN ROSE

Helianthemum 'Wisley White'
EVERGREEN SHRUB ZONES 6–9
This is a pretty sun rose with gray-green leaves, growing to 10in (25cm) high, with a spread of 12in (30cm); the white flowers of this cultivar have yellow centers, giving an overall effect of cream.
See also pages 141, 146, 161.

HYDRANGEA

Hydrangea
SHRUB ZONES 6–9
H. macrophylla 'Madame Emile Mouillère' is a fine white mophead hydrangea with a long flowering season, and is ideal for planting in a formal situation, such as in matched containers.

H.m. 'Lanarth White', a compact lacecap hydrangea, has flower heads with small fertile florets in the center, surrounded by large sterile florets.

Other deciduous hydrangeas suitable for containers include *H. quercifolia* (Z5–9) and *H. paniculata* (Z4–8). *H. quercifolia* has handsome lobed leaves, which color well in fall, and in mid-summer produces pyramid-shaped, milky white flower heads, which take on a purplish tint as they age. In containers it has a height and spread of about 4ft (1.2m). The most widely grown selection of *H. paniculata* is 'Grandiflora', which can reach 8ft (2.5m) or more in a container. Dense pyramids of sterile cream flowers are often 15in (38cm) or more long. The flowers take on a pink tinge as they age.

Plant in spring, using a soil-based potting mix. Repot every two or three years, top-dressing with fresh mix in other years. Prune in spring, cutting *H. paniculata* hard back.
See also pages 161, 175; illustrations pages 37, 45.

CANDYTUFT

Iberis
HARDY ANNUAL
Few plants add such startling whiteness to summer containers as candytuft. *I. amara* 'Giant Hyacinth Flowered White' has stems up to 15in (38cm) high, crowded with fragrant, long-lasting flowers. The globe candytuft (*I. umbellata*) is difficult to obtain in single colors, but it is often available in mixtures that include white. The Fairy Series, a color selection that includes pinks, reds, and lavenders as well as white, provides bushy plants 9in (23cm) high.

Raise from seed sown in fall or spring, or buy plants in spring. Use either a soil-based or a soil-less potting mix. Deadhead regularly in order to prolong the flowering season.

JASMINE

Jasminum
VINE ZONES 8–10
The summer-flowering common white jasmine (*J. officinale*) is a favorite deciduous or semi-evergreen vine, capable of twining up supports to a height of 30ft (9m) or more. Individual flowers, pink in bud but opening white, are small, but they bloom in pretty clusters over a long period and are deliciously scented. Although vigorous, and so not totally suitable as a container plant, it can be grown successfully in a big tub.

A more manageable vine in containers is the tender *J. polyanthum* (Z9–10), which reaches a height of about 10ft (3m). Where the climate is too harsh for it to be grown outdoors, it makes a superb greenhouse plant, with clusters of sweetly fragrant, white or pale pink flowers. It can start flowering in late winter, continuing into early summer, but in cooler conditions flowering does not usually begin before the spring.

Plant in a soil-based potting mix and ensure that there are adequate supports for the vine to climb up. Reduce congested growth if necessary, but avoid heavy pruning.

SWEET PEA

Lathyrus odoratus
HARDY ANNUAL/BIENNIAL VINE
POISONOUS
Sweet peas are most often sold in mixed pastel colors, but some named forms are available in single colors. Good whites include the fragrant 'White Supreme'.

Among the creams are 'Hunter's Moon', with sweetly scented and frilly flowers, and 'Lillie Langtry', lightly scented with prettily waved blooms. *See also pages 162, 169, 175.*

COMMON WHITE LAVENDER

Lavandula angustifolia 'Alba'
EVERGREEN SHRUB ZONES 5–9
The lavenders, easy sun-loving shrubs with aromatic foliage and flowers, are best known in their gray-blue or purple-blue forms, but *L. angustifolia* 'Alba' makes an attractive white variation. The eye-catching flower spikes produced in late summer cover a gray-green bush about 18in (45cm) high. *See also page 169.*

MALLOW

Lavatera trimestris 'Mont Blanc'
HARDY ANNUAL
One of the most brilliant whites in late summer to fall is the annual mallow 'Mont Blanc' (*below*), which is best appreciated when grown in groups in large planters or tubs in full sun.

Sow seed in spring. Thin to 6in (15cm) apart by early summer. *See also page 162.*

Mallow *Lavatera trimestris* 'Mont Blanc'

LILY

Lilium

BULB ZONES 3–9 POISONOUS

Lilies are the most important group of summer-flowering bulbs, and the majority are suitable for growing in containers. Ideally, lilies should be moved into an eye-catching position when they are coming into flower and withdrawn once their season is over. Place in sun or in partial shade.

In the following selection lilies are described as basal rooting or stem rooting. Basal-rooting lilies produce roots from only the bulb, while stem-rooting kinds also produce roots above the bulb and require deeper planting.

L. candidum (Z4–9), the Madonna lily, has been cultivated for centuries and still holds its own as a supremely beautiful ornamental. In early to mid-summer, stems up to 5ft (1.5m) tall bear numerous fragrant trumpets with golden anthers. It is basal rooting.

'Casa Blanca' (Z4–9) is a stem-rooting lily that flowers in mid- to late summer. Stems up to 4ft (1.2m) high carry several large fragrant flowers. Orange-brown anthers stand out against the white petals, which have wartlike bumps and a yellowish midrib.

'Mont Blanc', only 2ft (60cm) high, is a useful short-growing lily with creamy white flowers that are slightly spotted in the center. It is basal rooting.

L. regale (Z4–9), the regal lily (*below left*), is one of the easiest lilies to grow and one of the most splendid. Stems 4–6ft (1.2–1.8m) high carry clusters of fragrant trumpets in mid-summer. The glistening white flowers have a yellow center, and the backs of the petals are stained purple and deep pink. Purer whites can be found in the Album Group. All of these lilies are stem rooting.

L. speciosum is another richly fragrant, stem-rooting species. Between five and ten bowl-shaped flowers with turned-back, wavy petals are carried on stems that are 4–6ft (1.2–1.8m) high. In *L. s.* var. *album* (Z4–9) the flowers are clear white.

'Sterling Star' (Z4–9), a basal-rooting lily, has starry flowers in mid-summer on stems 3ft (90cm) high. Orange-brown anthers and dark speckling stand out against the white petals.

Buy undamaged, plump bulbs in fall and plant promptly, either singly or in groups of three or more. Consider stability as well as depth when choosing containers. The depth of potting mix needed above basal-rooting lilies is 5–6in (13–15cm) and above stem-rooting kinds is about 8in (20cm). Lilies planted in groups should be about 3in (8cm) apart. Use a soil-based potting mix and ensure free drainage. *L. candidum* is an exception: plant in late summer, just covering the bulbs with potting mix.

Repot lilies in small or medium-sized containers annually in late winter or spring. Repot those in tubs and other large containers every other year, and add more potting mix and apply a slow-release fertilizer in alternate years. Do not water lilies when dormant, and avoid overwatering during the growing season.

Viral diseases, transmitted by sucking insects such as aphids, can be a serious problem with lilies, so regular spraying against these pests is advisable. The most troublesome disease of lilies, especially of *L. candidum*, is botrytis, but fungicides can provide an effective control.

See also pages 142, 147, 153, 162; illustrations pages 7, 14, 18, 24, 50.

Regal lily *Lilium regale*

LOBELIA

Lobelia erinus 'Snowball'

HALF-HARDY ANNUAL POISONOUS

Lobelias are highly valued as trailing plants, especially in hanging baskets and as edging. 'Snowball' is a compact selection with large clear white flowers. An occasional rogue pale blue plant makes a pretty spot of color.

See also pages 153, 169, 175–76; illustration page 25.

SWEET ALYSSUM

Lobularia maritima

HARDY ANNUAL

The honey-scented sweet alyssum is a longstanding favorite and a useful filler for the edges of containers planted to last through summer and into fall. 'Carpet of Snow' makes a low mound up to 4in (10cm) high, with a spread of 15in (38cm). The flowers are small, giving an attractive white-and-green effect. 'Snow Crystal' is slightly more spreading with larger flowers. Sweet alyssum is often also sold in mixtures. Mixed Wonderland includes pinkish-red and purple as well as white.

Raise from seed or buy plants in spring. Use either a soil-based or a soil-less potting mix. To extend the season, trim off flowers as they fade.

See also page 162.

COMMON MYRTLE

Myrtus communis

EVERGREEN SHRUB ZONES 9–10

Glossy aromatic foliage is a year-round attraction of common myrtle (*below*),

Common myrtle *Myrtus communis*

which, in containers, rarely grows to more than 4ft (1.2m) high and 2ft (60cm) across. In late summer, it carries fragrant white flowers with a brush of thin stamens; these are followed by purplish-black berries.

M. c. subsp. *tarentina* is more compact than the species, and has small, narrow leaves.

Plant in late spring, using a soil-based potting mix. Choose a warm sheltered position, ideally against a sunny wall.

Flowering tobacco *Nicotiana* hybrid

FLOWERING TOBACCO

Nicotiana

HALF-HARDY ANNUAL POISONOUS

One of the most bewitching evening scents of the summer garden is that provided by flowering tobacco, *N. × sanderae* and *N. alata* (syn. *N. affinis*). This sticky perennial (*above*), usually treated as an annual, carries long-tubed flowers with starry mouths and grows to 30in (75cm). A well-positioned, large container that is thickly planted will make a major contribution to an intimate yard.

There is now a versatile range of flowering tobaccos. In 'Fragrant Cloud', the flowers are large and the evening scent powerful, but the height of plants – at 3ft (90cm) – limits their usefulness in the container garden. 'White Bedder', well scented and pure white, makes bushy plants only 16in (40cm) high, which can be used in window boxes and other small containers. Other compact flowering

tobaccos are available in color mixtures that include white. Domino Mixed are hybrids 12in (30cm) high with fragrant, upward-facing flowers in a range of colors. Even shorter growing are the Merlin hybrids, 10in (25cm) high; they branch freely and provide bright colors.

Raise from seed (sow in warmth in early spring, or buy plants in late spring). Use a soil-based or soil-less potting mix. *See also pages 142, 163; illustration page 113.*

OSTEOSPERMUM

Osteospermum

PERENNIAL ZONES 9–10

These sprawling evergreen daisies from South Africa flower freely throughout the summer. They are often grown as annuals or overwintered as cuttings on account of their tenderness.

O. ecklonis, up to 2ft (60cm) high and across, has white flowers, tinged blue on the reverse, and the disk itself is dark blue. 'Blue Streak', its petals washed with blue, and the variegated 'Silver Sparkler' are popular hybrids. 'Whirligig' is an arresting curiosity, with pinched, spoonlike petals. Osteospermums are also available in a wider color range, including pink ('Pink Whirls') and pale yellow ('Buttermilk'). All these daisies combine well with a wide range of sun-loving plants and are useful to lighten dark blues and purples.

If you raise from seed, sow in warmth in early spring and plant out in late spring; this is also the time to plant out overwintered cuttings or newly bought stock. Add soil-based or soil-less mix over a layer of drainage material. *See illustrations pages 101, 119.*

PELARGONIUM, GERANIUM

Pelargonium

EVERGREEN PERENNIAL ZONES 9–10

Although most familiar in bright red and many shades of pink, there are several white forms of these classic container plants. The wide color range among Zonal pelargoniums includes good whites such as 'Arctic Star' and 'Hermione', and there are some other whites available in the single colors of newly introduced seed strains.

Among the trailing, Ivy-leaved pelargoniums, few seed strains are available, but the many cultivars include the pure white 'Snowdrift'.

See also pages 147, 153–54, 163, 170, 181–82, 187, 190, 194; illustration page 108.

PETUNIA
Petunia
HALF-HARDY ANNUAL

Although there are brilliant whites among the petunias – the fringed double 'White Swan' is a dazzling example – the availability of separate colors is restricted and varies from year to year, many strains being sold only as mixtures. Buying plants just coming into flower may offer the surest way of obtaining whites to suit your needs.

White features prominently in a number of the bi-colored petunias, which can be used in extrovert and hectic displays. In the huge flowers of the Razzle Dazzle mixture, stars in strong colors overlay a white ground, while the Picotee Series has deep colors edged white.
*See also pages 142, 154, 163, 170, **176**; illustrations pages 19, 101, 113.*

ANNUAL PHLOX
Phlox drummondii
HALF-HARDY ANNUAL

A striking example of the taller varieties of annual phlox is the cultivar 'Brilliant', which grows to a height of 20in (50cm). Its petals are white, but the variable center is a deep rose.

MIGNONETTE
Reseda odorata
HARDY ANNUAL

Although in no way showy, mignonette (*below*) is much loved for the sweet scent of its flowers. Place pot-grown plants in sun among other containers,

in a position where the fragrance can readily be appreciated.

The plants are about 16in (40cm) tall with a spread of 10in (25cm), and they flower between summer and fall, depending on sowing time. Each loose spire contains a rich profusion of blooms with tiny creamy petals and orange-brown stamens.

For flowers in early to mid-summer, sow in containers during early spring. Use any soil-based or soil-less potting mix (mignonette does well in alkaline soils). Thin seedlings so that those retained are about 6in (15cm) apart. Pinch back the growing tips of young plants to encourage them to branch.

ROSE
Rosa
SHRUB ZONES 4–9

The modern ground-cover roses – low, mound-forming or prostrate shrub roses – include a number that do well in tubs or other large containers. 'Avon' is one example, with clusters of small, semi-double flowers that are pearly white, sometimes tinged pink. The shrub is only about 12in (30cm) high, but its trailing stems can have a spread of 3ft (90cm). The flowers produce little fragrance, but the season lasts throughout the summer and continues into fall.

'White Pet' is quite different in character, a lightly scented, 19th-century Polyantha rose with neat pompon flowers of pure white in summer. About 2ft (60cm) high and wide, it can also be grown as a short standard.
*See also pages 142, **154**, 164, 170, 203; illustration page 24.*

VERBENA
Verbena
HALF-HARDY ANNUAL

The hybrid verbenas flower over a long season in summer. They make useful container plants, and the mixtures usually include whites.

The purple-flowered trailing species *V. tenuisecta*, with stems about 18in (45cm) long, insinuates itself among other plants. The white form, *V. tenuisecta* f. *alba* has the same beguiling habit; it makes a lovely light touch at the edge of containers or trailing gracefully from a hanging basket.
*See also pages 149, 155, 165, **171**, 176–77; illustration page 108.*

VIOLET
Viola cornuta Alba Group
PERENNIAL ZONES 4–8

This white-flowered violet is a jaunty version of the blue-flowered species, and is pretty as an underplanting to shrubs or mixed with other perennials in large containers. It does well in sun or light shade, producing masses of spurred flowers in early summer. If clumps are cut back after flowering, they will bloom again later.

Plant in fall or spring in a soil-based potting mix.
*See also pages **143–44**, 149, 155, 167, 171, 177.*

YUCCA, SPANISH DAGGER
Yucca gloriosa
EVERGREEN SHRUB ZONES 7–10

Pointed leaves making a conspicuously jagged clump give this evergreen (*below*) its picturesque common name. The first flower spike, up to 6ft (1.8m) tall, may not emerge until the plant is five years old. The buds open in fall to pendulous, creamy white, fragrant flowers that are tinged red on the outside. This arresting plant is seen at its best growing on its own in a large pot placed in a sunny, sheltered position.

Plant in fall or spring, using a soil-based potting mix.

Mignonette *Reseda odorata*

Spanish dagger *Yucca gloriosa*

Crocus *Crocus chrysanthus* 'Cream Beauty'

FALL AND WINTER

CROCUS

Crocus
CORM ZONES 3–8
The winter-flowering crocuses are among the loveliest of all the bulbs that give a hint of spring. The white and cream crocuses recommended here all grow to a height of about 3in (8cm).

The many cultivars of *C. chrysanthus* are among the most reliable of the early crocuses. The buttermilk tone of 'Cream Beauty' (*above*) is softly appealing, while 'Snow Bunting' is a stronger white, although its outer petals are creamy with purplish feathering. Both these crocuses have yellow throats and vivid orange stigmas, as has *C. sieberi* 'Albus', whose petals are pure white and pointed.
*See also pages 128, **138**, 144, 149, 166, 171, 177.*

CYCLAMEN

Cyclamen hederifolium f. *album*
TUBER ZONES 5–9 POISONOUS
In fall the white flowers of this cyclamen have a freshness that matches the marbled beauty of the silvered leaves. Despite its small size – about 5in (13cm) high, with a foliage spread of 10in (25cm) – it is very effective in lightening shady corners.

Plant cyclamen on their own in a shallow pot, or include them as an underplanting to a shrub in a large container.
*See also page **165**.*

WINTER HEATH

Erica carnea 'Springwood White'
EVERGREEN SHRUB ZONES 5–8
'Springwood White' is a vigorous example of the many cultivars of this evergreen shrub. Not only is it a useful companion for other acid-loving plants but, unlike most heaths, it tolerates alkaline soil. It will also accept light shade, and so can be used to under-plant taller shrubs. Plants are about 6in (15cm) tall, often with a spread exceeding 18in (45cm). The brown stamens are conspicuous within the white flowers, which are produced in late winter and early spring.

Plant in fall, using a soil-based mix. Shear lightly after flowering.
See also pages 155, 165, 171, 183.

HEATH

Erica × *darleyensis* 'Silberschmelze'
EVERGREEN SHRUB ZONES 5–8
The named variants of this hybrid, like those of *E. carnea*, tolerate alkaline soil. 'Silberschmelze' ('Molten Silver') grows to about 2ft (60cm), but usually has a wider spread. It flowers throughout winter and into spring, when the pink tips of the young shoots are an added feature.

Plant in fall, in a soil-based potting mix. Shear lightly after flowering.
See also page 165.

SNOWDROP

Galanthus
BULB ZONES 3–8
Classic winter flowers that herald spring, snowdrops all share a strong family likeness, although subtle differences distinguish the species and the many named varieties. The white flowers dangle lightly, their three large outer petals enclosing three shorter inner ones, which are usually marked green. Snowdrops do well in shade and are suitable as an underplanting to shrubs in large containers, but growing clumps of plants separately allows their individual characteristics to be appreciated.

One of the largest snowdrops, up to 10in (25cm) high, is 'Atkinsii', which may be in flower by mid-winter. The outer petals are slender and pointed, the inner ones green tipped.

Another large snowdrop is *G. elwesii*, sometimes 12in (30cm) tall, which has broad gray-green leaves. The inner petals of the substantial flowers are green at the tip and also at the base. 'S. Arnott' also has blooms of good substance but is even more valued for its strong and pervasive scent.

The common snowdrop, *G. nivalis* (*below*), has much narrower, strap-shaped leaves and rarely exceeds a height of 6in (15cm). The inner petals are tipped green. In the double cultivar *G. n.* 'Flore Pleno', the numerous inner petals form a green-tipped rosette.

For best results, plant snowdrops "in the green," just after flowering but while still in leaf, during spring. Alternatively, plant dry bulbs in early fall. Use a soil-based potting mix with added leaf mold and keep it moist during the growing season. Divide congested clumps after flowering.
See illustration page 20.

Snowdrop *Galanthus nivalis*

YELLOW TO GREEN FLOWERS

Clear yellow flowers introduce sunny splashes that brighten the container garden in all seasons. Combined with orange blooms, yellow creates warm harmonies. For cooler schemes, hints of green are needed. Use yellow with violet for more dramatic effects.

SPRING

BASKET-OF-GOLD

Aurinia saxatilis
EVERGREEN PERENNIAL   ZONES 4–7
Basket-of-gold (sometimes known as *Alyssum saxatile*) produces a mass of flowers in the second half of spring and early summer. An attractive addition to a planter of easy sun-loving alpines, this evergreen is about 12in (30cm) high with a spread of 18in (45cm).

The species is bright gold, as is the dwarf cultivar 'Compacta', rarely more than 6in (15cm) in height. The lemon-yellow of *A. s.* var. *citrina* gives a lighter, cooler effect.

Plant in fall or early spring in a gritty, soil-based potting mix. Clip plants after flowering.

CROCUS

Crocus × *luteus* 'Golden Yellow'
CORM ZONES 3–8
The vigorous *C.* × *luteus* 'Golden Yellow' (*below*) comes into flower in early spring, when many crocus species and their hybrids have already finished.

Crocus *Crocus* × *luteus* 'Golden Yellow'

Its numerous rich gold flowers, 4–5in (10–13cm) high, look effective with other strong colors in sunny window boxes and other containers. This crocus is at its best, though, in a pot on its own, making dense clusters of golden cups.

Plant in fall, using a gritty, soil-based potting mix. Set corms just over 2in (5cm) deep and close to one another but not touching. Position in sun.
See also pages 128, 137, 144, 149, 166, 171, 177.

WALLFLOWER

Erisymum
BIENNIAL
The wallflowers, sometimes listed as *Cheiranthus*, are short-lived evergreen perennials usually grown as biennials. Bushy plants carry loose clusters of velvety flowers, which are deliciously fragrant, from late spring to early summer. Wallflowers are often mixed with other spring flowers, especially tulips, but they also look good on their own, especially when densely planted in a large container.

Both dwarf and taller wallflowers are often sold as mixtures that include yellow, but some good separate colors are also available. 'Cloth of Gold' is about 16in (40cm) tall and has rich yellow flowers. The more compact 'Primrose Bedder' is about 12in (30cm) high, its flowers a clear yellow.

To raise from seed, sow in a seed bed in late spring or early summer. When the plants are 6in (15cm) tall, pinch back the shoot tips in order to encourage bushy growth. Plant in containers in early to mid-fall, using a soil-based or soil-less potting mix.
See also pages 145, 150; illustration page 92.

SPURGE, EUPHORBIA

Euphorbia myrsinites
EVERGREEN PERENNIAL   ZONES 5–9
The woody but flopping stems of this member of the spurge family (*right*) are about 12in (30cm) long and clothed in fleshy gray-green leaves. They bloom in spring with a head of greenish-yellow flowers held in little saucers of the same color.

This unusual euphorbia, which needs sun and a gritty, soil-based potting mix, looks best sharing a large container with alpine-garden plants.

HYACINTH

Hyacinthus orientalis 'City of Haarlem'
BULB ZONES 4–8
This pale yellow hyacinth makes a useful variation on the pinks, blues, and white of the large-flowered hyacinths. The dense spikes of fragrant flowers seem tailor-made for sunny window boxes, but the bulbs also look attractive planted alone or mixed with other spring flowers in large containers.
*See also pages 129, 150, 156, **172**.*

DAFFODIL, NARCISSUS, JONQUIL

Narcissus
BULB ZONES 3–8
Daffodils are among the mainstays of the spring garden, the yellow-flowered species and cultivars introducing a sunny note that triumphs over uncertain weather. The daffodils best suited to containers are those of short or medium height with refined flowers. They include examples with a central cup as well as those with trumpets, some with several flowers to a stem, a few that are double, and many that are scented, some of which have an exceptionally sweet fragrance. All are easy to grow and do well in sun or partial shade.

Among the Cyclamineus daffodils of early spring, few last longer in flower than 'February Gold'. The blooms, with swept-back petals and elegant poise, stand about 12in (30cm) high. 'Tête-à-

Spurge *Euphorbia myrsinites*

Daffodil *Narcissus* 'Rip van Winkle'

'Tête', rarely more than 6in (15cm) high, is one of the earliest bloomers and has two or three golden flowers with reflexed lemon-yellow petals. A curiosity of similar height is 'Rip van Winkle', with double flowers of lemon-yellow shreds (*above*).

'Jack Snipe', which flowers a few weeks later than those already listed and is 10in (25cm) high, has a long cup rather than a trumpet. This is pale yellow, and its swept-back petals are creamy white.

All the following have several flowers per stem and bloom in mid-spring. 'Hawera', 8in (20cm) tall, has nodding lemon-yellow flowers; the petals ringing the small cups create a starry effect. Although fragrant, it does not have the delicious sweetness of 'Minnow', 8in (20cm) high, with lemon-yellow cups but creamier petals. Also beautifully scented is 'Yellow Cheerfulness', which blooms from mid- to late spring; the double creamy yellow flowers are carried on stems about 20in (50cm) tall.

Plant all daffodils in late summer or early fall, the sooner the better, because their roots develop long before there is any sign of growth above ground. Use any kind of potting mix, either soil-based or soil less, and plant so that bulbs are covered by mix to at least twice their own depth. Deeper planting is advisable for containers in exposed positions. Bulbs can be planted close together and in two layers if a really dense effect is required, but they should not be planted so close that they touch.

Deadhead but allow foliage to die down naturally. To avoid an untidy effect in containers and to allow for replacement planting, bulbs can be lifted as soon as flowering is over and replanted in the garden while their foliage dies down.

See also pages 129, 144, 145; illustration page 124.

POLYANTHUS, PRIMROSE
Primula
BIENNIAL/PERENNIAL ZONES 4–7
The English primrose (*P. vulgaris*), itself a plant of unaffected beauty and lovely in a pot, is the parent of a number of cluster-flowered hybrids that are grouped under the name polyanthus. These come in a color range that includes yellows as well as pinks, reds, blues, and white – most having a conspicuous eye. They are usually grown as biennials and discarded after flowering. Crescendo Mixed, with stems up to 12in (30cm) high, is a hybrid available as seed. For specific colors, it is better to buy young plants in fall or even early spring.

More refined plants in a wonderful range of colors, including dark spice shades, are available in Barnhaven strains, developed in Oregon in the 1930s. There is also a Barnhaven strain of gold-laced kinds, similar to those widely grown in the 19th century, which usually have dark red petals edged with yellow, matching the basal blotch. The perennial cowslip (*P. veris*) appears in early summer.

To raise from seed, sow in late spring or early summer. Pot young plants in fall, using any soil-based or soil-less potting mix. Grow in an open or lightly shaded position.

See also pages 166; illustrations pages 88, 89, 91.

AURICULA
Primula auricula
PERENNIAL ZONES 3–8
In the past, auriculas have enjoyed periods of great popularity: in the 18th and 19th centuries, they were raised for showing competitively. There is now renewed interest in this fascinating group of plants, which, as old lists show, covered a wide color range.

'Old Yellow Dusty Miller' is a border auricula but can be grown in a pot. The gray leaves, which appear to be dusted

Auricula *Primula auricula*

with white powder (farina), form a cluster through which the flower stem grows to a height of about 6in (15cm) in mid- to late spring. The fragrant clustered flowers are primrose-like but more rounded (*above*).

Plant singly in a gritty, alkaline, soil-based potting mix, and place in a cool, shady position.

See illustration page 14.

RHODODENDRON, AZALEA
Rhododendron
SHRUB ZONES 3–9
There are several fine yellow hybrids among the compact spring-flowering rhododendrons and azaleas.

'Bo-peep' (Z6–9) is an evergreen rhododendron flowering in early spring that grows 3–5ft (90–150cm) high and has a spread of about 3ft (90cm). The primrose-yellow, funnel-shaped flowers, tinged green, bloom in small clusters.

The hybrids of the evergreen *R. yakushimanum* (Z4–8) provide some of the best compact spring-flowering shrubs suitable for containers. 'Grumpy' (Z4–8), under 3ft (90cm) but with spreading growth, blooms in mid- to late spring, bearing clustered heads of yellow flowers, tinged pink.

One of the loveliest deciduous azaleas is 'Narcissiflorum' (Z4–8). This makes a bush up to 5ft (1.5m) high, which in spring bears clusters of pale yellow, sweetly scented, double trumpets. The foliage has bronze tints in fall.

See also pages 129, 145, 148, 150, 156–57, 167, 173.

SAXIFRAGE

Saxifraga

EVERGREEN PERENNIAL   ZONES 3–7

Among the saxifrages are many that are easy to grow and suitable for growing in containers mixed with other alpine-garden plants.

The following varieties all make tight rosettes of gray-green foliage that are hoary with an encrustation of lime. The cushions formed by *S. × apiculata* 'Gregor Mendel' (Z6–7) can be more than 12in (30cm) across, and its primrose-yellow flowers, blooming profusely in early to mid-spring, stand 4in (10cm) high. Even earlier flowering is *S. burseriana* 'Brookside' (Z4–9). Its cushion has a spread of about 6in (15cm), and the cup-shaped yellow flowers stand only 2in (5cm) high.

Plant between fall and early spring, using a gritty, preferably slightly alkaline, soil-based potting mix. *See also page 157.*

TULIP

Tulipa

BULB ZONES 3–8

Although some tulips start flowering in early spring, they reach their climax only in mid- to late spring. Within their color range are many strong yellows. Others offer attractive combinations and more subtle colors, including the Viridiflora group, with green markings.

Short-growing tulips under 10in (25cm) in height are especially suitable for window boxes. One of the earliest is *T. tarda* (*below*), with up to five flowers per stem, the yellow forming a broad band that leaves the points white. It is slightly more tender than most tulips (Z5–8). A little later comes 'Stresa', one of the water-lily tulips, whose flowers open out to a star-shape that is yellow inside but with a red base, and flushed red on the outside. A refined species, *T. clusiana* var. *chrysantha*, carries yellow flowers that are red on the outside in mid-spring.

Taller growing yellows include several sturdy singles and doubles. 'Yellow Purissima', 20in (50cm) high, flowers slightly before mid-spring, a satin sheen enhancing its golden single blooms. Mid-spring yellows include the fragrant single 'Bellona', 16in (40cm) high, the double 'Monte Carlo', 16in (40cm) high, with flowers that have deep yellow centers, and another double, 'Gold Medal', up to 20in (50cm) high. 'West Point' is a late-spring Lily-flowered tulip, 20in (50cm) high, with pointed petals that curve sharply outward at their tip.

All of the following tulips, in which yellow is combined with another color, flower in late spring and are 20–24in (50–60cm) high. The elegant *T. marjoletii* (Z6–8) has pale yellow petals bruised red at their edge, while 'Sweet Harmony' bears lemon-yellow petals with ivory margins.

The Viridiflora tulips flower in late spring. 'Groenland' ('Greenland') grows to 2ft (60cm) and has pink blooms with a green edge. 'Spring Green', 18in (45cm) high, has creamy flowers with green feathering.
See also pages 129–30, 145, 150–51, 157, 167; illustration page 93.

Tulip *Tulipa tarda*

SUMMER

GOLDEN MARGUERITE

Anthemis tinctoria

PERENNIAL ZONES 4–8

Above a clump of fernlike leaves, the golden marguerite produces a long succession of daisy flowers in summer. 'E.C.Buxton' is a cool, creamy yellow. *See illustration page 11.*

SNAPDRAGON

Antirrhinum majus 'Yellow Monarch'

HALF-HARDY ANNUAL

The Monarch snapdragons, often sold as mixtures in a wide range of colors, are rust-resistant and are of medium height, growing to about 18in (45cm). 'Yellow Monarch', one of the best single colors, is a good, clear yellow with upright sturdy spikes.
See also pages 130, 151, 158, 167.

PARIS DAISY, MARGUERITE

Argyranthemum

EVERGREEN PERENNIAL ZONES 9–10

Increasing numbers of Paris daisies in soft shades of creamy yellow and pink are steadily being added to the familiar white. 'Jamaica Primrose' makes a bush with fernlike leaves and a height and spread of 3ft (90cm), spangled with yellow daisies in summer and into fall. *A. callichrysum* 'Prado' is shorter growing, with flowers of rich yellow.
See also pages 130, 158; illustration page 119.

BIDENS

Bidens ferulifolia

ANNUAL/PERENNIAL   ZONES 9–10

Although a perennial and grown as such in frost-free areas, *B. ferulifolia* is most frequently treated as an annual. It throws out numerous lax stems up to 30in (75cm) long that carry light foliage of finely dissected leaves and work their way through other plants. When grown in full sun its airy display of small, bright golden flowers, looking like miniature single dahlias, is carried through summer and into fall. In full sun the astonishing succession of blooms hardly falters.

Raise from seed (sow in warmth in spring) or buy plants in late spring. Grow in either a soil-based or a soil-less potting mix. During the growing season, prune back unruly stems and any excessive growth.
See illustrations pages 9, 97, 119.

SLIPPER FLOWER

Calceolaria integrifolia

ANNUAL/PERENNIAL ZONES 9–10

The perennial slipper flower is often grown as an annual bedding or pot plant for its long summer display of pouched yellow flowers in crowded clusters at the end of stems. It displays bushy growth to a height of 2ft (60cm).

Plant in late spring, using either a soil-based or a soil-less potting mix.

POT MARIGOLD

Calendula officinalis

HARDY ANNUAL

Orange and yellow continue to be the dominant colors in the cultivars of this old-fashioned plant. All flower throughout summer and into fall, making bushy aromatic plants. Varieties range in height from 1–2ft (30–60cm).

'Kablouna Gold' is a tall cultivar in the yellow range, with double flowers that have brown tips to the inner petals. 'Sunglow', a dwarf yellow, has masses of bright golden daisies.

See also page 146.

TICKSEED

Coreopsis tinctoria

HARDY ANNUAL

Red centers give a special vividness to the tickseed's yellow daisies. It is an easy annual for full sun, growing to 30in (75cm) and flowering in summer and early fall. Sow in warmth in early spring. Harden off and plant out in late spring, using a soil-based potting mix.

See illustration page 120.

SUN ROSE

Helianthemum

EVERGREEN SHRUB ZONES 6–9

Among these low-growing alpine shrubs there are several with yellow flowers. 'Amy Baring' is a compact variety, usually less than 10in (25cm) high, with buttercup-yellow flowers covering the green foliage. 'Jubilee', slightly more spreading, has drooping double flowers of soft yellow. Plant in a gritty soil-based potting mix and position in sun. Clip after flowering.

See also pages 133, 146, 161.

SUNFLOWER

Helianthus annuus

HARDY ANNUAL

Although the annual sunflower is best known as a giant of the flower garden, short-growing cultivars are better suited

Sunflower *Helianthus annuus* 'Teddy Bear'

to cultivation in containers. All need sun. Music Box provides a mixture in a range from pale yellow to red-brown. Bushy plants no more than 30in (75cm) high produce medium-sized flowers about 5in (13cm) across. 'Teddy Bear' (*above*) is even shorter growing, no more than 2ft (60cm) high, but the fully double, rich yellow flowers are 6in (15cm) across. 'Valentine', up to 5ft (1.5m) high, has lemon-yellow flowers with black discs.

Raise from seed, sown in early to mid-spring, in their containers, one plant per medium-sized pot. Use either a soil-based or a soil-less potting mix, but include a generous layer of drainage material. Set two seeds where one plant is required, removing the weaker plant if both germinate.

See illustration page 120.

DAYLILY

Hemerocallis

PERENNIAL ZONES 3–9

The individual flowers of the daylilies, as their common name suggests, are short-lived, but many of the summer-flowering hybrids produce blooms over a long period. The strap-shaped leaves form clumps 18–24in (45–60cm) wide, and they are best planted singly or in small groups in large tubs.

The flowers come in a color range from yellow to orange-red. In the first half of summer 'Golden Chimes'

produces branching sprays of elegant yellow trumpets with a mahogany exterior. Stems are about 2ft (60cm) high. 'Stella de Oro', only 16in (40cm) high, is exceptional for its long flowering season, from mid-summer until well into fall. The taller *H. fulva* 'Kwanzo Variegata', 3ft (90cm) high, has white-variegated light green leaves and produces its tawny-orange flowers from mid- to late summer.

Plant daylilies during spring in a soil-based potting mix and position in sun or partial shade.

See illustration page 89.

LANTANA

Lantana camara

EVERGREEN SHRUB ZONES 7–11

POISONOUS

In tropical and subtropical regions, this plant is often considered a noxious weed. But it can be an attractive ornamental, the crowded heads of tubular flowers blooming profusely. Yellow is the most common flower color, but this ages to brick-red so that flower heads are bi-colored. In the variegated 'Samantha' (*below*) the flower color is a more consistent yellow. Lantanas can grow to 4ft (1.2m) with a spread of 3ft (90cm), and plants can be trained to make standards.

Lantana is often set out in late spring and discarded at the end of summer. Plant singly in a soil-based potting mix.

Lantana *Lantana camara* 'Samantha'

141

Lily *Lilium monadelphum*

LILY
Lilium

BULB   ZONES 3–9   POISONOUS

Many fine lilies flowering in early to mid-summer do well in containers. The following are about 3ft (90cm) in height.

The basal-rooting 'Connecticut King' is a vigorous lily with upward-facing flowers: a greenish tinge at the center shows off the clear yellow of the petals. The fragrant species lily *L. monadelphum* (*above*) has a sturdy stem that carries pendent pale yellow flowers, sometimes spotted deep purple or red inside, with purple at their base and the petal tips. *See also pages* **134**, *147, 153, 162.*

FLOWERING TOBACCO
Nicotiana 'Lime Green'

HALF-HARDY ANNUAL   POISONOUS

The flowering tobaccos are 30in (75cm) high and flower through summer into fall. In the steadily enlarging color range, 'Lime Green' has remained popular with flower arrangers and container gardeners. Its unusual pale yellowish-green works well with a surprising number of other colors. Used alone, it gives a cool, restrained effect. *See also pages* **135**, *163; illustrations pages 21, 111.*

WATER LILY
Nymphaea

PERENNIAL   ZONES 4–9

There are several diminutive water lilies ideal for tubs and similar containers with a depth of 12–18in (30–45cm). All need still, not flowing, water and an open, sunny position. Air temperatures are not relevant to plants such as water lilies, which have their roots some way beneath the water surface, but the water in which they are growing must not be allowed to freeze.

One of the best dwarf varieties is 'Aurora', which has purple mottling on olive-green leaves. The flowers have a curious color sequence, each color lasting a day. They open yellow from creamy buds and turn orange, then red. The truly pygmy *N.* × *helvola* will grow in less than 12in (30cm) of water.

The best time to plant water lilies is mid-spring. Grow them in open-sided baskets or, if the pool is very small, directly in soil on the bottom. The surface spread of the plants is usually slightly more than the growing depth. Thin the plants in mid- to late spring. *See also page 153; illustrations page 63.*

ONCOSIPHON
Oncosiphon grandiflorum

ANNUAL

This sun-loving annual (also listed as *Matricaria grandiflorum*), grows to a height of 18in (45cm) and produces buttonlike bright yellow flower heads in summer. Grow from seed sown outdoors in mid- to late spring, or start earlier under glass and transplant. Use a gritty soil-based potting mix. *See illustration page 120.*

PETUNIA
Petunia

HALF-HARDY ANNUAL

The few yellow petunias available as single colors are valuable for creating sunny color schemes. 'Brass Band' is a Multiflora that produces numerous small single flowers; 'Californian Girl', a Grandiflora with large flowers, is deep yellow with wavy petals; 'Summer Sun' is a strong yellow with large flowers. All three are 12in (30cm) or less in height. *See also pages 136, 154, 163, 170,* **176**; *illustration page 113.*

PHLOMIS
Phlomis chrysophylla

EVERGREEN SHRUB   ZONES 8–10

This stiff-branched shrub, with a height and spread of 3ft (90cm), has oval leaves that turn from gray-green to green-gold in summer, when it has two-lipped golden-yellow flowers. Plant in spring in a soil-based potting mix.

AZALEA, RHODODENDRON
Rhododendron 'Summer Fragrance'

DECIDUOUS SHRUB   ZONES 3–9

The deciduous azalea 'Summer Fragrance comes into its own in late spring or early summer. This beautifully scented shrub, usually less than 6ft (1.8m) in a container, bears clusters of white flowers that look yellow on account of their blotching. *See also pages 129, 139, 145, 148, 150,* **156–57**, *167, 173.*

ROSE

SHRUB   ZONES 4–9

Several yellow roses make fine additions to the container garden, and a valuable repeat-flowering characteristic is shared by the three roses described here.

Miniatures such as the unusual 'Baby Masquerade' with clusters of little flowers in a shifting combination of yellow, pink, and red are most suitable for window boxes and containers of similar size. Bushes grow to a height of 15in (38cm), but this rose may also be grown as a short standard, at about 30in (75cm) high. Slightly larger as a bush is 'Perestroika', a Patio rose that grows to about 18in (45cm) in height and spread. Small yellow double flowers bloom prolifically over dark foliage.

Much more substantial is the Shrub rose 'Graham Thomas', from the "English roses" group. These show good disease resistance and flower repeatedly throughout summer and into fall, carrying blooms in the style of the old-fashioned roses. 'Graham Thomas' can grow to a height of 8ft (2.5m), usually less in a container, and its double flowers are fragrant and rich yellow. It requires a large container, not less than 16in (40cm) deep. *See also pages 136,* **154**, *164, 170, 203.*

MARIGOLD
Tagetes

HALF-HARDY ANNUAL

Marigolds provide an unflagging display of flowers over several months. The color range includes rust-red, mahogany, and orange-brown, often with yellow mixed in. There are also plain yellows. A longstanding favorite among the African marigolds is 'First Lady', a compact plant up to 15in (38cm) high with clear yellow double flowers that are often more than 3in (8cm) across. 'Moonbeam' is similar, but with flowers of a paler yellow.

Marigold *Tagetes* hybrid

Nasturtium *Tropaeolum majus* 'Whirlybird Gold'

The large and massed blobs of color produced by these and other African marigolds are suitable for bold effects (*above*). More subtle are the small single flowers of 'Lemon Gem', a selection of *T. tenuifolia* var. *pumila* (*T. signata* var. *pumila*). This makes a feathery green mound 9in (23cm) high, almost covered by lemon-yellow stars. The small-flowered French marigold 'Naughty Marietta' is more assertive. Little bushes 12in (30cm) high carry a profusion of deep yellow flowers with a maroon blotch.
*See also page **148**; illustration page 33.*

GOLDEN FLEECE

Thymophylla tenuiloba
ANNUAL/BIENNIAL
This strongly scented, long-blooming plant with small yellow-orange flowers, a native of Texas and Mexico, may be perennial in frost-free areas, but is usually grown as an annual or biennial. Grown in full sun in a soil-based potting mix with added sand, it will reach a height of 20in (50cm). Raise from seed sown *in situ* in spring.
See illustration page 113.

NASTURTIUM

Tropaeolum majus
HALF-HARDY ANNUAL
The nasturtiums are easy and rewarding summer-flowering annuals. All the compact and climbing mixtures include yellows. The semi-double Whirlybird

Mixed, for example, has the vibrant 'Whirlybird Gold' (*above*). Another eye-catching semi-double readily obtainable as seed is 'Peaches and Cream'. This dwarf bushy cultivar bears numerous light yellow flowers with conspicuous scarlet blotches. Like all nasturtiums, it flowers most freely in full sun and in a poor potting mix.
*See also pages **149**, **155**; illustration page 97.*

CANARY CREEPER

Tropaeolum peregrinum
HARDY ANNUAL VINE
This short-lived perennial, usually grown as an annual, is a native of Peru. It grows rapidly, up to 12ft (3.7m) in a season. Prettily lobed blue-green leaves and curious yellow flowers with winglike fringed petals make this an attractive plant. It climbs by twisting leaf stalks around supports.

Raise from seed, sowing in warmth in early spring or outdoors in mid- to late spring. Sow two seeds where one plant is needed, subsequently removing the weaker seedling. Plants branch naturally, without pinching back.

VIOLET, PANSY

Viola
ANNUAL/BIENNIAL/PERENNIAL
ZONES 4–8
The summer-flowering garden pansies and violets are among the loveliest and most rewarding low-growing plants for containers. They are easy to please and

produce blooms in astonishing quantity over a long season. The classic pansy has a large rounded flower in a wide range of velvety colors, sometimes richly shaded and often with a conspicuous eye at the center of a bold mask. The Clear Crystal Series are strains with a wide range of clean colors, usually sold as a mixture but also by separate colors. There is a good bright yellow, with only fine dark rays marking the center of the flower. Plants have a height and spread of 8in (20cm).

The violets have smaller, less rounded flowers closer in character to the species from which they are derived. They are rarely more than 6in (15cm) high, although they spread to 8in (20cm). Their neat charm shows well in window boxes and as an underplanting to shrubs. 'Johnny Jump Up' is a good small-flowered yellow and purple bi-colored violet.

These pansies and violets are readily raised from seed, but others have to be propagated from cuttings, because they do not come true from seed. Among these is the unusually colored 'Irish Molly', with bronze-yellow flowers tinged green. 'Jackanapes' (*below*) is bi-colored, the lower petals yellow, the upper petals rusty red. Both these pansies grow to 5in (13cm).

Pansy *Viola* 'Jackanapes'

143

Pansies and violets are short-lived perennials. Those raised from seed are normally treated as biennials and sown outdoors in summer for flowering the following year. They can also be grown as annuals, sown under glass between mid-winter and early spring and planted out, after being hardened off, in late spring or early summer. Propagate plants that do not come true from seed by taking basal cuttings in mid-summer. Planted in a soil-based or a soil-less mix, they do well in sun or partial shade. *See also pages 136, 149, 155, 167, 171, 177; illustrations pages 90, 91, 92, 96.*

ZINNIA
Zinnia 'Envy'
HALF-HARDY ANNUAL

Zinnias, among the most colorful of the summer-flowering annuals, are mainly sold as mixtures. The unique pale green of 'Envy' is, however, so exceptional that it has become readily available as seed. 'Envy' is a sturdy plant 2ft (60cm) tall and belongs to the dahlia-flowered double zinnias with tiered blooms.
See also page 155; illustration page 33.

FALL AND WINTER

CROCUS
Crocus
CORM   ZONES 3–8

Like the other small crocuses of late winter, the yellows are best grown on their own in shallow pots; they can also be used as an underplanting to deciduous shrubs or in combination with alpine-garden plants.

C. chrysanthus 'Gipsy Girl' has small golden flowers with bronze feathering on the outside. 'E. P. Bowles' has larger flowers combining yellow and bronze markings. 'Zwanenburg Bronze' (*right*) is remarkable for its rich coloring: satiny purple-brown outer petals clasp a cup of orange-yellow. All these crocuses have flowers that stand about 3–4in (8–10cm) high.
See also pages 128, 137, 138, 149, 166, 171, 177; illustration page 125.

DWARF IRIS
Iris danfordiae
BULB   ZONES 5–9

This astonishing little bulb is one of the brightest flowers of mid- to late winter. No more than 4in (10cm) high, its

Iris *Iris danfordiae*

leaves develop fully only after flowering. The lemon-yellow of its sturdy blooms (*above*) catches the eye, but closer inspection reveals an orange crest and greenish spotting. It makes an attractive underplanting to deciduous shrubs or a first installment in a mixture of spring bulbs. For the purist it is best planted thickly on its own in a simple pot.

Plant in fall at a depth of 2–3in (5–8cm) in a gritty, soil-based potting mix. Deep planting may discourage bulbs from splitting into small bulblets after

Crocus *Crocus chrysanthus* 'Zwanenburg Bronze'

Daffodil *Narcissus bulbocodium*

flowering, but does not ensure success. Bulblets need to be grown for several years to reach flowering size. Container gardeners replace iris bulbs annually.
See also pages 171, 177; illustration page 124.

DAFFODIL, NARCISSUS
Narcissus
BULB   ZONES 3–8

A few dwarf daffodil species flower reliably in late winter, and they are among the loveliest bulbs to include in planters with alpines or, even better, to grow in shallow pots on their own.

Two are outstanding for their distinctive flower shape. The hoop petticoat daffodil, *N. bulbocodium* (Z6–9), has a funnel-shaped "petticoat," the petals being relatively insignificant (*above*). This delightful little plant, 3–6in (8–15cm) high, ranges in color from strong yellow to pale primrose.

Flowering a week or two earlier is the delicate-looking *N. cyclamineus* (Z6–8), the parent of many elegant short-growing hybrids. It is 4–8in (10–20cm) tall, with uniform rich gold flowers. The trumpet has an unevenly flared rim, and the petals sweep sharply back.

One of the earliest trumpet daffodils to flower is the bright yellow 'Rijnveld's Early Sensation', at 10in (25cm) tall.

Plant all these daffodils in fall, using a gritty, soil-based potting mix. Set bulbs close but not touching, 1–2in (2.5–5cm) deep. They like reasonably moist conditions during the growing season.
See also pages 129, 138–39, 145.

APRICOT TO ORANGE FLOWERS

The geniality and warmth of orange flowers, especially when tempered by green or gray-green foliage, can be a great asset in the container garden. More subtle but still warm-toned are the apricots, softer shades of orange that are deliciously flushed with pink.

SPRING

WALLFLOWER

Erysimum
BIENNIAL ZONES 7–9
Wallflowers, sometimes listed as *Cheiranthus*, bloom in mid- to late spring and are usually grown as biennials. Their warm colors and delicious fragrance give a hint of summer. Tall cultivars, up to 20in (50cm) high, and dwarf ones, 12in (30cm) high, are generally sold as mixtures that include shades of apricot and orange-brown, a color that looks lovely on their velvet-textured petals. A limited range of separate colors is available. 'Fire King Improved', a tall cultivar, has bright orange-red flowers. The vivid *E. × allionii* 'Orange Bedder' makes sturdy, compact plants 12in (30cm) high.
*See also pages **138**, 150.*

NARCISSUS, DAFFODIL, JONQUIL

Narcissus
BULB ZONES 3–8
'Jetfire', which flowers in early to mid-spring, is one of the most richly colored dwarf cyclamineus daffodils. The swept-back petals are a deep yellow, while the frilly-edged trumpet is orange. Usually less than 12in (30cm) high, it is a good choice for window boxes. 'Suzy' is an orange-cupped jonquil for mid-spring, with three to five large, sweetly scented flowers per stem. It grows to 15in (38cm). The Tazetta narcissi, renowned for their fragrance and with several flowers per stem, bloom in mid- to late spring. They include 'Geranium' and 'Cragford', both with tangerine cups surrounded by white petals, and 16–18in (40–45cm) high. The more tender 'Soleil d'Or', with yellow petals, is mainly used for forcing.
*See also pages 129, **138**, 144; illustration page 48.*

RHODODENDRON, AZALEA

Rhododendron
SHRUB ZONES 3–9
The Knap Hill hybrid rhododendrons, 5–7ft (1.5–2.2m) in height when grown in containers, carry trumpet-shaped flowers in a wide range of colors that includes strong oranges. Good examples of this group, which flower in late spring, are 'Gibraltar', and 'Ginger', a mixture of brilliant orange and rich yellow with dark red buds that open to reveal crinkled petals of blazing orange except for a yellow flash. Their foliage colors well in fall. The members of another group, the Mollis azaleas, are about 5ft (1.5m) high and bear scentless flowers, usually of intense color, in mid- to late spring. 'Spek's Orange' is deep orange in bud and when open slightly paler, with a green flash.

The compact rhododendrons also display shades of orange and scarlet. 'Vulcan' (Z7–9) has a height and spread of about 5ft (1.5m) and in late spring its flower clusters are of fiery orange.
*See also pages 129, 139, 148, 150, **156–57**, 167, 173.*

TULIP

Tulipa
BULB ZONES 3–8
Several of the wild tulips have contributed warm, even fiery colors to the hybrids that are such a welcome and conspicuous feature of the spring garden. Selection and breeding have provided a fine gradation in color from soft apricot to flaming orange.

The Batalinii Group of the dwarf *T. linifolia* are among the earliest tulips to flower and only 6in (15cm) high. 'Bright Gem' could be listed as yellow, but the reverse of the petals is brushed with orange. In 'Apricot Jewel' the outside of the petals shades from apricot through to orange-red.

'Prinses Irene' ('Princess Irene') is an unusual tulip for early to mid-spring: it grows to 14in (35cm) and the orange flowers have purple flames streaking from the base (*right*).

Mid-season tulips include 'Apricot Beauty', one of the loveliest in this range. It grows to 16in (40cm) and its flowers shade from peachy pink to cream. Another mid-spring beauty, 'Generaal de Wet', is remarkable for

the strength of the scent from its cupped, golden-orange flowers; it grows to 14in (35cm) high.

'Temple of Beauty', one of the late tulips, is also one of the tallest, growing to 26in (65cm) and therefore not suitable for an exposed position. Apricot-orange flowers stand above lightly mottled leaves.
*See also pages 129–30, 140, **150–51**, 157, 167; illustration page 23.*

SUMMER

AFRICAN DAISY

Arctotis
HALF-HARDY ANNUAL
Hybrid mixtures of African daisies are available as seed and provide a colorful range, including purple and crimson as well as many shades from cream to orange. In addition there are several hybrids (Z10–11) named for their color, including 'Apricot' and the vibrant 'Flame'. If deadheaded regularly they produce a long succession of daisies over deeply cut gray foliage on stems 16in (40cm) high.

These named hybrids must be propagated from cuttings, which can be overwintered under glass. All African daisies must be grown in full sun.
See also page 130; illustrations pages 9, 119.

Tulip *Tulipa* 'Prinses Irene'

Datura *Brugmansia × candida* 'Grand Marnier'

DATURA, ANGEL'S TRUMPET

Brugmansia × candida 'Grand Marnier'
EVERGREEN SHRUB ZONES 9–11
POISONOUS

Daturas are spectacular exotics for a yard or patio, but they need protection from frost and are large plants to overwinter. In containers they grow to 8ft (2.5m). They owe their name to their impressive flared-trumpet flowers, in many cases wonderfully fragrant, which hang among large leaves in summer. The trumpets of *B. × c.* 'Grand Marnier' (*above*) are pale green flaring to soft peach, with gracefully upturned points.

Plant singly, using a soil-based potting mix. Grow either as a bush or as a standard trained on a stem to a height of about 4ft (1.2m). Water generously during summer but sparingly at other times. In frost-prone climates, position in a frost-free greenhouse or sunroom from fall to late spring. Plants can be hard pruned in early spring.
See illustration page 7.

POT MARIGOLD

Calendula officinalis
HARDY ANNUAL

The aromatic pot marigold is widely available in numerous mixtures as well as a few single colors (*right*). Fiesta Gitana Mixed are dwarf bushy plants, with a height and spread of 12in (30cm), bearing a long succession of double flowers in the full color spectrum, from creamy yellow to glowing orange. A more subtle range of colors can be found in the taller Art Shades Mixed, which includes soft cream and apricot. In 'Apricot Bon Bon', the double flowers have a soft warm tone.

Raise from seed, sowing in spring in the container where plants are to flower, and thin the seedlings after germination. Use a gritty, soil-based potting mix. Pinch back the growing tips to encourage bushy growth and deadhead regularly for a long flowering season. *See also page 141.*

CIGAR PLANT

Cuphea ignea
EVERGREEN SHRUB ZONES 9–11

The Mexican cigar plant is a useful subshrub in mixed plantings based on warm and hot color schemes in sunny spots. On a bush about 12in (30cm) in height and spread, orange-red, narrowly tubular flowers, 1in (2.5cm) long, flash among mid-green leaves. The mouth of the tube is curiously finished with a purplish-black band and white ring. The plant blooms from spring to fall, and in ideal conditions it continues throughout much of the year.

In frost-prone areas the cigar plant is commonly treated as an annual and planted in late spring. Cuttings taken during the growing season can be overwintered under glass. Grow in any soil-based or soil-less potting mix. *See illustrations pages 25, 119.*

Pot marigold *Calendula officinalis* 'Orange Gitana'

BLANKET FLOWER

Gaillardia
ANNUAL/PERENNIAL ZONES 3–9

The perennial blanket flowers tend to be short-lived and are often used like annuals for summer displays. Their daisylike flowers are in arresting combinations such as orange and flame-red or yellow and maroon. The short-growing 'Kobold' ('Goblin'), up to 12in (30cm) high, with flowers combining yellow and rusty orange, is useful in pots.

Buy nursery-raised stock and plant out in spring, using either a soil-less or a soil-based potting mix. Apply liquid fertilizer every two weeks, starting three to four weeks after planting. *See illustration page 121.*

SUN ROSE

Helianthemum
EVERGREEN SHRUB ZONES 6–9

Some of the rock rose cultivars in the orange range are exceptionally vivid. The incandescent orange-scarlet of 'Fire Dragon' demands attention, even though the plant itself is usually under 12in (30cm) high, with a spread of 18in (45cm). Its foliage is gray-green.
See also pages 133, 141, 161.

EVERLASTING FLOWER

Helichrysum bracteatum
ANNUAL

Usually grown for cutting and drying, *H. bracteatum* (syn. *Bracteantha bracteata*) has a height and spread of 12in (30cm). It requires moist soil in sun. 'Hot Bikini' has flowers in shades of orange, red, yellow, and pink.
See illustration page 120.

IMPATIENS

Impatiens
HALF-HARDY ANNUAL

These tender perennials, normally grown as annuals, include some of the most strongly colored plants for containers. One of the most startling is 'Mega Orange Star'. Although only 10in (25cm) high and wide, it is eye-catching throughout summer, with vivid orange flowers overlaid by a white star.

The New Guinea hybrid impatiens bear large flowers of dazzling color against attractive, sometimes variegated foliage. In 'Tango' the searing orange of the flowers is set against dark green leaves on a plant with a height and spread of 2ft (60cm).
See also pages 161–62.

Lily *Lilium* 'Enchantment'

Coral gem *Lotus berthelotii* × *maculatus*

LILY
Lilium
BULB ZONES 3–9 POISONOUS
Among the most vivid of the lily species and hybrids are some of orange coloring, while those in softer shadings are highly unusual.

One of the most strongly colored is 'Enchantment' (Z5–9), a stem-rooting hybrid that blooms in early summer (*above*). The fiery orange-red flowers, borne clustered at the end of stems 3ft (90cm) high, are cup-shaped and outward-facing.

'African Queen' (Z5–9), also stem-rooting and blooming in mid- to late summer, is spectacular. Stems, which can be more than 5ft (1.5m) tall, bear large fragrant trumpets that flare widely to show their orange interiors; the outsides of the petals are mahogany and yellow.

Much quieter than either of these is the Nankeen lily (*L.* × *testaceum*, Z5–9), which flowers in mid-summer. This is an old basal-rooting hybrid, with stems 4–6ft (1.2–1.8m) high, bearing hanging flowers in an unusual shade of pale apricot. These scented blooms carry a few reddish spots, and the pollen sacs are a conspicuous bright red. *L. henryi* (Z5–9), with pale apricot flowers spotted red, flowers a little later. This stem-rooting species may reach 8ft (2.5m) and bears numerous downward-facing flowers with petals that curve outward.
*See also pages **134, 142, 153, 162**.*

CORAL GEM
Lotus berthelotii
SEMI-EVERGREEN PERENNIAL ZONES 9–10
This trailing perennial has beautiful foliage and unusual flowers, making it a splendid addition to a hanging basket of mixed sun-loving plants. It looks lovely, too, grown on its own in a tall pot or basket. The stems, which may be 2–3ft (60–90cm) long, trail needlelike but soft, gray-green leaves and in summer bear clusters of dark orange, clawlike flowers. The similar hybrid *L. b.* × *maculatus* has yellow flowers with orange-brown shading (*above*).

Plant in mid- to late spring, using a gritty, soil-based potting mix. These plants are frequently grown as annuals and discarded in fall, but rooted cuttings are easily overwintered in frost-free conditions under glass.
See illustration page 97.

MIMULUS, MONKEY FLOWER
Mimulus
HALF-HARDY ANNUAL
The modern mimulus hybrids, perennials that are quick to flower when grown from seed, are usually treated as annuals. Provided they receive adequate water, these moisture-loving plants thrive in sun or partial shade, producing flowers throughout the summer, and are well suited to both window boxes and hanging baskets. Their flowers are a pretty snapdragon shape, each flared trumpet having two upper and three lower lobes.

Mimulus is available not only in a bright range of colors including orange, red, and yellow, but also as pastel shades of apricot, salmon, and cream, and as bi-colors too. Many flowers produce arresting rusty blotches and dots. Young plants can often be selected for color, but seed is normally sold as mixtures. In Malibu Mixed, 6in (15cm) high and with a spread of 12in (30cm), the flowers are mainly single colors in orange, red, and yellow. Calypso Mixed (*below*), up to 9in (23cm) high, has a wider color range.

If raising from seed, sow under glass in late winter or early spring in frost-prone areas. Buy young plants in late spring or early summer. Do not plant until there is negligible risk of frost. Use either a soil-based or a soil-less potting mix.
See illustration page 96.

PELARGONIUM, GERANIUM
Pelargonium
EVERGREEN PERENNIAL ZONES 9–10
Among the many modern hybrids, especially of Zonal and Regal pelargoniums, there are several in the apricot to orange range. 'Springtime' ('Springtime Irene') has short-jointed stems, making a bushy plant about 18in (45cm) high, and the salmon-pink flowers, like those of all the Irene Zonals, are semi-double.

Less conventional is *P. frutetorum* 'The Boar'. This trailing cultivar is ideal for hanging baskets, with a height and

Monkey flower *Mimulus* Calypso Mixed

RED FLOWERS

Reds include some of the most eye-catching, extroverted, even aggressive colors in the gardener's palette. But there are cooler reds, too, and flowers of astonishingly deep and rich color in which the velvet texture of petals seems to intensify an inner glow.

SPRING

CAMELLIA

Camellia japonica
EVERGREEN SHRUB ZONES 7–9
Many camellias are surprisingly tough, but early-flowering ones may have their magnificent blooms damaged by frost. A striking old cultivar with semi-double red flowers up to 5in (13cm) across is 'Adolphe Audusson': gold stamens stand out against the deep red of the petals. 'Bob Hope' is a more recent semi-double, with blood-red flowers and yellow stamens. In containers both will grow to about 6ft (1.8m), with a spread of 4ft (1.2m).
See also pages 128, 156.

WALLFLOWER

Erysimum
PERENNIAL ZONES 7–9
Most wallflower mixtures (sometimes listed under *Cheiranthus*) include rich colors in the red range, and several cultivars in separate colors are also available. 'Blood Red' carries velvety flowers drenched in a wonderfully deep hue, and is a tall wallflower, as is 'Vulcan', 12–15in (30–38cm) high, with deep crimson blooms. Dwarf cultivars suitable for window boxes include mixtures such as the Tom Thumb Series and 'Scarlet Bedder', all under 12in (30cm) high.
See also pages 138, 145; illustration page 8.

HYACINTH

Hyacinthus orientalis
BULB ZONES 4–8
In mid- to late spring red hyacinths produce spikes 8in (20cm) high so densely packed with heavily scented, waxy flowers that they form a column of highly concentrated color. 'Jan Bos' has white centers to its carmine-red flowers, while 'Hollyhock' is slightly deeper in color and its double flowers strengthen the effect of the red coloring

Hyacinth *Hyacinthus orientalis* 'Hollyhock'

even more (*above*). Both these hyacinths flower early.
See also pages 129, 138, 156, 172.

RHODODENDRON, AZALEA

Rhododendron
SHRUB ZONES 3–9
Compact rhododendrons and azaleas include some of the best flowering shrubs for containers, and there exists a wide choice of red-flowered hybrids. The evergreen rhododendron May Day, which makes a spreading dome under 5ft (1.5m) high, bears loose clusters of scarlet-red flowers in late spring. The underside of the leaves is pale and felted. *R. yakushimanum* hybrid 'Dopey' (Z4–7) is an evergreen spreading shrub that grows up to 4ft (1.2m) high, and produces its red flowers from late spring into summer.

The popular 'Hinodegiri' (Z7–9), an evergreen azalea, grows to about 30in (75cm) but has a wider spread. Its small crimson flowers bloom in great profusion in mid- to late spring.

Many deciduous azaleas have flowers in strong reds and oranges, most blooming in mid- to late spring. The trumpet-shaped flowers of 'Royal Lodge' (Z5–9) are vermilion but they turn crimson as they age; in a container this variety is usually less than 6ft (1.8m) tall.
See also pages 129, 139, 145, 148, 156–57, 167, 173.

TULIP

Tulipa
BULB ZONES 4–8
Centuries of breeding have provided an astonishing range of color among modern tulips, and the vivid reds of several species have been passed on to some of the showiest hybrids. All the following are easily grown in containers and, according to the selection, provide splashes of eye-catching color between early and late spring.

Kauffmanniana tulips are among the first to flower and, being less than 10in (25cm) high, are ideal for window boxes. Their leaves have attractive purple stripes. The pointed petals of 'Alfred Cortot' are deep scarlet, radiating from a central black blotch.

The single tulips that flower in early spring are a taller group, most being about 14in (35cm) high. 'Couleur Cardinal' is a splendid crimson tinged with purple. A double with the same flowering season is the long-lasting, vivid scarlet 'Carlton', 10in (25cm) high.

Several early tulips are derived from the spectacular *T. fosteriana* and of these one of the most brilliant is 'Madame Lefeuer' ('Red Emperor'). It is sheeny scarlet-red with a yellow base and grows to 15in (38cm).

Sturdy tulips for mid- to late spring include 'Bing Crosby' (*below*), with long-lasting, lustrous, scarlet flowers on stems 16in (40cm) high. Quite different

Tulip *Tulipa* 'Bing Crosby'

in character is the species *T. linifolia*. At a height of 4–6in (10–15cm) this can easily be grown with alpines. The flowers open wide over narrow, wavy leaves to show a silky scarlet interior with a center of dark purple.

T. greigii is a parent of numerous, brilliantly colored, late-flowering, dwarf tulips, most being less than 12in (30cm) high. To many of its offspring, it has passed on magnificent red flowers and purple-brown striping of the foliage. The scarlet 'Red Riding Hood', for example, is deservedly popular.

Plant tulips in late fall, preferably in a soil-based potting mix (they thrive in alkaline conditions). Large-flowered hybrids should be covered by at least 4in (10cm) of potting mix. Plant small species such as *T. linifolia* at a depth of 2–4in (5–10cm). Planting closely and in two layers will create a dense display, but avoid bulbs touching one another.

Remove flower heads as soon as the petals begin to drop, but leave stems and leaves to die down before lifting, drying, and storing bulbs. If containers are needed for other plants, lift tulips after flowering and replant in the fall. For containers it is worth buying fresh stock annually.

See also pages 129–30, 140, 145, 157, 167; illustrations pages 8, 49, 92.

SUMMER

LOVE-LIES-BLEEDING

Amaranthus caudatus
HALF-HARDY ANNUAL
This tropical annual, much prized in gardens of the 17th century, is worth growing in pots, as it often was then, to make a handsome curiosity for decorating steps, paths, and patios. Growing to 4ft (1.2m) tall, it bears crimson tassels of dangling flowers between mid-summer and early fall. The individual flowers are minute, but the ropelike stems of clustered blooms are up to 18in (45cm) long.

Raise these plants from seed, in frost-prone areas sowing under glass in early spring. Plant hardened seedlings and bought stock outdoors in late spring. Use any soil-based or soil-less potting mix, preferably enriched with organic matter, because these plants thrive on a rich diet. Apply liquid fertilizer generously. These plants must have full sun to thrive.

Snapdragon *Antirrhinum majus* 'Black Prince'

SNAPDRAGON

Antirrhinum majus
HALF-HARDY ANNUAL
The snapdragons, perennials that are usually grown as annuals, are available as tall, intermediate, and dwarf cultivars in a wide range of colors, including various shades of red, and with several variations on the flower type. All have erect, densely packed flower stems, creating an impact throughout summer when planted in groups; they are also attractive as vertical accents in mixtures of other flowers.

Tall snapdragons such as Madame Butterfly, a mixture 2–3ft (60–90cm) high with lance-shaped leaves and spikes of double flowers superficially resembling azaleas, are suitable only for containers in sheltered spots.

Monarch, an intermediate, rust-resistant, and sturdy series that grows to a height of 18in (45cm), is readily available in single colors. 'Scarlet Monarch' produces brilliant scarlet flowers. Plants form several lateral spikes, giving a long season.

'Black Prince' (*above*) is one of the darkest snapdragons available as a separate color. Growing to 18in (45cm), it has deep crimson flowers and bronze foliage.

Dwarf varieties, particularly good in window boxes, include the rust-resistant Royal Carpet, a mixture up to 12in (30cm) high.

Raise from seed in late winter or early spring, sowing under glass in frost-prone areas. Plant hardened seedlings and bought stock outdoors in late spring or early summer. Use any soil-based or soil-less potting mix.

Pinch back the growing points of young plants to encourage bushy growth, and remove side shoots to produce impressive flower spikes. Snap off the spikes when the blooms have faded in order to prolong the flowering season.

See also pages 130, 140, 158, 167.

THRIFT, SEA PINK

Armeria maritima
EVERGREEN PERENNIAL ZONES 4–8
Grassy evergreen hummocks, thickly studded in the first half of summer (and often later) with tightly packed flower heads, make the thrifts an attractive addition to alpine collections grown in full sun. Although wild plants are usually pink or white, deeper-colored cultivars include rose-red 'Vindictive' and crimson-magenta 'Düsseldorfer Stolz' ('Dusseldorf Pride'). Both are under 6in (15cm) in height, with a spread of 10–18in (25–45cm).

Plant between fall and mid-spring, using a gritty, soil-based potting mix.

ASTILBE

Astilbe × arendsii
PERENNIAL ZONES 5–8
Hybrids of the moisture-loving astilbes, producing feathery sprays of long-lasting flowers over attractive divided foliage, include some strong reds.

The short-growing 'Fanal', up to 2ft (60cm) high, carries deep crimson-red flowers in early summer. 'Red Sentinel' blooms at the same time and is of similar color, but its plumes are more open and may be 3ft (90cm) tall. 'Feuer' ('Fire') attains the same height but produces its feathery coral-red plumes in mid- to late summer. The beautifully bronzed young leaves of all three varieties are dark green with a hint of red throughout summer.
See also page 158–59.

BEGONIA

Begonia × tuberhybrida
TUBER ZONES 9–10
Tuberous begonias are often sold in flamboyant mixtures that include reds, such as the erect Nonstop Series and

the trailing kinds of the Pendula group. In addition there are numerous named cultivars in red: 'Allan Langdon', for example, is an erect bush, 12–24in (30–60cm) high, bearing large double flowers of cardinal-red from mid-summer to early fall.

BOUGAINVILLEA
Bougainvillea × buttiana
EVERGREEN VINE ZONES 9–10
In California, the Mediterranean region, and many other parts of the world where the climate is hot, bougainvillea is a widely grown scrambler that may reach a height of 15ft (4.5m) or more outdoors. In cool temperate regions, however, it needs to be grown in a greenhouse or sunroom.

Its profuse flowers are surrounded by attractive and flamboyantly colored papery bracts. Many cultivars of the hybrid *B. × buttiana* are magenta, scarlet, orange, or yellow: 'Scarlett O'Hara' ('San Diego Red'), for example, has magenta-red bracts; those of 'Scarlet Queen' are, predictably, scarlet.

Plant in a soil-based potting mix and position in full sun. Tie growths into supports. In early spring prune the previous season's growth, leaving spurs with one or two buds.

CHOCOLATE COSMOS
Cosmos atrosanguineus
PERENNIAL ZONES 7–10
In late summer this slightly tender perennial, which grows to a height of 2ft (60cm), produces numerous small dahlialike flowers of an exceptionally rich maroon (*below*). What is rather surprising is that there is a chocolatelike fragrance to match.

In late winter, plant the tubers individually 6in (15cm) deep, using a soil-based potting mix to which leaf mold or other humus has been added. Keep frost-free until the container is moved outdoors in early summer. Water generously in the growing season and apply a liquid fertilizer every two weeks, starting two to three weeks after growth begins to show in late spring. Overwinter in a frost-free environment and repot annually.
See also pages 132, 159–60.

DAHLIA
Dahlia
HALF-HARDY ANNUAL/
TUBEROUS PERENNIAL ZONES 8-10
Modern hybrid dahlias are among the best plants to give the container garden a lift in the second half of summer and early fall. All need a sunny, open spot.

Chocolate cosmos *Cosmos atrosanguineus*

Dahlias are grown from tubers, which are planted and lifted annually, or, in the case of the bedding dahlias, raised from seed each year. Many of those grown from tubers are too large for containers. However, the bushy 'Bishop of Llandaff', which grows to 40in (1m), is manageable and is an appealing plant with dark foliage and semi-double scarlet flowers.

The shorter-growing bedding dahlias raised from seed are generally the most suitable for tubs and even window boxes. They are usually sold as mixtures in which red is an important constituent. Bambino Mixed, for example, grows to 18in (45cm) and their small semi-double flowers cover a wide color range. In Coltness Mixed, which grows to 2ft (60cm), the flowers are single, while the dark bronzy foliage of Redskin, under 16in (40cm) in height, makes a good foil for double flowers in a mixture of vivid colors.

Grow all dahlias in a fertile, soil-based or soil-less potting mix. Plant un-sprouted tubers in mid-spring, sprouted tubers in late spring, at a depth of 4in (10cm). After two or three weeks, pinch back growing tips to encourage bushy plants and provide stakes for large ones, tying in as stems develop. Lift tubers in fall and store in a frost-free place.

Sow seed of bedding dahlias under glass in late winter or early spring. Plant hardened seedlings or bought stock outdoors during late spring.
See also page 168.

PINK
Dianthus
PERENNIAL ZONES 4–8
Dwarf pinks are among the loveliest summer-flowering, alpine-garden plants. The alpine pink (*D. alpinus*), only 4in (10cm) high, is variable in color, ranging from pink to purple, and flowers in early summer. The rose-red flowers of 'Joan's Blood' have red-purple centers. The maiden pink (*D. deltoides*) is 6–9in (15–23cm) high, with masses of small flowers. Several named selections, including 'Leuchtfunk' ('Flashing Light') and 'Samos', have crimson flowers. All of them bloom in early to mid-summer.

Old-fashioned and modern hybrid pinks grow 12in (30cm) tall. 'Brympton Red', with its single fragrant flowers of bright crimson overlaid with a deeper shade, has all the charm of the old

hybrids. 'Ian', a modern pink with flowers of deep velvet red, darker at the petal edges, blooms in early to mid-summer and sometimes again in late summer or fall.
*See also pages 132, **160***.

FUCHSIA
Fuchsia
DECIDUOUS SHRUB ZONES 8–10
All the following fuchsias have red petals. 'Marinka' is a longstanding favorite among fuchsias with trailing stems and almost-uniform red flowers, as also is 'Golden Marinka', which produces golden foliage. Another trailing hybrid with almost-uniform red flowers is 'Red Spider', with its long sepals that surround the petals. In 'Cascade' the white sepals curve back, fully exposing the carmine petals. The trailing stems of all of these may easily grow 3ft (90cm) long.

Most of the upright hybrids form bushes up to 3ft (90cm) high. 'Rufus', which has small flowers of almost-uniform red, is also suitable for training as a standard. 'Gartenmeister Bonstedt' has red-brown petals and sepals. 'Thalia' is a bushy plant with velvety foliage. Throughout summer it bears slender flowers with red sepals and orange-scarlet petals.
*See also pages 132–33, 160–61, **168**; illustrations pages 8, 97, 116.*

LILY
Lilium
BULB ZONES 4–8 POISONOUS
Among the numerous hybrid lilies – an outstanding group of summer flowers – are some that produce strong reds. The richly fragrant 'Star Gazer' (Z4–9), for example, blooms in mid- to late summer: it grows to 3ft (90cm) and bears large, outward-facing flowers, the broad crimson petals, curving back at the tips, edged with white, and heavily spotted maroon. Similarly colored and also strongly scented is *L. speciosum* var. *rubrum*, a variety of a stem-rooting species that needs a warm position to thrive. Stems may be more than 4ft (1.2m) high and bear many nodding waxy flowers in late summer.

Very different in character is the short-stemmed 'Red Carpet'. It is 12in (30cm) high, with yellow buds opening in mid-summer to upward-facing flowers of intense scarlet.
*See also pages **134**, 142, 147, 162.*

LOBELIA
Lobelia erinus
HALF-HARDY ANNUAL POISONOUS
Variations on the familiar blue and purple lobelias make a welcome change. The Fountain Series, often sold as a mixture, includes 'Rose Fountain', 6in (15cm) or so high, with long, slender stems bearing masses of small rose-red flowers. Plants in the Cascade Series are also trailing: 'Red Cascade' produces purple-red flowers with white eyes and 'Rosamund' has wine-red flowers with white eyes.
*See also pages 135, 169, **175–76**.*

SCARLET TRUMPET HONEYSUCKLE
Lonicera × brownii
DECIDUOUS VINE ZONES 3–9
The scarlet trumpet honeysuckle, which grows to 12ft (3.7m), is a beautiful hybrid, with blue-green leaves showing off clusters of scarlet flowers. These have two lips opening to an orange throat. There are several varieties, 'Dropmore Scarlet' (*right*) being richly colored and flowering throughout most of summer.

Plant in fall or early spring, using a soil-based potting mix. Provide supports. Prune lightly and top-dress with fresh mix in spring.

NEMESIA
Nemesia strumosa
HALF-HARDY ANNUAL
Much of the charm of nemesias lies in the pretty form of the flowers, funnel-shaped and pouched, and in the bright colors of the seed mixtures in which they are generally sold. Carnival, with large flowers, and Tapestry, which includes many subtle shades, both mixtures under 12in (30cm) high, draw on a range that covers crimson, scarlet, pink, orange, yellow, cream, and blue. Markings in the throat often add a cheering dash. The unusual bicolor 'Mello Red and White' combines two colors with dazzling effect.

Raise from seed, sowing under glass in early spring in frost-prone areas. Plant hardened seedlings or bought stock outdoors in late spring, using any soil-based or soil-less potting mix. Nemesias need sun – they are especially lovely in sunny window boxes and hanging baskets – but do not flower for long in hot weather.
See also pages 169–70, 176.

Scarlet trumpet honeysuckle *Lonicera × brownii* 'Dropmore Scarlet'

WATER LILY
Nymphaea 'Laydekeri Purpurata'
PERENNIAL
Many of the small water lily hybrids may be grown in 12–24in (30–60cm) of water, making them suitable for tubs and other small containers. The tulip-shaped flowers of *N.* 'Laydekeri Purpurata', deep pink to wine-red with orange stamens, are produced freely throughout summer. Its small leaves are purple on the undersides and occasionally blotched maroon.
*See also page **142**.*

PELARGONIUM, GERANIUM
Pelargonium
EVERGREEN PERENNIAL ZONES 9–10
Pelargoniums are mainstays of the container garden, justly popular for being easy plants that tolerate more neglect than most while producing bright flowers over a long season, provided they are grown in sun. In frost-free areas they will flower almost the whole year round. Elsewhere, they are commonly grown as annuals, though they may be overwintered under cover (*see page 85*). There are four main groups of pelargoniums.

The Scented-leaved kinds are grown for their aromatic foliage. The Regals (sometimes listed under *Pelargonium* × *domesticum*) have large, showy flowers, but only a few of them are robust enough to be cultivated outdoors. 'Dubonnet', with repeating wine-red flowers, and 'Grand Slam', scarlet with red markings, are worth trying in sunny sheltered spots. Both varieties grow to about 2ft (60cm).

The two most important groups for the container gardener are the Zonal and the Ivy-leaved pelargoniums. The Zonals are shrubby plants, usually less than 3ft (90cm) high, and often show a distinctive dark zone on the leaf. Their single, semi-double, or double flowers are borne in dense clusters, usually well above the foliage. Their wide color range includes many dashing reds: 'Irene', a parent of many other good Zonals, is semi-double and rich crimson; also semi-double is the scarlet 'Gustav Emich', while 'Madame Dubarry' is a resplendent coral-red single and 'Paul Crampel' (*below*), a bright scarlet single. There are miniatures, too, usually less than 8in (20cm) in height: 'Caligula' has double crimson flowers. The seed strains available, such as the Pulsar Series, are generally mixtures that include reds.

Ivy-leaved pelargoniums, derived from *P. peltatum*, have flowers similar to those of the Zonals, but the plants are trailing, sometimes having a spread of 4ft (1.2m) or more, and their somewhat fleshy leaves are similar in shape to ivy foliage. 'Rote Mini-Cascade' is a short-jointed example with single red flowers. Others include 'Mexican Beauty' and 'Yale', both deep crimson semi-doubles, and 'Tavira', also semi-double but light crimson. A few seed strains are available.

Plant in soil-based or soil-less potting mix, and prune plants that have flowered in summer before overwintering them. Take cuttings in early fall, or, if raising from seed, sow in late winter at a temperature of 61–64°F (16–18°C). Keep overwintered plants just moist until they are started into growth in spring. Pelargoniums are usually bought for planting in late spring, when overwintered stock should also be planted outdoors. Deadhead regularly to keep plants in flower.
See also pages 135, 147–48, 163, 170, 181–82, 187, 190, 194; illustrations pages 8, 9, 21, 25, 111.

Pelargonium 'Paul Crampel'

PETUNIA
Petunia
HALF-HARDY ANNUAL
Most mixtures available as seed contain reds, including the extravagant Fluffy Ruffles Mixed (veined and splashed flowers that are waved and ruffled) and the bright but more sober Super Cascade Series, which is ideal for hanging baskets.

The range of separate colors available as seed is limited, although occasionally an unusual shade is picked out. 'Flame Carpet', a dwarf single usually less than 12in (30cm) high, produces yellow-throated flowers of vibrant coral. Color selections are more readily available in young plants.
*See also pages 136, 142, 163, 170, **176**.*

ROSE
Rosa
SHRUB ZONES 4–9
Among the hundreds of rose hybrids with red blooms are many that may be grown in containers. Most suitable as container plants are the Cluster-flowered bush roses (Floribundas) and their dwarf forms, the so-called Patio roses. 'Red Rascal', 18in (45cm) high, is a double with scarlet-crimson blooms.

Smaller still, and better in containers than in the open garden, are Miniature roses, which rarely exceed 12in (30cm). 'Red Ace' is a tested cultivar with semi-double flowers in deep red. It repeats well but has little scent.

Ground-cover roses, too, are useful for growing in pots and tubs. 'Scarlet Meidiland', for example, which makes a mound up to 4ft (1.2m) high with an ultimate spread of 6ft (1.8m), bears large clusters of small but double scarlet flowers in several flushes.

Plant roses between fall and early spring, using a soil-based potting mix. Apply a liquid fertilizer every two weeks. Deadhead regularly and prune in late winter, Cluster-flowered and Large-flowered hard, others lightly. Repot every second year, but top-dress with fresh mix in alternate springs.
See also pages 136, 142, 164, 170, 203.

SALVIA
Salvia
ANNUAL
One of the most vivid of all bedding plants is *S. splendens*. This tender perennial, usually grown as a half-hardy annual, has spikes 12–24in (30–60cm)

Salvia *Salvia splendens*

Mixed dwarf zinnias *Zinnia* Miniature Pompon

ZINNIA
Zinnia
HALF-HARDY ANNUAL
Among the most colorful of the summer-flowering annuals, zinnias stand up well to heat and drought, but the large-flowered forms may be damaged by rain. They are mainly sold as mixtures in which there are often several shades of red as well as pink, purple, maroon, orange, yellow, and white. Cactus-flowered and dahlia-flowered hybrids produce large blooms as much as 6in (15cm) across, the former shaggy, the latter dense and neat. Plants grow to 30in (75cm). There are also more compact hybrids such as Persian Carpet, under 12in (30cm), with semi-double and double flowers, and Miniature Pompon (*left*), up to 9in (23cm) high.

Sow seed in warmth in early spring. Plant hardened seedlings outdoors during late spring. Use soil-based or soil-less potting mix. Deadhead the blooms regularly.
See also page 144.

FALL AND WINTER

WINTER HEATH
Erica carnea
EVERGREEN SHRUB ZONES 5–8
Numerous cultivars of the winter heath are available. This dwarf evergreen shrub has needlelike leaves. In the flowering season, stems are tipped with clusters of small bells in pink, white, or red. The nearest to a deep red is 'Vivellii', which flowers from mid-winter to early spring. The dark green foliage assumes a bronze tint in winter.
See also pages 137, 165, 171, 183.

PANSY
Viola
BIENNIAL/ANNUAL
Shades of red are found in a few named selections of winter-flowering pansy and one of the most valuable is the 'Redwing', which brings cheer to containers and window boxes throughout the bleakest season. The two upper petals are rich rust, and there are touches of the same color as well as a dark mask on the yellow of the other petals. It grows to 6in (15cm).
See also pages 136, 143–44, 149, 167, 171, 177.

---

high, densely packed with scarlet flowers surrounded by long-lasting bracts of the same color (*above*). There are also white, pink, and purple forms. The cardinal sage (*S. fulgens*, Z9–10) is a perennial with spikes of vivid red flowers 2ft (60cm) high.

The evergreen shrub *S. microphylla* needs frost-free conditions. It grows to 4ft (1.2m), and from mid-summer to mid-fall carries a succession of small but conspicuous crimson or scarlet flowers.
See also pages 170, 176; illustration page 111.

NASTURTIUM
Tropaeolum majus
HALF-HARDY ANNUAL
Climbing, semi-trailing, and compact nasturtiums are commonly sold as mixtures in which reds feature prominently. The range of separate colors sold as seed is limited, but 'Empress of India', a long-standing favorite of compact growth, is often listed. It has a height and spread of 9in (23cm) and produces a long succession of deep crimson, single flowers set among blue-green leaves.
See also pages 143, 149; illustrations pages 97, 103.

VERBENA
Verbena
HALF-HARDY ANNUAL
Most color mixtures of verbena include reds. Separate colors are often available as bedding plants and a limited range

---

also as seed. 'Blaze' is a compact hybrid, 9in (23cm) high, carrying the characteristic tight clusters of tubular flowers, in this case scarlet. 'Valentine' makes a larger plant, up to 15in (38cm) high, a white eye giving a sprightly touch to the clear red florets. Verbenas that do not come true from seed, and which therefore must be propagated from cuttings, include the scarlet perennial 'Lawrence Johnston' (Z8–10).

These versatile verbenas combine well with other plants, especially in window boxes and hanging baskets.
See also pages 136, 149, 165, 171, 176–77.

PANSY, VIOLET
Viola
BIENNIAL/ANNUAL
These invaluable plants flower recklessly over a long period, especially in areas where the summers are on the cool side. They are charming whether grown on their own or combined with other plants. Dusty, velvety, and rich reds feature prominently in many pansy and violet seed mixtures. Color selections are often best made from nurseries and garden centers in late spring, when plants are sold as they come into bloom. From time to time, seed is also available of pansies and violets with names, such as 'Alpen Fire' and 'Flame Princess', that suggest their color range.
See also pages 136, 143–44, 149, 167, 171, 177.

PINK FLOWERS

Many pinks, especially those associated with traditional flowers, are soft pastels, which have a fresh delicacy. At the other extreme, some vivid pinks can be shocking. Combining them with gray foliage helps almost all pinks; the more aggressive shades are subdued, while the pale ones appear brighter and more intense.

SPRING

ENGLISH DAISY
Bellis perennis
BIENNIAL   ZONES 4–9
Before the range of ornamentals was dramatically increased by successive waves of plant introductions, double forms of familiar flowers such as the common English daisy held a special place in the affection of gardeners. 'Dresden China', which some claim dates from the 18th century, has flowers that are densely packed pink pompons. Although small, they are in scale with the 4in (10cm) high plant, making it a perfect companion for dwarf spring bulbs such as blue grape hyacinths (*Muscari*) and scillas.

Seed mixtures in a range covering pink, red, and white include several small-flowered doubles, such as 'Pomponette', and others with blooms more than 2in (5cm) across, such as Goliath Mixed (*below*) and Habanera Mixed. The large-flowered cultivars are up to 8in (20cm) high.

'Dresden China', which does not

English daisy *Bellis perennis* Goliath Mixed

produce seed, is propagated by division. To raise other kinds from seed, sow in early summer and grow until ready to plant out in fall in soil-based or soil-less potting mix. Daisies are suited to window boxes and low containers in sunny spots.
See illustrations pages 41, 89, 93.

CAMELLIA
Camellia
EVERGREEN SHRUB   ZONES 7–9
Camellias are outstanding container shrubs, beautiful on account of their polished dark green leaves as well as their elegant flowers, which open in late winter and spring. The flower color is predominantly pink or red, but there is considerable variation in shape, elaborately categorized by specialists, from single to fully double. In containers, most of the numerous cultivars of *C. japonica* and its hybrids grow up to 6ft (1.8m) high, with a spread of 4ft (1.2m).

'Hagoromo', also listed as 'Magnoliiflora', is a beautiful semi-double cultivar of *C. japonica*, with pale pink, magnolialike flowers. The much darker 'Elegans' ('Chandleri Elegans') is an anemone-centered double.

The various hybrids listed under *C. × williamsii* often start flowering in winter, and they have an advantage over *C. japonica* cultivars in that they drop their blooms as they fade rather than turn brown. The free-flowering 'Donation' is a bright pink semi-double, and 'J. C. Williams' is a lighter pink and single.

Plant camellias singly in large pots or tubs, using a neutral or acidic-soil potting mix like those suitable for rhododendrons. Camellias like a cool, moist root run, but their potting mix should not be soggy. Place containers in partial shade or even in the unrelieved shade cast by a wall. In frost-prone areas, do not place plants where flowers are exposed to early morning sun. To reduce the risk of blooms being damaged by frost, give plants overhead protection or, in the case of those flowering very early, bring them under cover. Prune after flowering, but only to cut out diseased or damaged wood and to maintain a good shape.
See also pages 128, 150.

CLEMATIS
Clematis macropetala
VINE   ZONES 5–9   POISONOUS
Among the most beautiful of the spring-flowering species is the delicate *C. macropetala*. The cultivar 'Markham's Pink' grows to 12ft (3.7m), its nodding flowers a soft but rich shade of pink.
*See also pages 128, **131–32**, 159, 167, 174; illustration page 75.*

LENTEN ROSE
Helleborus orientalis
EVERGREEN PERENNIAL   ZONES 4–9
The Lenten roses sometimes ignore their name and flower in winter but they are usually at their peak in early spring. Stems up to 2ft (60cm) high carry several saucer-shaped flowers above the old foliage, which is soon replaced by glossy, dark green leaves. Flower color ranges from greenish white to deep purple, the interior often beautifully speckled. The richest colors have a grapelike bloom.

The Lenten roses do well in full or partial shade. Plant individually in mid-fall, using a soil-based potting mix to which leaf mold has been added. Plants resent root disturbance, so should be repotted only when this is absolutely essential.
See illustration page 88.

HYACINTH
Hyacinthus orientalis
BULB   ZONES 4–8
The Dutch hyacinths are among the most highly bred of all spring bulbs, with fragrant waxy flowers clustered in dense spikes from mid- to late spring. Pinks are represented in a broad color range. One of the deepest, 'Pink Pearl', is tinged with carmine. Paler pinks include 'Anna Marie' and 'Lady Derby' – the latter has larger flowers carried less stiffly than the others and blooms slightly later. All are approximately 8in (20cm) in height.
*See also pages 129, 138, 150, **172**; illustration page 88.*

RHODODENDRON, AZALEA
Rhododendron
SHRUB   ZONES 3–9
The vast genus *Rhododendron*, which also includes deciduous and evergreen azaleas, contains many outstanding

Rhododendron *Rhododendron* 'Bow Bells'

flowering shrubs that are suitable for containers. Their preference for shade makes them an ideal choice for large pots in small shady spots. The broad color range includes many pinks.

A superb evergreen species, *R. williamsianum* (Z7–9), makes a dome 4–5ft (1.2–1.5m) high with bronze young leaves turning to deep green. The bell-shaped flowers, borne in small clusters or singly in mid-spring, are carmine in bud but on opening fade to soft pink. A popular, more compact species, *R. yakushimanum* (Z4–8), up to 30in (75cm) high but spreading, flowers in late spring, as do most of its outstanding hybrids. Its leathery leaves, silvery when young, are felted brown on the underside. Upright flower trusses are deep pink in bud, but the blooms are an apple-blossom mixture on opening and then pure white.

One of the earliest spring-flowering hybrid rhododendrons is 'Cilpinense' (Z6–8). This semi-evergreen, generally less than 4ft (1.2m) in height and spread when grown in a container, bears masses of pink buds that open to near-white flowers with rose spots. 'Bow Bells' (Z6–8), slightly later to flower, is similarly compact; its blooms are borne in loose clusters, deep pink in bud but opening to show a soft pink interior, and the young leaves are copper colored (*above*). 'Anna Baldsiefen', less than 30in (75cm) high, and a vivid

pink, also flowers early. Its leaves are bronzed in winter. 'Temple Belle' (Z6–8), under 5ft (1.5m) in height and spread, flowers in mid- to late spring, the open bunches of clear pink blooms attractive against rounded leaves that are gray-green on the underside.

Many of the hybrid evergreen azaleas have been introduced from Japan. 'Hinomayo' is a tall example of the group known as the Kurume azaleas, most of which are under 4ft (1.2m) in height but with a spread of about 5ft (1.5m). The vivid pink, funnel-shaped flowers are borne in mid- to late spring.

There are also numerous pink-flowering deciduous hybrids. 'Homebush' (Z5–8), under 5ft (1.5m) in height and spread, produces dense clusters of semi-double flowers in late spring. They are purplish pink with paler shading. Few of the hybrid azaleas can match the beauty of *R. schlippenbachii* (Z5–7), a deciduous species up to 6ft (1.8m) high. The soft pink flowers bloom profusely between mid- and late spring, preceding the leaves, which are purplish red when young and color well in fall.

Plant single specimens of azaleas and rhododendrons in large pots or tubs using an acidic-soil mix. Little pruning is needed except to tidy straggly growth, but remove faded flowers to prevent seed production. The blooms of even hardy rhododendrons and azaleas, especially of those that flower early, may be spoilt by frost. Overhead protection from trees or an overhanging roof will reduce the risk of damage. *See also pages 129, 139, 142, 145, 148, 150, 167, 173; illustration page 45.*

SAXIFRAGE

Saxifraga

EVERGREEN PERENNIAL   ZONES 3–7

Many saxifrages are remarkably slow growing, with tight rosettes of small leaves gradually building up to domes or flatter mats. *S. × irvingii* 'Jenkinsiae' is a suitable one for adding to a collection of alpine-garden plants in free-draining soil. It forms a cushion only 1in (2.5cm) high but as much as 12in (30cm) across. In early to mid-spring this saxifrage is covered with stemless pink flowers.

The mossy saxifrages make more substantial and denser hummocks of green leaves and require moist growing conditions. The foliage of 'Peter Pan'

stands 3in (8cm) high, with a spread of 12in (30cm), above which crimson stems carry pink flowers in early to mid-spring. *See also page **140**.*

TULIP

Tulipa

BULB   ZONES 3–8

The traditional association of pink tulips and blue forget-me-nots (*Myosotis*) remains one of the most pleasing and reliable standbys for spring gardens. The classic tulip for this combination is 'Clara Butt', 2ft (60cm) tall but with rather small, globular, rosy-pink flowers in late spring. Other single tulips flowering in late spring and about 20in (50cm) high include 'Palestrina', salmon-pink but with a green tinge to the outside of the petals, and 'China Pink', a Lily-flowered tulip with petals less markedly curved outward than many in the group. 'Garden Party', 18in (45cm) tall, has single flowers whose white petals are edged with a strong reddish pink; it blooms in mid-spring. Two fine doubles flowering in mid- to late spring are deep pink 'Peach Blossom' (*below*), 12in (30cm) high, and softer-colored 'Angélique', 16in (40cm) high.

Several multi-flowered pink tulips are also available. 'Toronto', which flowers in mid- to late spring, is 12in (30cm) high and has two or three long-lasting flowers of brilliant pink. 'Happy Family', slightly later to flower and a strong rose-pink, is 18in (45cm) high. *See also pages 129–30, 140, 145, **150–51**, 167; illustration page 89.*

Tulip *Tulipa* 'Peach Blossom'

157

SUMMER

STONECRESS

Aethionema 'Warley Rose'

EVERGREEN PERENNIAL   ZONES 4–8

In early summer, this easy alpine-garden plant produces many short spikes of deep pink flowers over gray-green foliage. It grows to 6in (15cm) high, but can have a spread of 15in (38cm), and is a suitable companion for other vigorous dwarf plants that like a free-draining soil and enjoy a position in full sun.

Plant between fall and early spring, using a gritty, soil-based potting mix. Trim off the faded flower stems in summer.

BLUE HIBISCUS

Alyogyne huegelii

EVERGREEN SUBSHRUB   ZONES 9–11

From spring to fall, furled buds open to flowers that, despite their name, are a satiny purple-pink. Sometimes more than 4in (10cm) across, they make a sensational display on an evergreen bush that in containers is usually under 5ft (1.5m). Plant in spring, using a soil-based potting mix. In cold areas give the plant, or cuttings, winter protection. *See illustrations pages 10, 109.*

ANISODONTEA

Anisodontea capensis

EVERGREEN SHRUB   ZONES 9–11

Dark veining intensifies the pink of the small flowers borne through summer on this sun-loving shrub (*below*). Reaching 3ft (90cm) tall, the tips of the shoots need pinching back in order to encourage bushiness. Grow them as individual specimens or in combination with other plants needing full sun.

Plant in spring, using a soil-based potting mix, but do not place outdoors until there is negligible risk of frost.

Water generously throughout summer. Water plants or rooted cuttings kept under glass during winter sparingly. *See illustration page 105.*

SNAPDRAGON

Antirrhinum majus

HALF-HARDY ANNUAL

Separate colors of tall, intermediate, and dwarf snapdragons are often more readily available as young plants than as seed. The Monarch Series, being of intermediate height and rust-resistant, offers one of the best ranges of seed available in single colors. 'Coral Monarch', up to 18in (45cm) high, is a bright coral-pink.

*See also pages 130, 140, **151**, 167.*

PARIS DAISY, MARGUERITE

Argyranthemum

EVERGREEN PERENNIAL   ZONES 9–10

All the color variations of the Paris daisy are worth trying, most sharing its easy-to-please, free-flowering ways. There are several good pinks: 'Petite Pink' ('Pink Delight') and 'Pink Australian' are pretty singles and 'Vancouver' and 'Mary Wootton' are good doubles, the former being strongly colored, and with anemone-centers. Plants are 12–24in (30–60cm) in height, and they can be trained successfully as standards.

*See also pages **130–31**, 140; illustrations pages 98, 109, 115.*

ASTILBE

Astilbe

PERENNIAL   ZONES 5–8

Astilbes are among the loveliest perennials for containers provided their potting mix is kept moist. Their beautiful ferny foliage is often deeply bronzed or copper, especially when young, and their long-lasting flower plumes remain attractive even in their dry state during winter. Most astilbes thrive in partial shade as well as full sun, but it is easier to keep container-grown plants adequately watered if they are grown in shade.

The species and hybrids include many good pinks. The dwarf *A. chinensis* 'Pumila' sends up stiff spikes, 18in (45cm) high, of mauve-pink flowers in late summer and early fall. *A.* 'Bronce Elegans', which rarely exceeds 12in (30cm), has looser spikes of tiny pink and cream flowers, also produced late in the season, arching

Anisodontea *Anisodontea capensis*

over handsomely bronzed foliage.

A much larger plant than either of these and flowering in early to mid-summer is *A.* 'Straussenfeder' ('Ostrich Plume'). This grows to 3ft (90cm), bearing graceful, coral-pink plumes.

Plant between fall and early spring, using a soil-based potting mix to which leaf mold has been added. Keep the potting mix moist. Flower spikes retained through the winter should be cut down in early spring.
See also page 151.

LING, SCOTCH HEATHER
Calluna vulgaris
EVERGREEN SHRUB   ZONES 4–7
Many cultivars of ling have pink flowers, which usually bloom in late summer and often well into fall. Most are 12–18in (30–45cm) in height, but several useful cultivars are shorter. 'County Wicklow', for example, rarely exceeds 9in (23cm) but has a spread of 14in (35cm) or more. Its flowers are double and pale pink. The salmon-pink 'J. H. Hamilton' is also compact. Plant in spring or summer, using an acidic-soil mix. Trim plants in spring and top-dress with fresh mix.
See also pages 131, 183.

CLARKIA, FAREWELL-TO-SPRING
Clarkia amoena
HARDY ANNUAL
The satin-textured, frilled flowers of farewell-to-spring, blooming profusely in sunny spots, are full of charm. The seed of these plants, sometimes listed under *Godetia*, is normally bought as mixtures in which pink is the predominant color. Some mixtures are dwarf, under 12in (30cm) high, while the tallest are as much as 2–3ft (60–90cm) high. Among intermediates are the Azalea-flowered Mixed, which grow to 15in (38in) high, with semi-double flowers.

Several color selections are available. One of the prettiest is the dwarf 'Salmon Princess' (*below left*), in which an overall pink color is warmed by a peachy tone.

The best results are achieved by sowing seed directly in the container, using soil-based or soil-less potting mix, and then thinning to leave plants 4–6in (10–15cm) apart. Avoid excessive fertilizing, which will encourage leaves to thrive at the expense of flowers.

CLARKIA
Clarkia unguiculata
HARDY ANNUAL
This clarkia (sometimes listed as *C. elegans*) is a bushy plant about 2ft (60cm) in height, and in seed mixtures is usually available with double flowers closely clustered on slender stems. Double Mixed, for example, covers a range of pink shades but also includes scarlet, purple, salmon, and white.

Sow seed thinly in the container in early spring, thinning subsequently to leave plants 6in (15cm) apart. Pinch back the tips of shoots to encourage bushy growth. In sheltered areas, sow in early fall for a display in early summer.

CLEMATIS
Clematis
VINE   ZONES 3–9   POISONOUS
Many large-flowered hybrid clematis bloom at various times in summer in shades of pink. When grown as vines, for which supports are needed, the following may reach a height of 12ft (3.7m). They are also beautiful when allowed to trail from a tall container.

'Bees' Jubilee' flowers in early summer and may repeat later in the season. The mauve-pink of the single flowers is made vivid by carmine shading down the center of the sepals, which surround creamy stamens. Grow this plant in light shade to avoid the risk of the flowers bleaching. Cut out a proportion of the old wood in spring.

A very prolific flowerer in late summer is 'Comtesse de Bouchaud', with its bright pink single flowers tinted mauve with cream stamens. 'Hagley Hybrid', also late flowering, has single mauve-pink blooms, up to 4in (10cm) wide, with purple-red anthers. Cut both hybrids hard back in spring.
*See also pages 128, **131–32**, 156, 167, 174.*

SPIDER FLOWER
Cleome hassleriana
HALF-HARDY ANNUAL
The fast-growing spider flower (*below*), sometimes listed as *C. spinosa*, needs full sun and heat to reach 4ft (1.2m). From mid-summer to early fall, it carries large heads of unusual flowers, with narrow petals and conspicuous protruding stamens. The normal color is white with a pink flush, but there are mixtures including pure white, purple, carmine, and strong pinks. 'Rose Queen', a deep pink, is one of several separate colors available.

Raise from seed, in frost-prone areas starting under glass in early spring. Harden off before planting outdoors in late spring. Deadhead faded flowers throughout the summer.

COSMOS
Cosmos bipinnatus
HALF-HARDY ANNUAL
Cosmos is an easy and rewarding annual for full sun, providing an airy display of dahlialike flowers, usually single, over finely cut leaves in summer and fall. They are most commonly grown as mixtures of pink, red, and white flowers. *C. bipinnatus* Sonata Mixed is especially useful for containers. The plants, up to 20in (50cm) in height, bear masses of flowers, including bi colors in red and

Clarkia *Clarkia amoena* 'Salmon Princess'

Spider flower *Cleome hassleriana*

Cosmos *Cosmos* 'Sea Shells'

pink. Most cosmos grow to 3ft (90cm) and when grown in containers usually need staking. 'Daydream' produces striking white flowers with a strong pink stain around the yellow center. The flowers of Sea Shells (*above*), also in a mixture of predominantly pink colors, have curiously fluted rays.

Raise from seed, sowing under glass in early spring in frost-prone areas. Plant in groups for maximum effect, using soil-based or soil-less potting mix. Avoid excessive fertilizing, which will encourage foliage at the expense of flowers. Deadhead regularly to keep the plants flowering over a long period. *See also pages 132, 152.*

PINK
Dianthus
PERENNIAL ZONES 4–8
With their gray-green, grasslike foliage, neat flowers that are often beautifully patterned, and, in some cases, a deliciously spicy scent, pinks have been an inspiration to gardeners for centuries. They are not difficult to grow, and are remarkably tolerant of drought, but need full sun to do well.

A traditional way of growing the larger pinks is in terracotta pots with hooped stakes inserted around the edge to prevent the plants from flopping.

There are true species and numerous hybrid alpine pinks suitable for growing in troughs with other alpine-

garden plants. 'Inshriach Dazzler' makes a tight mound of foliage studded with carmine-pink flowers in summer. 'Pike's Pink' has semi-double flowers with a strong color. Both are typically no more than 4in (10cm) high. Taller than these is the Cheddar pink (*D. gratianopolitanus* Z5–8), which can grow to 12in (30cm). It bears single fringed flowers, fragrant and fresh pink, from late spring to mid-summer.

The old-fashioned pinks, usually 12in (30cm) or so tall, flower only in early summer. They include singles and doubles, most with a ravishing scent. 'Inchmery' is a pretty pale pink double.

The modern pinks are faster growing than the old-fashioned kinds, although similar in height. The main flowering season of these hybrids is early to mid-summer but they often flower again in fall. Not all are scented but 'Doris' (*below*), a pale salmon-pink semi-double, is very fragrant.

Grow pinks in a gritty, soil-based, alkaline potting mix. Modern pinks need to be propagated every two or three years and old-fashioned pinks every four or five years. This is easily done from cuttings taken in the first half of summer. To encourage well-branched pinks, pinch back young plants, especially modern pinks, in mid- to late spring. Snap off the main shoot just above a joint.
See also pages 132, 152–53.

Pink *Dianthus* 'Doris'

TWINSPUR
Diascia
PERENNIAL ZONES 8–9
The perennial twinspurs are full-sun plants that produce masses of small, more or less tubular flowers over a long period in summer. They are often treated as annuals, but rooted cuttings of all the following twinspurs can be overwintered under glass.

The stiff stems of *D. rigescens* initially sprawl before growing upward, to 12in (30cm), and displaying dense spikes of salmon-pink flowers over a long summer season. From mid- to late summer 'Ruby Field', a smaller plant up to 6in (15cm) high, carries flowers of the same color but in open sprays. Two more that bloom in the second half of summer are *D. vigilis* (Z7–9), with spires up to 18in (45cm), loosely clustered with pale pink flowers that have a dark eye, and *D. cordata*, 8in (20cm) tall, with bright pink flowers.

Plant in mid- to late spring, using a soil-based potting mix. If plants are retained for the following season, cut out old stems in mid-spring.
See illustrations pages 22, 101, 104, 105.

DICENTRA, BLEEDING HEART
Dicentra
PERENNIAL ZONES 4–8
There are several compact dicentras with beautifully divided leaves and dangling lockets of mauve or pink flowers in late spring and early summer. 'Stuart Boothman' makes a fernlike clump of blue-gray, 18in (45cm) high and with a spread of 12in (30cm), and the flowers are soft pink. It thrives in partial shade.

Plant in fall or early spring, using a soil-based potting mix.
See illustration page 89.

FUCHSIA
Fuchsia
DECIDUOUS SHRUB ZONES 8–10
A few hybrid fuchsias produce flowers of uniform pink, but an attractive feature of many is the contrast between the color of the petals and that of the tube and sepals.

The trailing 'Pink Galore' has double flowers that are soft pink all over, whereas 'Lena', also trailing, is a semi-double with the tube and sepals flesh-pink and much darker petals. In 'Pink Marshmallow', another trailing double, it is the tube and sepals that are pink, while the petals are white. 'Jack Shahan' is a trailing fuchsia with large, single flowers, the petals deep pink and the sepals paler. All four grow to 18in (45cm) but can have a spread of more than 3ft (90cm).

'Brilliant', a small upright shrub, has rose-scarlet petals and purplish-pink sepals. 'Other Fellow' is another upright hybrid, growing 2–3ft (60–90cm) in a season. Its small single flowers have pink petals beneath the white tube and sepals. 'Leonora', a more vigorous hybrid that is eminently suitable for training as a standard, is a pink single with green-tinged sepals.
*See also pages 132–33, 153, **168**; illustrations pages 87, 114.*

Cranesbill *Geranium cinereum* 'Ballerina'

CRANESBILL

Geranium

PERENNIAL   ZONES 4–9

Several of the smaller cranesbills are attractive among alpine-garden plants. One of the most free-flowering is *G. cinereum* 'Ballerina' (*above*). A long succession of cup-shaped mauve-pink flowers, with purple veins running to a dark eye, is carried on lax stems over its 4in (10cm) mound of decorative gray-green leaves.

Another dwarf cranesbill, *G. sanguineum* var. *striatum* (*G. s.* var. *lancastrense*), up to 5in (13cm) high, can also be grown on its own but is especially useful for planting under shrubs. The flowers are pale pink with crimson veining.

Plant between fall and mid-spring, using a gritty, soil-based potting mix. Cut back plants after flowering to encourage a second flush of blooms.
See also page 168.

SUN ROSE

Helianthemum 'Rhodanthe Carneum'

EVERGREEN SHRUB   ZONES 6–9

This sun rose, perhaps better known as 'Wisley Pink', is free-flowering over a long season provided it has full sun and is grown in free-draining potting mix. It makes a gray-green mound, 12in (30cm) in height and spread, covered in small, soft pink saucers of flowers with orange-yellow centers.
*See also pages 133, **141**, 146.*

HYDRANGEA

Hydrangea

DECIDUOUS SHRUB   ZONES 6–9

In neutral or alkaline potting mixes, the mophead hydrangeas or hortensias, cultivars of *Hydrangea macrophylla*, are pink or red. In these conditions 'Générale Vicomtesse de Vibraye', pale blue in acid soils, is soft pink. It comes into flower in mid-summer. 'Mariesii', also pink or blue according to the potting mix in which it is grown, is a lacecap hybrid in which the mixture of sterile and fertile flowers creates a light effect overall.

Another mophead hydrangea, *H.* 'Preziosa', has foliage that colors well in fall. In early summer the flowers are deep pink but they take on red tones as they age, which also make attractive dried flowers.

All of these make bushy plants that grow to 3–4ft (90–120cm) high in containers and their flowering season continues into the fall.
See also pages 133, 175.

IMPATIENS

Impatiens

HALF-HARDY ANNUAL

These tender perennials, usually grown as half-hardy annuals, come in a wide range of eye-catching colors (*below*). Seed is available as mixtures that feature many shades of pink, some of them shocking. Accent Mixed is a luminously dazzling selection up to 6in (15cm) high with a spread of 8in (20cm). Super Elfin Mixed has bushy plants up to 12in (30cm) high carrying large blooms in a range of vibrant colors. Intermediate in height between these is Eye Eye Mixed, the pastel colors of the flowers being intensified by a bright eye.

The New Guinea hybrids are invaluable for the container gardener, their large flowers in arresting colors being presented against dark or variegated foliage. These plants grow to a height of 14in (35cm) and have a spread of up to 18in (45cm). They are usually bought as plants in mid- to late spring, but are also available as seed.

Sow seed of impatiens in spring, starting plants under glass in frost-prone areas. Harden off before planting outdoors in late spring, using a soil-based or soil-less potting mix. The

Impatiens *Impatiens*

New Guinea hybrids do well in full sun, but other kinds are better in partial shade. Water regularly. Apply a liquid fertilizer every two weeks, starting three or four weeks after planting.
See also page 146; illustrations pages 53, 110.

CHILEAN BELLFLOWER
Lapageria rosea
EVERGREEN VINE   ZONES 9–11
The Chilean bellflower is a twining vine of sublime beauty, usually less than 12ft (3.7m) high, that is often grown as a greenhouse plant in temperate regions. It can also be planted outdoors in a warm, sheltered spot in the shade. This attractive vine produces dangling, waxy, deep pink bells in the second half of summer and into fall.

Plant singly in spring, using an acidic-soil potting mix such as that formulated for rhododendrons, adding organic material such as leaf mold. Provide supports. Water generously during the growing season and apply weak liquid fertilizer every two weeks.

SWEET PEA
Lathyrus odoratus
HARDY ANNUAL/BIENNIAL VINE
ZONES 5–9 POISONOUS
Their fragrance and butterfly appeal make sweet peas favorites for summer floral arrangements (the more they are cut, the more they flower). They are highly ornamental and can be grown successfully in containers. These annuals climb using tendrils and can reach a height of 10ft (3m). In the container garden they can be trained to grow up sunny walls or fences to which netting has been fixed. Another option is a large tub or similar container with its own framework of a stake wigwam, positioned in a sunny, sheltered spot.

Seed is commonly available as color mixtures, including a good range of pastel shades – pinks and mauves featuring prominently – and dark reds and purples. The large-flowered Spencer sweet peas are the most commonly grown, while Antique Fantasy is a mixture of old-fashioned kinds, smaller in flower but strongly scented. There are also dwarf mixtures: Knee Hi Mixed and Jet Set Mixed, up to 3ft (90cm) in height, provide a good color range of compact plants which require minimal support.

New additions appear every year among large-flowered sweet peas.

Good examples include: 'Memories', with white petals flushed a warm shade of rose-pink, and 'Mrs Bernard Jones', with large, reddish-pink, frilled flowers.

Sow seed in fall or early spring, pinching back the growing tips of seedlings when they are 4in (10cm) high to encourage branching. Plant in pots between mid- and late spring, using soil-based or soil-less potting mix. Fertilize generously during the growing season and guide young plants onto supports. Cut flowers or deadhead regularly to extend the flowering season.
See also pages 133, 169, 175.

MALLOW
Lavatera trimestris
HARDY ANNUAL
The annual mallow forms an upright bush, 20–36in (50–90cm) high, that in summer to fall bears large, satiny flowers with a wide, funnel shape. These plants need full sun, and tall cultivars should be planted in sheltered positions.

'Sunset' ('Loveliness'), with flowers of deep pink, is 30in (75cm) or more tall. Even more useful in a planter is the compact 'Silver Cup', up to 2ft (60cm) high, with glowing pink flowers (*below*).

Sow seed in spring in the container, using soil-based or soil-less potting mix. Thin by early summer so that plants are about 6in (15cm) apart. Avoid excessive fertilizing.
See also page 133.

LILY
Lilium
BULB   ZONES 3–9   POISONOUS
Almost all of the pink lilies make excellent container plants. Outstanding is the stem-rooting 'Pink Perfection', whose strong stem, 4–5ft (1.2–1.5m) high, carries up to 20 highly scented, trumpet-shaped, dusty pink blooms, 6in (15cm) across, in mid- to late summer. The spectacular 'Journey's End' is another fragrant lily, which flowers slightly later. Stems 3–4ft (90–120cm) high carry large star-shaped blooms with deep pink midribs; maroon spotting intensifies the color but the tips and edges of the petals are pale pink.

By comparison, 'Joy' (syn. 'Le Rêve') is lightly scented; its soft pink, mauve-tinged, funnel-shaped flowers, blooming on strong stems 3ft (90cm) high, make it one of the most enchanting hybrid lilies for mid-summer. 'Cote d'Azur', also flowering in mid-summer, is a useful compact hybrid, the upward-facing flowers of rich pink carried on stems about 2ft (60cm) high.
See also pages 134, 142, 147, 153.

SWEET ALYSSUM
Lobularia maritima
HARDY ANNUAL
Several good selections of sweet alyssum are available, providing a color range in addition to the familiar white that is useful when choosing an edging

Mallow *Lavatera trimestris* 'Silver Cup'

plant for a container. One of the loveliest is 'Rosie O'Day', which bears clusters of fragrant deep-pink flowers over a long season. It is under 6in (15cm) in height and has a spread of 12in (30cm).
See also page 135.

Oleander *Nerium oleander*

OLEANDER

Nerium oleander
EVERGREEN SHRUB   ZONES 9–11
POISONOUS
The leathery evergreen leaves give a clue to the drought- and heat-tolerance of the oleander, one of the most familiar shrubs of Mediterranean-type gardens (*above*). Pink-flowered oleanders are common, but there are numerous single and double cultivars in red, yellow, and white, as well as intermediate shades. The propeller shape of the five-petaled singles is particularly appealing. These plants have an exceptionally long flowering season in summer and fall.

Plant singly in late spring, using a soil-based potting mix. Cut back the tips of shoots on young plants to encourage bushy growth. Water freely during the growing season but sparingly from fall to mid-spring.

FLOWERING TOBACCO

Nicotiana
HALF-HARDY ANNUAL   POISONOUS
Pink flowers are conspicuous in many flowering tobacco mixtures, while in the limited range of separate colors 'Domino Salmon Pink' stands out as an unusual warm shade. Bushy plants grow

to 12in (30cm), and the flowers are open all day rather than (as with many flowering tobaccos) just in the evening. *See also pages 135, 142.*

PELARGONIUM, GERANIUM

Pelargonium
EVERGREEN PERENNIAL   ZONES 9–10
There is a good range of pinks to choose from in all categories of pelargoniums, especially among the Ivy-leaved and Zonal kinds.

Good Ivy-leaved examples include 'The Crocodile', a semi-double with cream-variegated leaves, 'Hederinum Variegatum' ('Duke of Edinburgh') (*below*), a single pink with silvery foliage, 'Madame Crousse', a semi-double with pale pink flowers, and 'Galilee', a double with bright pink flowers. These can trail from hanging baskets with stems 30in (75cm) or more in length.

'Rio', one of numerous single pink Zonals, has bright pink flowers, each petal marked by a crimson dot. 'Party Dress' is a semi-double with more delicate coloring. Most Zonals reach 3ft (90cm) high, but there are also Dwarf and Miniature kinds: 'Bridesmaid', a fancy-leaved double with soft pink flowers, has a height and spread of only 9in (23cm).

An impressive Regal pelargonium for sheltered positions is 'Aztec', whose large pink blooms have brown markings.
See also pages 135, 147–48, 153–54, 170, 181–82; illustrations pages 115, 119.

Pelargonium *Pelargonium* 'Hederinum Variegatum'

PETUNIA

Petunia
HALF-HARDY ANNUAL
Almost all petunia mixtures include a range of pinks, from soft peachy colors to more assertive shades that are near magenta, while a limited range of single colors is also available. 'Pastel Salmon' looks particularly beautiful when shown off by its silver foliage.
See also pages 136, 142, 154, 170, 176.

MOSS PHLOX

Phlox subulata
EVERGREEN PERENNIAL   ZONES 3–9
In mid- to late spring, the moss phlox is a mound of flat, starry flowers, mainly in pinks, mauves, and reds. The mat of small linear leaves obscured at this season is only 4in (10cm) high with a spread more than twice this. 'Alexander's Surprise', a fine pink, makes a lovely addition to a collection of alpine-garden plants.

Grow in gritty, soil-based potting mix with the container positioned in full sun. Trim plants after flowering to keep them compact.
See also page 129.

PERSIAN RANUNCULUS

Ranunculus asiaticus
PERENNIAL   ZONES 5–8 POISONOUS
When grown as a perennial, this is usually considered a flower of early summer. However, the magnificent doubles, with layers of tissue-paper petals in white and shades of red, orange, yellow, and pink are raised in quantity by nurserymen for the spring trade. In their relatively short season, few flowers are more showy (*below*).

For extravagant spring displays it is advisable to buy plants as the buds are

Persian ranunculus *Ranunculus asiaticus*

Rose *Rosa* 'The Fairy'

BUTTERFLY FLOWER, POOR MAN'S ORCHID
Schizanthus pinnatus
HALF-HARDY ANNUAL

The butterfly flower is often grown in containers to provide spring displays in a cool greenhouse, but it can also be effective placed outdoors for flowering in summer. Usually available in pink-dominated mixtures, its orchidlike flowers have contrasting markings and conspicuous veining in the throat. Tall cultivars grow to 3ft (90cm) or more, while the shorter ones are more suitable for containers. The Disco mixture grows to 15in (38cm), the compact plants covered with prettily marked flowers for weeks on end.

Raise from seed in early spring, under glass in frost-prone areas. Plant outdoors in late spring, in soil-based or soil-less potting mix, placing container in a sunny, sheltered spot. Water regularly and apply liquid fertilizer every two weeks, starting in early summer. Pinch back the tips of shoots on young plants to encourage bushy growth.
See illustration page 13.

STONECROP, SEDUM
Sedum 'Autumn Joy'
PERENNIAL   ZONES 3–9

Several of the fleshy-leaved stonecrops carry tightly packed heads of small flowers in late summer or early fall. 'Autumn Joy' ('Herbstfreude') (*below*)

opening, so that you can choose the colors. Plant in soil-based or soil-less potting mix and keep well watered. Apply a liquid fertilizer about two weeks after planting. These highly bred plants are rather prone to disease, so take off flowers as they fade and discard the plants when they have finished blooming.
See illustrations pages 13, 89.

ROSE
Rosa
SHRUB   ZONES 4–9

Within the range of modern Patio roses, 'Gentle Touch' is one of the most free-flowering. Lightly scented, double, pale pink flowers, like a Hybrid Tea rose in shape, bloom all summer long on bushes with a height and spread of 15in (38cm).

Several much older roses are also suitable for containers. The 19th-century 'Cécile Brünner', sometimes known as the sweetheart rose, forms a twiggy bush up to 30in (75cm) high. The pale pink double flowers, only lightly scented, are exquisite miniature Hybrid Teas in bud, although untidy on opening. Long established but more modern in style is 'Mevrouw Nathalie Nypels', a Polyantha rose with lightly scented, semi-double, deep pink flowers, which grows to 30in (75cm) high. Larger than these is Hybrid Musk 'Ballerina', up to 4ft (1.2m) in height and spread, bearing large sprays of single flowers in an apple-blossom mixture of pink and white. Again, unfortunately, they have little scent. 'The Fairy', 2–3ft (60–90cm) in both height and spread, is a Polyantha that comes into flower rather late but bears masses of small double flowers in pretty sprays (*above*).
*See also pages 136, 142, **154**, 170, 203.*

Stonecrop *Sedum* 'Autumn Joy'

forms a striking clump of gray-green foliage, topped in late summer by pink flowers that take on bronze and copper tints as they age. When in bloom, the plant has a height and spread of about 2ft (60cm). The dead flowers remain attractive through winter: 'Autumn Joy' looks wonderful covered with frost.

Plant between early fall and mid-spring, using a soil-based potting mix. Place containers in a sunny spot. Avoid excessive watering and fertilizing as this will result in lax growth, and the stems will then flop.

VERBENA
Verbena
HALF-HARDY ANNUAL
Many of the verbenas are useful trailing plants, those with pink blooms looking especially beautiful combined with blue flowers and gray foliage.

The seed mixtures of brightly colored bedding verbenas usually include pinks. There are also good verbenas that do not breed true from seed. 'Silver Anne', spreading to 30in (75cm) but with stiff stems to a height of 18in (45cm), has clusters of large flowers that are deep pink on opening and fade to near-white. 'Sissinghurst' (*below*) has rounded heads of bright pink flowers on plants up to 8in (20cm) in height with a spread of 18in (45cm).
See also pages 136, 149, 155, 171, 176–77; illustrations pages 22, 27, 98, 101, 105.

Verbena *Verbena* 'Sissinghurst'

FALL AND WINTER

CYCLAMEN
Cyclamen
TUBER   ZONES 5–9   POISONOUS
The cyclamen are remarkably consistent in appearance and in their pink, white, and red color range. The large-flowered cyclamen, giant forms of *C. persicum* (Z9), are mainly used as houseplants, but where the climate is mild enough they can give an outdoor display lasting four to eight weeks from mid-winter to early spring. They are usually 9–14in (23–35cm) high.

Two dwarf species make lovely additions to alpine-garden mixtures. The flowers of *C. hederifolium* (syn. *C. neapolitanum*) bloom from late summer to early winter over marbled leaves. The plant is 5in (13cm) high with a spread of 10in (25cm). The leaves of *C. coum* (*below*) are rounded, and some varieties have a variegation that gives them a pewterlike finish. Plants are rarely more than 3in (8cm) high, and the pink, carmine, or white flowers appear from early winter to early spring.

Plant tubers when cyclamen are dormant, using a soil-based potting mix with added leaf mold. Barely cover the tubers of the dwarf species, but set the large-flowered cyclamen so that the tubers are just bedded into the potting mix. Water regularly when cyclamen

Cyclamen *Cyclamen coum*

are in growth and apply weak liquid fertilizer every two weeks after the leaves start to show. Stop watering and fertilizing completely as the leaves begin to die down.
See also page 137.

WINTER HEATH
Erica carnea
EVERGREEN SHRUB   ZONES 5–8
Most of the numerous cultivars of the winter heath (*below*) are 6–12in (15–30cm) high but may have a spread of more than 2ft (60cm). They flower between early winter and late spring. 'Pink Spangles' is one of many with pink flowers. Although all winter heath cultivars prefer acid soil and so are useful companions for other acid-loving plants, they do tolerate alkaline soil and, because they stand light shade, can be used to underplant a wide range of taller shrubs.

Plant in fall, using a soil-based mix. Trim the shrub all over once it has finished flowering.
See also pages 137, 155, 171, 183.

Winter heaths *Erica carnea*

HEATH
Erica × darleyensis
EVERGREEN SHRUB   ZONES 5–8
The many cultivars of the hybrid *E. × darleyensis*, like those of *E. carnea*, prefer acid soil but will generally tolerate alkaline ones, and they can be used in much the same way.

'Arthur Johnson' grows to about 2ft (60cm) but usually has a wider spread. It flowers through winter into spring, when the cream-pink tips of the young shoots are an attractive feature. Plant in fall, using a soil-based potting mix. Trim the shrub all over after flowering.
See also page 137.

To raise from seed, sow in warmth in early to mid-spring. Pinch back young shoots to encourage bushy growth. Harden off and plant outdoors in late spring, using soil-based or soil-less potting mix. Apply liquid fertilizer every two weeks, starting three to four weeks after planting.

See also illustrations pages 22, 113, 119.

BROWALLIA

Browallia

HALF-HARDY ANNUAL/
PERENNIAL   ZONES 9–11

The browallias are tropical perennials that are usually grown as annuals. The most widely cultivated are compact cultivars such as 'Blue Troll', which makes a ball-shaped plant, 10in (25cm) high, carrying masses of white-eyed, violet-blue flowers. It can flower at almost any season and is often used in hanging baskets for winter display in sunrooms and greenhouses. Grown outdoors in a sunny sheltered position, it will flower throughout summer and into fall.

To raise from seed for outdoor display, sow under glass in early to mid-spring. Plant outdoors in late spring, using a soil-based or soil-less potting mix. Keep well watered during the flowering season and apply liquid fertilizer every two weeks, starting three to four weeks after planting.

See also page 131.

BELLFLOWER

Campanula

PERENNIAL   ZONES 4–7

Blue is the predominant color of bellflowers, including the numerous low-growing species that are especially attractive when mixed in troughs and similar containers with other alpine-garden plants that thrive in sun or partial shade. Bellflowers are invaluable because most bloom after the spring flowering season of many alpine-garden plants.

All forms of *C. carpatica* are worth growing for their generous display of saucer-shaped flowers. Most have a height and spread of 8–12in (20–30cm). Particularly beautiful is the compact *C. c.* 'Blaue Clips', with its violet-blue flowers, while 'Birch Hybrid', only 4in (10cm) high but producing a long succession of purple-blue flowers, is a pretty bellflower to combine with dwarf alpine-garden plants. Also long-

flowering is *C. poscharskyana* 'Stella', rarely more than 6in (15cm) high but making a spreading plant that is covered for weeks in star-shaped dark blue flowers.

More tender than these and often grown as a biennial for indoor decoration is the Italian bellflower (*C. isophylla*). Its trailing stems, 12in (30cm) or so long and massed with star-shaped blue flowers, are delightful in a hanging basket.

With the exception of the Italian bellflower, which needs frost-free conditions in winter and a warm position outdoors in summer, plant between mid-fall and mid-spring, using gritty, soil-based potting mix. Apply weak liquid fertilizer two or three times during the growing season.

See also page 131.

CLEMATIS

Clematis

VINE   ZONES 3–9 POISONOUS

Although the blue of clematis is usually tinged with mauve or purple, this does not lessen the splendor of some of the large-flowered hybrids. One of the most spectacular of those that flower in early summer and then repeat later, with smaller flowers, is 'Lasurstern'. The blooms, with seven to nine "petals" and creamy stamens, are blue-purple at first, fading to blue-mauve. (The flowers are bleached by strong sunlight.) 'Perle d'Azur', which flowers lavishly in the second half of summer, usually has six pale blue "petals" that show a hint of mauve around the greenish stamens.

*See also pages 128, **131–32**, 156, 159, 167.*

CONVOLVULUS

Convolvulus sabatius

PERENNIAL   ZONES 9–10

The tumbling growth and long succession of purplish-blue trumpet flowers through summer and into fall make *C. sabatius* (also known as *C. mauritanicus*) an exceptionally valuable container plant. *C. sabatius* (*above right*) rarely stands more than 8in (20cm) high, but the slender trailing stems can be 18in (45cm) or more long. It needs a sunny position and, because it is tender, in temperate regions it is generally treated as an annual. Cuttings can be overwintered under glass.

Plant in late spring, using either soil-

Convolvulus *Convolvulus sabatius*

based or soil-less potting mix. Apply liquid fertilizer every two weeks, starting approximately three to four weeks after planting.

See illustration page 108.

WATER HYACINTH

Eichhornia crassipes

PERENNIAL

The water hyacinth, a tropical free-floating aquatic, is a slender plant that in temperate areas needs to spend the winter under glass in frost-free and well-lit conditions in shallow water. However, it can be moved to a sunny spot in an outdoor container pool for the summer once risk of frost has passed. The stems of its glossy evergreen leaves act as buoys, keeping afloat plants that produce spikes 4in (10cm) high of mauve-blue flowers with a yellow eye. Thin the plants if they increase too vigorously.

BLUE DAISY

Felicia

EVERGREEN SHRUB   ZONES 9–10

In temperate regions, these small-flowered blue daisies are usually treated as annuals and discarded in fall, although rooted cuttings taken in summer are easily overwintered under glass. They bear a long display in summer and fall, provided they have sun and well-drained potting mix.

The compact *F. amoena* (also known as *F. pappei*) has narrow leaves. The large-flowered 'Santa Anita', which grows to 24in (60cm), is a widely available selection of the bushy

Blue daisy *Felicia amelloides*

F. amelloides (*above*). There are variegated forms of both the species and the cultivar.

Plant in late spring, using free-draining soil-based or soil-less potting mix. During the growing season, trim plants if they become untidy and apply liquid fertilizer every two weeks, starting three to four weeks after planting.
See illustration page 10.

HYDRANGEA
Hydrangea
DECIDUOUS SHRUB   ZONES 6–9
Hortensias or mophead hydrangeas, which are cultivars of *H. macrophylla*, produce blue or pink flower heads, up to 8in (20cm) across. Their color is also influenced by the soil or potting mix in which these cultivars are grown – blue is intensified on acid or neutral soil, while in alkaline soils flowers have a pink or red coloring. Brand-name preparations can be applied to the growing medium to bring out the blue coloring. 'La France' and 'Générale Vicomtesse de Vibraye' (*right*) are capable of producing good blues.

In the lacecap hydrangeas, also cultivars of *H. macrophylla*, the flower heads consist of small fertile florets in the center surrounded by large sterile florets. Their color is also affected by the chemistry of the soil. 'Blue Wave' is outstanding in an acidic-soil mix.

Most container-grown hydrangeas reach 3–5ft (90–150cm) and have a spread of 2–4 ft (60–120cm). They flower from mid-summer to early fall.

See also pages 133, 161.
MORNING GLORY
Ipomoea tricolor 'Heavenly Blue'
ANNUAL/PERENNIAL   ZONES 8–11
POISONOUS
This fast-growing, twining perennial, usually grown as an annual, can attain 8ft (2.5m) or more, provided it has a suitable support and is grown in a sheltered sunny spot. The cultivar 'Heavenly Blue' deserves its name – the white-throated, trumpet flowers, as much as 5in (13cm) across, being a clear sky-blue.

To raise from seed, sow in warmth in early spring. Plant outdoors in late spring or early summer, using soil-based or soil-less potting mix. Apply liquid fertilizer every two weeks.

SWEET PEA
Lathyrus odoratus
HARDY ANNUAL VINE   POISONOUS
Pastel and dark blues are an attractive component of many sweet pea mixtures, and there are also numerous named selections in this color range, to which new additions are constantly being made. Established examples include 'Blue Danube', with prettily waved, mid-blue flowers, and the richly fragrant 'North Shore', which combines a navy blue standard with paler wings.
*See also pages 133, **162**, 169.*

LOBELIA
Lobelia erinus
HALF-HARDY ANNUAL   POISONOUS
Lobelia is one of the most familiar of all container plants. This perennial, usually treated as an annual, is easy to grow. It produces quantities of neat little flowers over a long season and, because it tolerates light shade, is suitable as an underplanting. Trailing forms are especially useful for softening the edge of a container and are good fillers in a hanging basket.

Compact lobelias, making neat rounded plants about 6in (15cm) high, include 'Cambridge Blue' with sky-blue flowers, 'Crystal Palace Compacta' with

Hydrangea *Hydrangea* 'Générale Vicomtesse de Vibraye'

dark blue flowers and bronze foliage, and 'Mrs Clibran Improved', which has dark blue flowers with a white eye. Trailers, with slender stems about 12in (30cm) long, include 'Sapphire', with white-eyed flowers of deep blue, and the Fountain Series, available as mixed seed and in separate colors that range from blue or white to pink and red.

To raise from seed, sow in warmth in early to mid-spring. Harden off and plant outdoors in late spring. Use soil-based or soil-less potting mix and apply liquid fertilizer every two weeks, starting three weeks after planting. *See also pages 135, 153, 169; illustration page 116.*

NEMESIA
Nemesia
HALF-HARDY ANNUAL/PERENNIAL   ZONES 9–10
In addition to the familiar range of yellow, orange, red, and cream from mixed seed, there is also an attractive sky-blue nemesia, 'Blue Gem'. The compact plant, 8in (20cm) high, grows quickly and bears prettily formed flowers with white touches at the center. They are smaller than the flowers of other annual nemesias but are borne in great profusion.
See also pages 153, 169–70.

CATMINT
Nepeta
PERENNIAL   ZONES 4–9
The catmints, aromatic plants with gray-green foliage and sprays of soft mauve-blue flowers, are ardent sun-lovers and tolerate dry conditions. They have a long main flowering season in early summer and, if plants are cut back lightly in mid-summer, there is usually a second good flush. The compact *N. × faassenii* has a height and spread of 18in (45cm) and the slightly hardier *N.* 'Six Hills Giant' can grow to 3ft (90cm). Both can be used in tubs and other large containers as part of a semi-permanent planting of perennials and shrubs that like sun and good drainage.

Plant in mid-spring, using a gritty, soil-based potting mix. Cut plants back in early to mid-fall.

PETUNIA
Petunia
HALF-HARDY ANNUAL
Plant breeders have produced such an astonishing variety of long-flowering,

rain-resistant hybrid petunias in a range of colors that these plants have become one of the first choices for the container garden. Two broad groups of petunias have been recognized: the Grandifloras, with large flowers, sometimes more than 4in (10cm) across; and the Multifloras, which produce a large number of smaller flowers. The availability of hybrids, doubles, ruffled flowers and cascading kinds has opened up even wider choices. Plants usually have a height and spread of about 12in (30cm), while dwarf cultivars are more compact and cascading petunias have a wider spread.

There are shades of blue in most of the mixtures, and separate seed is available for some blue selections. 'Blue Daddy' is a single Grandiflora with flowers 4in (10cm) across that are light blue with heavy violet veining. 'Blue Skies' is another single with slightly smaller pale blue flowers.

To raise from seed, sow in warmth in early spring. Plant outdoors in late spring or early summer, using soil-based or soil-less potting mix. Excess moisture or heavy fertilizing and shade will encourage foliage at the expense of flowers. Deadhead regularly.
See also pages 136, 142, 154, 163, 170.

SALVIA
Salvia
ANNUAL/PERENNIAL   ZONES 9–10
Among the salvias are several blue-flowered species that are tender perennials commonly grown as annuals in sunny sheltered spots. One of the loveliest is the slender *S. patens*, which grows to 60cm (2ft) and in late summer produces widely spaced, eye-catching, bright blue flowers. *S. p.* 'Cambridge Blue' (*above right*) is similar, but has flowers of a paler blue. Another perennial almost invariably grown as an annual is *S. farinacea*. Its numerous stems grow to a height of 20in (50cm) – the upper part, like the flowers, furry and richly colored. *S. f.* 'Victoria' is midnight-blue. Of even darker blue are the flowers of *S. discolor*, which make a startling contrast with the white backs of the leaves. The plants have a height and spread of about 18in (45cm).

To raise from seed, sow in warmth in early spring. Harden off and plant outdoors in late spring or early summer, using soil-based or soil-less potting mix. Apply liquid fertilizer

Salvia *Salvia patens* 'Cambridge Blue'

every two weeks, starting three to four weeks after planting.
See also pages 154, 170; illustrations pages 22, 87, 97,100, 114.

FAN FLOWER
Scaevola aemula
ANNUAL/PERENNIAL   ZONES 10–11
This drought-resistant, trailing plant from coastal regions of Australia has proved a useful container plant. Stiff stems, clothed with coarsely toothed, dark green leaves, carry clusters of purplish-blue, fan-shaped flowers from early summer to early fall. Plants can have a spread of 3ft (90cm) or more, yet, unless stems seek support by working their way up through other plants, their height is usually less than 16in (40cm). 'Blue Wonder' and 'Blue Fan' are two good named selections.

Plant in late spring, using a soil-based potting mix. Do not fertilize generously, since this will encourage leafy growth at the expense of flowers. Overwinter rooted cuttings under glass.
See illustration page 112.

VERBENA
Verbena
HALF-HARDY ANNUAL
Among the hybrid verbenas, which are usually grown as annuals, there are several good blues. 'Amethyst', one of the best, has a height and spread of 12in (30cm) and bears clusters of white-eyed, cobalt-blue flowers. The more compact 'Blue Lagoon' has a

height and spread of 9in (23cm); there is no eye to the violet-blue flowers. *See also pages 136, 149, 155, 165, **171**.*

VIOLET, PANSY

Viola

ANNUAL/BIENNIAL & PERENNIAL

ZONES 4–8

Although the violets and pansies are short-lived perennials, most are grown as biennials or annuals. The reliably perennial horned or tufted violet (*V. cornuta*), evergreen and up to 12in (30cm) high, produces masses of spurred blue flowers in early summer and, if they are cut back, again later. The deep color of several violets is as near black as is found in any flower. *V.* 'Mollie Sanderson' has mat black flowers 1in (2.5cm) across, which are brightened by a yellow eye. 'Penny Black' (*below*) has smaller flowers of darkest blue-black velvet. Both grow to 6in (15cm).

Many of the large-flowered pansies, most of which grow 6–10in (15–25cm) high, have blue or partly blue flowers. The striking 'Ullswater Blue' has a yellow eye and a blue-black mask imposed on sky-blue petals. It can be raised from seed, as can the blue-flowered violet 'Baby Lucia', only 4–5in (10–13cm) high.

*See also Pansy, below, and pages 136, **143–44**, 149, 155, 167, 171.*

Viola 'Penny Black'

WISTERIA

Wisteria

DECIDUOUS VINE   ZONES 6–8

All wisterias are vigorous vines. When grown in open ground and given the support of a pergola or a stout tree, the Chinese wisteria (*W. sinensis*) is capable of extending 100ft (30m). It bears drooping clusters of fragrant mauve-blue flowers in early summer, some-times with a lesser display in late summer. The Japanese wisteria (*W. floribunda*) is less rampant but also a strong climber, and in beauty its scented flowers almost match those of its Chinese cousin. Specimens grown in containers do not make the phenomenal growth of plants in the open garden, and in any event are best restricted. They can be kept to almost any size by pruning and training and are frequently grown as standards.

Between mid-fall and early spring, plant in a large container at least 20in (50cm) deep, using soil-based potting mix incorporating slow-release fertilizer. Insert a stake to support the vine. To control growth and promote the development of short stems that will produce flowers, cut back shoots in late summer, leaving stubs about 2in (5cm) long extending from the framework of main stems. Additional pruning may be needed in winter. Top-dress with fresh mix in mid-spring.

Reticulata iris

FALL AND WINTER

CROCUS

Crocus chrysanthus

CORM   ZONES 3–8

The most versatile of the crocuses flowering in late winter, *C. chrysanthus* is available in a wide range of colors, including shades of blue. The popular, 'Blue Pearl', is pale blue with a bronze-yellow base and orange stigmas. As with other cultivars, the leaves appear at the same time as the flowers, which stand about 3in (8cm) high.

*See also pages 128, 137, **138**, 144, 149, 166, 171.*

IRIS

Iris

BULB   ZONES 5–9

There are many blue sections of the exquisite Reticulata iris (*below left*), which are easy bulbs to grow and particularly valuable on account of their early flowering season, in mid- to late winter. Good examples include: 'Cantab', pale blue with an orange blotch on the falls; 'Clairette', with pale blue standards and each fall with a dark blue blotch at the tip; and 'Harmony', sky-blue with deeper blue falls and conspicuous golden markings. All grow to about 6in (15cm) high.

I. histrioides 'Major' belongs to the same broad group of dwarf irises. Usually only 4in (10cm) high, its sturdy build and its intense blue, with a paler area around the orange crest, make it one of the most arresting small flowers of late winter.

*See also pages **144**, 171; illustration page 125.*

PANSY

Viola

BIENNIAL

The winter-flowering pansies, sown in late spring or early summer for flowering in winter and early spring, are commonly sold as mixtures. Universal Mixed includes a wide range of clear and blurred colors, among them several shades of blue. Separate colors are also available, including 'Beaconsfield', a bi-color with upper petals of pale blue and lower petals of rich purple blue, and 'True Blue', a clear mid-blue. All grow 6–8in (15–20cm) high.

*See also Violet ,above, pages 136, **143–44**, 149, 155,167, 171, 177; illustrations pages 8, 13.*

GREEN FOLIAGE

In container gardening, foliage is the most frequently overlooked component. Many flowering plants have attractive green leaves, and there are many others that are outstanding for their foliage alone. In the vast range of green shades, some serve best as background or fill, which prevents flower colors from appearing as a congested mass. Many foliage plants can be grown successfully on their own. The evergreens are invaluable for providing continuity throughout the year.

JAPANESE MAPLE

Acer palmatum

DECIDUOUS SHRUB   ZONES 5–8

Few deciduous shrubs can match the variety of leaf shape and color available in the numerous cultivars of the Japanese maple (*below*). Many have a moment of supreme beauty when the foliage colors in fall; most have a

delicate charm as the leaves unfold in spring; and the summer mantle of all is exceptionally refined. Japanese maples can be grown either in sun or partial shade, but they need shelter from wind. Most produce their best fall color in acid or neutral soil.

The slow-growing *A. palmatum* var. *dissectum* does well in containers, building up a mound of intricate weeping branches carrying finely dissected leaves. Those of the Dissectum Viride Group are the brightest green.

Plant between mid-fall and early spring, using an acidic-soil mix to which leaf mold or other humus has been added. Keep the mix moist. Repot in spring only if the roots are congested; otherwise, just top-dress with fresh potting mix annually in early to mid-spring.

See also pages 183, 188.

MAIDENHAIR FERN

Adiantum

EVERGREEN/DECIDUOUS FERN

ZONES 3–8

In temperate regions, maidenhair fern (*A. capillus-veneris*, Z7–10) is usually grown indoors, where its elegantly lacy fronds, up to 10in (25cm) long, remain evergreen. It can reach 3ft (90cm) in height and spread. The hardier *A. pedatum* is deciduous and produces wiry black stems from which appear sprays of delicate fronds. This species, which rarely exceeds 18in (45cm) high, with a spread of 12in (30cm), needs full or partial shade.

Plant *A. pedatum* in mid-spring, using soil-based potting mix to which leaf mold or other humus has been added. Set the rootstock at a depth of about 1in (2.5cm). Keep plants well watered during the growing season and remove fronds as they fade.

LADY'S MANTLE

Alchemilla mollis

PERENNIAL   ZONES 3–7

All through a long summer season lady's mantle (*below*) bears sprays of tiny yellow-green flowers on plants with a height and spread of about 16in (40cm). It is also a superb foliage plant: when fanned open, the downy leaves hold beadlike droplets of water. Suitable for sun or shade in a wide range of conditions, it is excellent grown under shrubs.

Japanese maple *Acer palmatum*

Lady's mantle *Alchemilla mollis*

Plant between mid-fall and early spring, using soil-based potting mix. Remove the flower heads as they fade; if left, plants self-seed freely. Lift and divide every two years, and in other years top-dress with fresh potting mix.

HART'S-TONGUE FERN
Asplenium scolopendrium
EVERGREEN FERN ZONES 4–8
The hart's-tongue fern (*below*) produces a bold shuttlecock of evergreen strap-shaped leaves that makes a good background to flowers. The Crispum Group has fronds that are crested and waved, while in the Undulatum Group the waviness of the leaf edges is very pronounced. All are about 20in (50cm) in height with a spread of 15in (38cm).

Plant these ferns in early to mid-spring, using an alkaline, soil-based potting mix to which leaf mold or other humus has been added. Place in full or partial shade and keep well watered during the growing season. *See also illustrations pages 52–53, 110.*

LADY FERN
Athyrium filix-femina
DECIDUOUS FERN ZONES 4–9
The lady fern has lacy, fresh green fronds up to 3ft (90cm) high, giving it a light elegance. Although it tolerates fairly dry soil, its delicately refined beauty lasts longer in moist conditions.

Plant in early to mid-spring, using a soil-based potting mix to which leaf mold or other humus has been added. Place plants in full or partial shade and water well during the growing season.

Hart's-tongue fern *Asplenium scolopendrium*

Common boxwood *Buxus sempervirens*

BERGENIA
Bergenia
EVERGREEN PERENNIAL ZONES 4–8
The foliage of some bergenias is more remarkable for its purple and red tints in winter than for its solid greens in summer. One that remains more or less green throughout the year, however, is *B. cordifolia*, a useful underplanting to shrubs and is attractive planted on its own. Growing to 2ft (60cm), it bears sprays of pinkish-mauve flowers in spring, and its large, rounded leaves have wavy edges.

Plant between mid-fall and early spring, using a soil-based potting mix. Cut down flower stems when the blooms have faded. Lift and divide plants every two years and top-dress in spring in other years.
See also page 189.

COMMON BOXWOOD
Buxus sempervirens
EVERGREEN SHRUB ZONES 6–8
This small-leaved, glossy evergreen has long been cultivated and valued for the ease with which it can be trimmed into dense shapes, either geometric or fanciful representations. Although capable of eventually reaching a height of 10ft (3m) or more, this slow-growing shrub (*above*) is generally restricted to a height of 3ft (90cm) when grown in containers. Common boxwood's pale green flowers, which appear in mid-spring, are inconspicuous. The dwarf form 'Suffruticosa', often used as an edging plant, can easily be kept at a height of 2–3in (5–8cm).

Plant in mid-fall or early to mid-spring, using soil-based potting mix into which slow-release fertilizer is incorporated. Cut back in mid-spring to promote bushy growth and trim established specimens in late summer or early fall. Top-dress in mid-spring. *See also page 186; illustrations pages 13, 17, 19, 20, 70, 82, 95.*

FALSE CYPRESS
Chamaecyparis obtusa 'Nana Gracilis'
EVERGREEN CONIFER ZONES 3–8
Although eventually reaching a height of 6ft (1.8m) or more, this slow growing, semi-dwarf conifer is most commonly seen as a dense cone with a height and spread at the base of less than 3ft (90cm). The foliage of false cypress is an exceptionally rich dark green, arranged in upright sprays.

Plant in mid-spring, using a soil-based potting mix. Top-dress annually in early to mid-spring. Repot, in mid-spring, if the roots are congested. *See also page 183.*

GRASS PALM
Cordyline australis
EVERGREEN TREE ZONES 8–10
In cold areas this palm-like member of the lily family is often grown under glass, but where the climate is mild enough its spiky head makes a bold centerpiece to a large planting. Plants used for this purpose are normally about 3–4ft (90–120cm) high, but are insufficiently mature to flower. Grass palms are useful near the sea, since they stand up well to wind and salt spray.

Grass palm *Cordyline australis*

Plant grass palm (*above*) in mid- to late spring, using a soil-based potting mix incorporating slow-release fertilizer. Top-dress with fresh potting mix in mid-spring .

See also page 189; illustrations pages 21, 111.

MALE FERN
Dryopteris filix-mas
DECIDUOUS FERN ZONES 4–8
The male fern is one of the easiest ferns to grow, tolerating a wide range of conditions and forming a graceful clump of much-divided fronds above stalks that are covered with rust-colored scales (*right*). It can grow to 3ft (90cm) or more, and in very mild conditions may be semi-evergreen. There are several forms, usually more compact, with crested fronds.

Plant in early to mid-spring, using a soil-based potting mix with added humus. Place in shade and water well.

BAMBOO
Fargesia
EVERGREEN BAMBOO ZONES 4–9
The fountain-like effect of several clump-forming bamboos is nicely displayed when they are grown in containers. Among the most graceful of evergreens, bamboos are tall and airy, and give a patio or yard an established, subtropical look.

Two of the best for this purpose have recently undergone name changes. The bamboo now known as *F. nitida* (previously known as *Arundinaria nitida* or *Sinarundinaria nitida*) has purplish stems up to 10ft (3m) high that arch with the plentiful mass of small leaves. The slender stems, up to 8ft (2.5m) high, and the larger leaves of *F. murieliae* (*Arundinaria murieliae, A. spathacea, Thamnocalamus spathaceus*) create a more pronounced arching clump that sways in even a light breeze.

Plant in tubs or in other large containers during the second half of spring, using a soil-based potting mix, which should be kept moist at all times. These bamboos (*right*) can be grown in sun or partial shade, but need shelter from cold winds. Top-dress with fresh potting mix in mid-spring.
See also illustration page 23.

FATSHEDERA
× *Fatshedera lizei*
EVERGREEN SHRUB ZONES 7–11
Although often grown as an indoor plant, this hybrid between *Fatsia* and an ivy makes a handsome foliage plant for growing outdoors in containers and will thrive in sun or shade. Growing to 5ft (1.5m) or more high, its leathery, five-lobed leaves are dark green and glossy. The pale green flowers, which

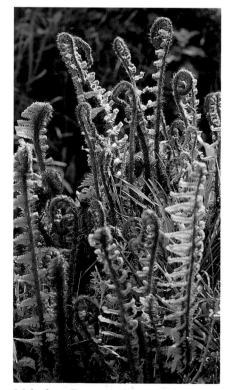

Male fern *Dryopteris filix-mas*

Bamboo *Fargesia*

appear in fall, are rarely significant on specimens grown outdoors.

Plant in fall or early to mid-spring, using soil-based potting mix. Fatshederas (*opposite*) tend to flop if unsupported, so insert a stake when planting and tie in the leading shoot as it develops. Top-dress annually in early to mid-spring.

FATSIA
Fatsia japonica
EVERGREEN SHRUB ZONES 8–10
The large, glossy, fingered leaves of the fatsia suggest subtropical luxury, and this upright plant is capable of exceeding 10ft (3m). Clusters of creamy, rounded flower heads appear in fall and are followed in spring or early summer by bunches of black berries.

Plant in fall or mid-spring, using a soil-based potting mix. In early spring, repot if the roots are congested; otherwise top-dress with fresh potting mix. Extensive pruning is not normally required, but cut back any weak or straggly growth in mid-spring.
See also page 186.

COMMON ENGLISH IVY
Hedera helix
EVERGREEN VINE ZONES 5–9
Ivies are a very versatile group of evergreens, most flourishing in sun or shade. In containers they are

sometimes used as vines but more often as trailers. When allowed to climb, they cling to whatever surface is available by means of aerial roots and often pass through a long juvenile stage before producing the nonclimbing shoots that carry flowers and berries. The small-leaved cultivars are the most suitable as trailers, and when grown in this way they normally do not flower.

Common English ivy, whose green leaves have three or five lobes, has numerous cultivars, both green-leaved and variegated. Green-leaved cultivars include: 'Duckfoot', with small leaves that have three rounded lobes; 'Green Ripple', with small leaves, coppery in winter, with three or five lobes elegantly pointing forward; 'Donerailensis', which has three-lobed leaves that are a somber green with white veins in summer, and in winter turn copper with the veins showing green; 'Manda's Crested' ('Curly Locks'), with medium-sized leaves that take on a red tinge in winter; 'Spetchley', with very small leaves of dark green; and 'Triton' ('Green Feather'), with much dissected, dark green leaves.

Plant ivies between early fall and early spring, using a soil-based potting mix. It may take several months before ivies grown as vines start to cling. To get them started, tie young shoots close to their support. To encourage trailing ivies to branch, pinch back the growing tips of stems. All ivies do better if given liquid fertilizer every three or four weeks during the growing season.
See also pages 184, 186; illustrations pages 55, 72–73, 88.

CORKSCREW RUSH
Juncus effusus 'Spiralis'
EVERGREEN PERENNIAL   ZONES 3–7
This curiosity is an aquatic perennial, suitable for the edges of a container pool. Tightly spiraling or more loosely twisted stems up to 18in (45cm) long make a knotted clump. The corkscrew rush bears inconspicuous clusters of brown flowers in early to mid-summer.

Plant in mid- to late spring, using an aquatic potting mix in a basket or perforated pot. Set in water at a depth of 2–3in (5–8cm). Tidy plants during the growing season and remove any straight leaves.

JUNIPER
Juniperus sabina 'Tamariscifolia'
EVERGREEN CONIFER   ZONES 4–8
Junipers provide a large number of dwarf or semi-dwarf evergreen shrubs that can be grown in containers. Many have gray-green or gray-blue foliage. The sprawling *J. s.* 'Tamariscifolia', which is green-leaved, makes a flat-topped bush 18in (45cm) high with horizontal branches 2–3ft (60–90cm) long.

Plant in mid-spring, using a soil-based potting mix. Repot only when the roots are congested; otherwise top-dress in early to mid-spring.
See also page 194.

OSTRICH FERN
Matteuccia struthiopteris
DECIDUOUS FERN   ZONES 2–8
A short stem supports a perfect shuttlecock 3–5ft (90–150cm) high, of yellow-green, sterile fronds surrounding a circle of shorter, dark brown fronds

that are fertile. The symmetry of the ostrich fern is appealing but it requires a regular supply of moisture to achieve perfection.

Plant in early to mid-spring, using a soil-based potting mix to which leaf mold or other humus has been added. Grow in full or partial shade and keep well watered. Cut down dead fronds in mid- to late fall.

ROYAL FERN
Osmunda regalis
DECIDUOUS FERN   ZONES 4–9
This splendid fern lives up to its regal name, since its copper-tinted fronds unfold with great elegance. Bright green and leathery in summer, when they sometimes attain a height of 6ft (1.8m), they turn bronze in fall. Mature royal ferns can have a spread of over 4ft (1.2m). They will grow in sun or shade but require permanently moist conditions.

Plant in early to mid-spring, using a soil-based potting mix, to which leaf mold or other humus has been added. Set the crowns so that their tops are level with the soil surface. Clear the foliage away in mid- to late fall, and top-dress annually in early to mid-spring by replacing the top 2–3in (5–8in) of potting mix.

PELARGONIUM, GERANIUM
Pelargonium
EVERGREEN PERENNIAL   ZONES 9–10
Many pelargoniums have attractive foliage, and in some cases the ornamental and aromatic qualities of the leaves count for more than the flowers. Those with scented leaves, pungent as well as sweet-smelling, will normally release their fragrance when lightly touched. These excellent pot plants deserve to be more widely grown for this reason alone.

One of the most splendid is the peppermint pelargonium (*P. tomentosum*), which can make a mound, 4ft (1.2m) high and wide, with large, pale green, downy-soft leaves that release a powerful peppermint scent when bruised. This pelargonium is unusual because it prefers light shade. Its white flowers are inconspicuous.

The oak-leaved pelargonium (*P. quercifolium*), usually less than 3ft (90cm) high, has narrow, dark-veined, aromatic leaves, deeply lobed and with a serrated edge. The flowers, blooming in late

Fatshedera × *Fatshedera lizei*

181

spring and summer, are pink with purple markings. 'Graveolens', with a height and spread of 2–3ft (60–90cm), has deeply lobed and toothed lemon-scented leaves. All through summer it carries pink flowers with purple spots on the upper petals. The purple-flowered 'Radula' (*below*), of similar size, has foliage smelling of rose and lemon. The more compact 'Prince of Orange', with darkly veined pink flowers, has leaves with the most intense orange fragrance.
See also pages 135, 147–48, 153–54, 163, 170, 187, 190, 194; illustrations pages 104–105, 127.

Pelargonium *Pelargonium* 'Radula'

PINE
Pinus
EVERGREEN CONIFER   ZONES 3–7
Many dwarf pines are easy to grow in containers and they are valuable for their striking evergreen needles. They are best placed in full sun on their own or combined with alpine-garden plants.

The slow-growing mountain pine (*P. mugo*) may eventually exceed 6ft (1.8m) in height and spread while developing into an attractively gnarled specimen (*right*). Several dwarf forms are sold as grafted plants: 'Mops' makes a gray-green ball 2ft (60cm) high and wide.

Dwarf forms of the Scots pine (*P. sylvestris*) include 'Beuvronensis', with a height of 3ft (90cm) and slightly broader spread. Its short needles are gray-green and the buds have a red tinge in winter.

Plant in fall or early spring, using soil-based potting mix. Top-dress annually in early to mid-spring.

SHIELD FERN
Polystichum
EVERGREEN FERN   ZONES 5–8
The soft shield fern (*P. setiferum*) may form a sprawling clump 4ft (1.2m) wide, but has a more upright habit in cool, moist conditions. Light green fronds up to 3ft (90cm) high are soft in texture, and the stems are covered with gray-brown scales. The Acutilobum Group has particularly elegant, narrow fronds about 2ft (60cm) high. The hard shield fern (*P. aculeatum*) has leathery fronds, up to 3ft (90cm) high, with a glossy upper surface and mat underside. The Christmas or sword fern (*P. munitum*) has lustrous evergreen fronds that taper to a fine point. In containers this fern rarely exceeds 3ft (90cm) in height.

Plant in mid-spring, using an alkaline-based potting mix to which leaf mold or other humus has been added. Place in full or partial shade and keep well watered during the growing season.

PORTUGAL LAUREL
Prunus lusitanica
EVERGREEN SHRUB OR SMALL TREE
ZONES 8–9
The Portugal laurel is a somber but beautiful shrub or small tree that is capable of reaching to more than 15ft (4.5m) but is easily restricted to 8ft (2.5m) or less. In a container it is best grown as a tree, on a single stem, with the head sheared to a rounded or

Pine *Pinus mugo*

domed shape. Unclipped bushes bear cream flowers in early summer, followed by strings of black fruit. The red stalks of the glossy dark leaves are also an attractive feature.

Plant in early fall or mid-spring, using a soil-based potting mix incorporating slow-release fertilizer. Top-dress annually in mid-spring after removing the top 2–3in (5–8cm) of potting mix. Use pruners to trim the foliage in late summer.

FRINGECUP
Tellima grandiflora
SEMI-EVERGREEN PERENNIAL   ZONES 4–8
The heart-shaped, purplish-green leaves of the fringecup make an interesting addition to a container planting, with the small, bell-shaped cream flowers providing a late spring bonus.

Plant in fall or early spring, in a soil-based potting mix.
See illustration page 96.

AMERICAN ARBORVITAE
Thuja occidentalis 'Holmstrup'
EVERGREEN CONIFER   ZONES 3–7
The species *T. occidentalis* is too large for containers, but numerous dwarf and compact forms are suitable. 'Holmstrup' makes a rich green pyramid, packed with upright sprays of foliage, that can eventually exceed 5ft (1.5m). It needs full sun and is best in a sheltered spot.

Plant in fall or early to mid-spring, using a soil-based potting mix. Top-dress annually in mid-spring.
See also page 185.

DWARF CATTAIL
Typha minima
PERENNIAL   ZONES 6–9
The cattails have a reputation for being invasive, yet the dwarf cattail is a well-behaved waterside plant, suitable for small pools of any kind, including those in containers. Growing to a height of 18–24in (45–60cm), it has thin grassy leaves and long stalks. The brown flower heads produced in mid- to late summer are succeeded by decorative seed heads.

Plant in spring in a basket or perforated pot, using an aquatic potting mix. Set in water at a depth of 2–6in (5–15cm); such a covering of water reduces the risk of plants being killed by cold weather in winter.

GOLD TO CHARTREUSE FOLIAGE

There are numerous plants with greenish-yellow foliage or leaves that are variegated in shades ranging from cream to gold. They are plants to use with discretion, but the sunny warmth of their coloring can create a cheerful mood in the container garden just as it can on a larger scale. Yellow foliage is most pronounced when plants are grown in an open, sunny position, although some yellow foliage scorches under a fierce sun.

MAPLE

Acer

DECIDUOUS SHRUB ZONES 5–7

The foliage of the golden-leaved maples is likely to be scorched by strong sun, yet it will lose its glow if plants are positioned in full shade. A sheltered position in partial shade is best.

The slow-growing *A. shirasawanum* f. *aureum* (often listed as *A. japonicum* 'Aureum') will eventually reach a height of 4–5ft (1.2–1.5m). Its yellow leaves, beautiful when unfolding at the same time as the clusters of red flowers are showing, turn rich crimson in fall. Also slow growing is the golden form of the Japanese maple (*A. palmatum* 'Aureum'), which may eventually exceed 6ft (1.8m) high, and has dense fan-shaped sprays of rich yellow-green foliage.

*See also pages **178**, **188**.*

SPOTTED JAPANESE AUCUBA

Aucuba japonica 'Picturata'

EVERGREEN SHRUB ZONES 7–10

Although the aucuba tolerates the most unpromising conditions, the variegated forms are worth growing in good potting mix in an open spot. Plants are either male or female, but only female plants bear berries. The male plant 'Picturata' can grow to more than 6ft (1.8m) and be as broad as it is high. Its large, leathery leaves are dark green with a central yellow splash. The female plant 'Crotonifolia' is a similar size. Its leaves are boldly splashed with yellow, and its scarlet berries often persist through winter and into spring.

Plant in early to mid-fall or early to mid-spring, using a soil-based potting mix. Top-dress annually in spring with fresh potting mix; repot only when the roots are congested.

See also page 202.

LING, SCOTCH HEATHER

Calluna vulgaris

EVERGREEN SHRUB ZONES 5–7

Among the many cultivars of ling there are a number that have strongly colored foliage. Its long-lasting, ornamental value, however, is sometimes undermined by mismatched flower colors. Worthwhile exceptions include 'Gold Haze', which has bright gold foliage with white flowers. In spring the young growths of 'Orange Queen' are rich yellow, but in summer they age to deep orange. Both these cultivars grow to 2ft (60cm) and flower in late summer or early fall.

See also pages 131, 159.

FALSE CYPRESS

Chamaecyparis

EVERGREEN CONIFER ZONES 5–8

Numerous dwarf cultivars of *Chamaecyparis* species produce gold foliage. The Lawson false cypress (*C. lawsoniana*) makes a large, vigorous, conical tree, yet the cultivar 'Aurea Densa' reaches its height of 6ft (1.8m) only slowly. The conical bush is packed with short, stiff sprays of golden foliage. More compact is a cultivar of the Hinoki false cypress (*C. obtusa*) called 'Nana Aurea'. This plant makes a dome about 2ft (60cm) high of dense, fan-shaped sprays of rich yellow-green foliage.

*See also page **179**.*

WINTER HEATH

Erica carnea

EVERGREEN SHRUB ZONES 5–8

The vivid yellow foliage of some heaths and heathers is highly ornamental. However, as with the golden-leaved lings (*Calluna*), flower and foliage color do not always go well together, which makes the exceptions even more valuable.

Among useful container heaths is 'Ann Sparkes': by winter, when the rose-pink flowers are borne, the golden foliage has turned to a rich bronze. 'Aurea' bears bright gold foliage in spring and summer, which changes to light green in winter, during the flowering season. Its flowers are pink, fading to near white. These two cultivars grow 6–8in (15–20cm) high.

*See also pages **137**, **155**, **165**, **171**.*

EUONYMUS

Euonymus

EVERGREEN SHRUB ZONES 5–8

There is a surprising range of variegation among *E. fortunei* cultivars, most of which make useful small shrubs for containers, although the species itself can be semi-prostrate or even a self-clinging vine. One of the brightest cultivars is *E. f.* 'Emerald 'n' Gold', with its rich yellow edging to glossy green leaves, which assume a red tinge in winter. The leaves of the slightly more subdued 'Sunspot' (*below*) have a green edge and a cream or golden-yellow center. Both make hummocks of foliage about 18in (45cm) high by 2ft (60cm) wide, and bear small sprays of greenish-white flowers from early to mid-summer.

Japanese spindle (*E. japonicus*, Z7–9) also has several good variegated forms. 'Ovatus Aureus' has glossy, dark green leaves with bold yellow edging. This useful shrub tolerates salt spray; it grows to 6ft (1.8m) or more.

Plant in early to mid-fall or mid-spring, using a soil-based mix. Pruning is not usually necessary, but plants can be shaped in late summer or early fall. Top-dress with fresh mix in spring; repot when the roots are congested.

See also page 186.

Euonymus *Euonymus fortunei* 'Sunspot'

Hakonechloa *Hakonechloa macra* 'Aureola'

Common English ivy *Hedera helix* 'Buttercup'

HAKONECHLOA

Hakonechloa macra

EVERGREEN PERENNIAL GRASS   ZONES 6–9

The variegated forms of this Japanese, clump-forming genus are more widely grown than the green-leaved species itself. 'Alboaurea' makes a softly arching clump about 12in (30cm) high, the leaves variegated white and yellow and showing very little green. Even more striking is 'Aureola' (*above*), its ribbonlike, bright yellow leaves having only a few narrow lines of green. Both make lovely specimens planted on their own, positioned in an open or partially shaded spot.

Plant in mid-fall or early to mid-spring, using a soil-based potting mix. The rhizomes spread slowly, but if necessary divide in spring; otherwise give an annual topdressing of fresh potting mix.

COMMON ENGLISH IVY

Hedera helix

EVERGREEN VINE   ZONES 5–9

The somber green of many common English ivy cultivars is relieved by gold variegation, but in most cases the full richness of the variegation develops only when plants are grown in sun.

'Californian Gold' has medium-sized leaves with yellow blotches and speckles over green, while 'Midas Touch' bears yellow leaves with gray-green splashes and bright green speckling. 'Buttercup' has small to medium-sized leaves, which are bright greenish yellow (*above*). They tend to burn in full sun, yet lose their yellow tint if heavily shaded. One of the most popular in this group is 'Goldheart', which has small to medium-sized dark green leaves with a rich gold splash in the center. Its variegation remains vivid even when the plant is grown in shade. Another ivy with sunny variegation is 'Golden Ingot', its yellow splashed with shades of green.

*See also pages **181**, **186**; illustration page 124.*

HELICHRYSUM

Helichrysum petiolare 'Limelight'

EVERGREEN SHRUB   ZONES 8–10

This yellow-green, trailing shrub is as useful as the more familiar, gray-leaved helichrysum and, like it, is normally grown as an annual. Its felted leaves, covering a plant with a spread of 4ft (1.2m) or more, cool down hot color schemes and fill out, but do not clutter, mixed plantings in hanging baskets, window boxes, and other containers.

*See also page **193**; illustrations pages 106, 115.*

HOSTA

Hosta

PERENNIAL   ZONES 3–9

Hostas provide some of the finest foliage plants that can be grown in temperate gardens, and many make superb container plants – generally seen at their best when grown alone. The hosta cultivars cover a wide range of leaf shapes, sizes, and colors: gold, yellow, and cream are found in both plain-leaved and variegated forms.

'Sum and Substance' has impressively large, heavily textured leaves that are greenish gold and stand 30in (75cm) high. *H. fortunei* 'Aurea' makes a clump of soft yellow leaves, 2ft (60cm) high, which gradually turn to green.

Of those with yellow edges to the leaves, *H. sieboldiana* 'Frances Williams' is outstanding. A quilted blue leaf standing up to 30in (75cm) tall is outlined by an irregular cream edge that deepens to yellow in fall. In *H. fortunei* 'Aureomarginata', green leaves edged with yellow make a clump 2ft (60cm) high. Of the smaller hostas, one of the best is 'Golden Tiara'. It grows to 12in (30cm) and has gold edges to its heart-shaped, green leaves.

In *H. fortunei* 'Gold Standard' it is the edge that is green, the center of the leaf gradually changing from green to rich yellow. It makes a clump up to 30in (75cm) high.

The lilylike flowers of these hostas, an added attraction in summer, may be white, as with *H. sieboldiana* 'Frances Williams', or shades of lavender, mauve, or purple.

Plant hostas in fall or spring, using a soil-based potting mix to which leaf mold or other humus has been added. Apply liquid fertilizer every two to three weeks during the growing season. Slugs and snails relish the foliage of hostas and need to be controlled. Top-dress hostas generously with fresh potting mix in spring.

See also pages 187, 193.

GOLDEN HOP

Humulus lupulus 'Aureus'

PERENNIAL VINE   ZONES 5–9

Less vigorous than the common hop, but even so capable of climbing to 15ft (4.5m) or more, the golden hop makes an unusual foliage for containers. The leaves, with three or five elegantly cut lobes, are a beautiful shade of yellow-green until mid-summer, when the green becomes more pronounced. The yellow is strongest in full sun.

Plant in fall or spring, using a soil-based potting mix. Provide supports for the twining stems.

See illustration page 75.

DEAD-NETTLE
Lamium maculatum 'Aureum'
PERENNIAL   ZONES 4–8
Many dead-nettles have silvery foliage: in 'Aureum' the leaves are a strong yellow-green with a white stripe. It also carries pink flowers in early summer. Plants are 6in (15cm) high, and the stems, up to 20in (50cm) long, root as they spread. This slow-growing cultivar can make an attractive underplanting to a large shrub or as a filler in a mixed planter. Plant in spring, using a soil-based potting mix.
See also page 187.

CREEPING JENNY
Lysimachia nummularia 'Aurea'
PERENNIAL   ZONES 4–8
In summer this creeping perennial (*below*), only 2in (5cm) high but with trailing stems as long as 18in (45cm), happily combines bright yellow, cup-shaped flowers and greenish-yellow leaves, which are carried in neat pairs along the stems. It is best planted so that it spills over the edge of a pot.

Plant in spring, in a soil-based or a soil-less potting mix. Although moisture-loving, it will tolerate dry conditions. The foliage turns green in shade.
See illustration page 96.

OSMANTHUS
Osmanthus heterophyllus
EVERGREEN SHRUB ZONES 7–9
This slow-growing, hollylike shrub, with inconspicuous but fragrant flowers in fall, has several variegated forms. 'Goshiki' has bold yellow mottling and its young growth is colored a rosy bronze.

Plant in spring, using a soil-based potting mix.
See illustration page 124.

NEW ZEALAND FLAX
Phormium 'Yellow Wave'
EVERGREEN PERENNIAL   ZONES 5–9
Phormiums are grown mainly for their clumps of leathery, sword-shaped leaves, which are sometimes colored with linear yellow variegation. Unlike some phormiums, 'Yellow Wave' has lax leaves, about 3ft (90cm) high, which are yellow, bordered by fine green edges.
*See also page **190**; illustration page 12.*

BAMBOO
Pleioblastus auricomus
EVERGREEN BAMBOO   ZONES 5–9
This dwarf bamboo (sometimes listed as *P. viridistriatus*) is extraordinarily beautiful when grown on its own and placed in full sun. In shade much of its golden radiance is lost. Growing to 30in (75cm), its downy, ribbonlike leaves are a rich gold that is unevenly striped with green (*below*).

Plant in mid-spring, using a soil-based potting mix. Cut out old stems in early spring to encourage fresh growth. Top-dress generously with fresh potting mix in spring; repot only if the roots become congested.
See also pages 180, 187.

PICK-A-BACK PLANT
Tolmiea menziesii 'Taff's Gold'
EVERGREEN PERENNIAL   ZONES 7-10
The common names of the species refer to the way plantlets develop where leaves join stems. This zestful characteristic is also found in the cultivar 'Taff's Gold', in which the leaves are prettily speckled green and soft yellow. This is a hearty filler for hanging baskets and other containers, forming a dense clump 1ft (30cm) or more high, and trailing elegantly. There are spikes of tiny, green-brown flowers in spring.

Plant in early spring, using a soil-based potting mix. Renew plants every year or two, propagating from plantlets.
See illustration page 25.

ARBORVITAE
Thuja
EVERGREEN CONIFER   ZONES 3–8
One of the most widely grown of all golden-leaved conifers is the dwarf cultivar of the American arborvitae, *T. occidentalis* 'Rheingold'. This slowly forms a loose cone, eventually more than 3ft (90cm) in height, its old-gold richness standing out particularly well in the winter garden.

Among the many dwarf cultivars of the Chinese arborvitae (*T. orientalis*) is 'Aurea Nana', which makes a dense, globular bush, packed with sprays of yellow-green foliage.
*See also page **182**.*

THYME
Thymus
EVERGREEN SHRUB   ZONES 4–9
Thymes are grown mainly as aromatic herbs, yet several also make attractive foliage plants. The golden thymes offer more showy alternatives to those such as *T. vulgaris* 'Silver Posie', with creamy variegation that creates a cool silvery effect. Lemon thyme (*T. × citriodorus*), for example, has cultivars with yellow foliage or gold variegation: 'Aureus' is a springy dwarf shrub, about 4–8in (10–20cm) high, forming a dense, spreading mat up to 18in (45cm) across of tiny, fragrant bright golden leaves and bearing lilac flowers in summer. Another attractive thyme is 'Doone Valley'. Its low mat, only 3in (8cm) high, displays gold mottling running through dark green. Heads of mauve flowers are an inconspicuous feature in late summer.
*See also page **197**; illustration page 125.*

Creeping jenny *Lysimachia nummularia* 'Aurea'

Bamboo *Pleioblastus auricomus*

WHITE AND CREAM IN LEAVES

The detailed beauty of variegated foliage is often lost in the open garden. This is one reason for growing plants in a way that allows them to be seen up close. Variegated plants also add sparkle to ambitious plantings and introduce a light note to shady areas.

VARIEGATED GROUND ELDER

Aegopodium podagraria 'Variegatum'
PERENNIAL   ZONES 4–9
The variegated form of ground elder is less invasive than the plain green species, and the clumps of cream-splashed leaves, about 10in (25cm) high, are ornamental in shade. Plant in spring, using a soil-based potting mix.
See also illustration page 17.

ORNAMENTAL CABBAGE

Brassica oleracea Capitata Group
ANNUAL
As well as the edible cabbages, there are some that have been bred specifically for their ornamental value. Many have creamy white and green heads, and the leaves of the flowerlike rosettes are often waved or crinkled (*below*). These biennials grown as annuals are most frequently used for long-lasting fall and winter planting. Most have a height and spread of 12–18in (30–45cm).

To raise from seed, sow outdoors in spring. Plant in containers in late

summer or early fall, using an alkaline-rich, soil-based potting mix.
See also page 189; illustration page 95.

COMMON BOXWOOD

Buxus sempervirens 'Elegantissima'
EVERGREEN SHRUB   ZONES 6–8
There are several variegated forms of boxwood – the touches of white, cream, or gold lightening the somber green of these plants, especially those grown in shade. 'Elegantissima' is a slow-growing, dense, dome-shaped cultivar with creamy white edges to the leaves, which create a silvery effect. It rarely exceeds 4ft (1.2m).
See also page 179; illustration page 70.

EUONYMUS

Euonymus fortunei
EVERGREEN SHRUB   ZONES 5–8
Several cultivars of *E. fortunei* display white or cream variegation. 'Silver Queen' has young foliage that is yellow in spring but later changes to gray-green with a creamy white edge. This plant is up to 3ft (90cm) high but often wider. 'Emerald Gaiety', of similar dimensions, has rounded dark green leaves edged in startling white. Both of these cultivars grow in sun or shade.
See also page 183.

FATSIA

Fatsia japonica 'Variegata'
EVERGREEN SHRUB   ZONES 8–10
The plain-leaved fatsia is handsome, but the addition of random, creamy white splashes on the tips of the fingered leaves puts this cultivar in a higher class. It will thrives in a container in a sheltered, partially shaded position.
See also page 180.

VARIEGATED GROUND IVY

Glechoma hederacea 'Variegata'
EVERGREEN PERENNIAL   ZONES 8–10
Trailing stems, which can be 3ft (90cm) or more long, and prettily variegated, heart-shaped leaves make ground ivy ideal for window boxes and hanging baskets. It grows well in sun or shade. Plant in spring, using any soil-based or soil-less potting mix. The ground ivy is often treated as an annual but it can be salvaged from summer displays, cut back and used the following year.
See illustrations pages 105, 115.

IVY

Hedera
EVERGREEN VINE   ZONES 5–9
Several large-leaved, variegated ivies make impressive vines, climbing to 15ft (4.5m) or more. They also look attractive trailing from a large container. One of the most widely grown is *H. canariensis* 'Gloire de Marengo' (Z9–10). Its handsome green leaves, usually unlobed, have gray mottling and a creamy white edge.

Although the white-variegated cultivars of common English ivy (*H. helix*) are numerous, few match the cool beauty of 'Glacier', with three- or five-lobed leaves edged with creamy white and overlaid with patches of gray-green and silver-gray. Other good selections include 'Caecilia', with frilly, three-lobed leaves that are green and creamy white; 'Kolibri', which has small green leaves boldly splashed and speckled with white; and 'Little Diamond', bushy, with silvery leaves.
See also pages 181, 184.

HEUCHERA

Heuchera 'Snow Storm'
EVERGREEN PERENNIAL   ZONES 4–8
The fresh delicacy of *H.* 'Snow Storm' (*below*) creates a beautiful lightness among plants that enjoy dappled shade. Forming a clump with a height and

Ornamental cabbage *Brassica oleracea*

Heuchera *Heuchera* 'Snow Storm'

spread of 12in (30cm), it is composed of overlapping, heart-shaped leaves that have a scalloped, ruffled edge. While their base color is ivory, the edges are green, as is the speckling, which varies in intensity from leaf to leaf. The leaf veins turn deep pink in winter. Red flower sprays appear in early summer.
*See also page **189-90**.*

Hosta *Hosta fortunei* 'Francee'

HOSTA
Hosta
PERENNIAL   ZONES 3–9
The crisp combination of white and green is found in a number of variegated hostas. A classic in this group is *H. undulata var. albomarginata* (*H.* 'Thomas Hogg'). This makes a clump 2ft (60cm) high of deeply veined, green leaves with a wavy white edge tapering to a fine point. Another good choice for containers is *H. fortunei* 'Francee', with its clump, 2ft (60cm) high, of large, rich green leaves edged in white (*above*). Both these hostas have mauve flowers in summer. In 'Sugar and Cream', the edge to the wavy leaves has a warmer tone. This hosta stands 2ft (60cm) high and bears fragrant white flowers in summer.
*See also pages **184**, 193; illustration page 23.*

ENGLISH HOLLY
Ilex aquifolium 'Argentea Marginata'
EVERGREEN SHRUB OR TREE   ZONES 7–9
Many hollies are grown simply for the beauty of their glossy, usually prickly and often variegated foliage. Male and female flowers usually bloom on separate bushes, and female plants

produce berries only if there is a male plant nearby. One of the loveliest of the English hollies is the white-variegated 'Argentea Marginata'. The white edge combined with the lustrous foliage creates a silvered effect that is beautiful in sun or shade. Mature plants can bear good crops of berries. When grown as container specimens, many hollies – even though slow growing – may need shaping to keep them to a height of 5–8ft (1.5–2.5m).

Plant hollies in mid- to late spring, using a soil-based potting mix. Clip topiary specimens in mid-summer. Top-dress with fresh mix annually in spring; repot only when the roots are congested.
See also page 184.

DEAD-NETTLE
Lamium maculatum
SEMI-EVERGREEN PERENNIAL   ZONES 4–8
The adventurous habits of the dead-nettles have made them valued ground-cover plants, but they are also useful as trailing fillers in containers. The foliage of 'Beacon Silver' has a metallic white, mauve-tinged variegation. This cultivar carries heads of small mauve flowers.
*See also page **185**.*

PELARGONIUM, GERANIUM
Pelargonium
EVERGREEN PERENNIAL   ZONES 9–10
Among the several handsome pelargoniums with white or cream variegation, 'Lady Plymouth' is an understated aristocrat. Elegantly cut, gray-green leaves that are sweetly aromatic have an irregular creamy margin. The lemon-scented *P. crispum* 'Variegatum' is more assertive, with upright stems carrying tightly crinkled leaves edged with cream. 'Atomic Snowflake' has rose-scented leaves of velvety pale green edged with cream.
*See also pages 135, 147–48, **153–54**, 163, 170, 181, 190, 194; illustration page 104.*

GARDENER'S GARTERS
Phalaris arundinacea var. *picta*
EVERGREEN PERENNIAL   ZONES 4–9
This notoriously invasive grass is highly ornamental, with a cream and bright green variegation that runs the length of the narrow leaf blades. The flower panicles are a subsidiary feature but add to the plant's overall appeal. In a densely planted container, the spreading tendencies are to some

extent controlled, and the grass is a useful foil for more showy plants. It also looks distinctive planted on its own. Plant in spring, in a soil-based mix. When dismantling plantings in fall, retain vigorous clumps of the grass for planting the following spring.
See illustration page 113.

PLECTRANTHUS
Plectranthus madagascariensis 'Variegated Mintleaf'
EVERGREEN PERENNIAL   ZONES 9–10
The scented variegated foliage of the tender perrennial *P. madagascariensis* 'Variegated Mintleaf' (*below*) is useful for summer displays in the container garden. This tender perennial does well in partial shade. Bushy plants are covered in scalloped leaves with an irregular white edge. White and purple flowers sometimes appear in summer.

Plant in late spring, using a soil-based or soil-less potting mix. Pinch back young shoots to encourage bushy growth. Keep well watered and apply liquid fertilizer every two weeks, starting three to four weeks after planting. Rooted cuttings can be overwintered.
See also illustrations pages 101, 110.

Plectranthus *Plectranthus madagascariensis* 'Variegated Mintleaf'

DWARF WHITE-STRIPE BAMBOO
Pleioblastus variegatus
EVERGREEN SHRUB   ZONES 5–9
Whether grown in sun or shade, this dwarf bamboo makes dense clumps, up to 3ft (90cm) high and 18in (45cm) across, of variegated leaves. Some leaves are almost entirely dark green, others nearly white, others more balanced.
*See also pages 180, **185**.*

RED, PURPLE, AND BRONZE FOLIAGE

Red foliage tints are usually associated with seasonal change, either the time when the leaves unfurl in spring or the brief period in fall before the leaves drop. Those plants that retain the red, bronze, or purple coloring of their foliage for weeks or months provide an unusual feature and make a useful contrast to other foliage in a container garden. They add depth to plantings, but need the companionship of lighter colors in foliage or flowers to relieve their somber tendencies.

JAPANESE MAPLE

Acer palmatum
DECIDUOUS SHRUB ZONES 5–8
The Japanese maple has produced a large number of cultivars with purplish, coppery, or bronze foliage. One of the most richly colored is 'Bloodgood', which can grow to 8ft (2.5m) or more. Clothed in summer with tiers of elegant, five-lobed leaves of rich

purplish red, in fall the glowing red foliage is even more outstanding. The name *A. palmatum* Dissectum Atropurpureum Group covers several forms with finely divided leaves that are bronze-purple in summer turning to vivid red in fall (*below*). These slowly form a mound about 3ft (90cm) high but spreading to 5ft (1.5m) or more.

The fall tints of the maples must be taken into account when choosing plants for foliage color. The seven-lobed leaves of the cultivar 'Osakazuki', a small tree under 10ft (3m) high, provide an exceptionally fiery display. *See also pages* **178**, **183**, **185**; *illustrations pages 46–47.*

CARPET BUGLE

Ajuga reptans
EVERGREEN PERENNIAL ZONES 4–8
Carpet bugle, suitable as an underplanting to shrubs, makes low rosettes of overwintering leaves and

Carpet bugle *Ajuga reptans* 'Burgundy Glow'

sends up spires 4–6in (10–15cm) high of purple-blue, tubular flowers in early summer. The purple foliage of *A. r.* 'Atropurpurea' has a metallic sheen, while in 'Burgundy Glow' (*above*) the leaves are an appealing mixture of wine-red, pink, bronze, and cream.

Plant in fall or spring, using a soil-based potting mix. Divide and replant in spring.

BURNING BUSH, SUMMER CYPRESS

Bassia scoparia f. *tricophylla* 'Childsii'
HALF-HARDY ANNUAL
The narrow pointed leaves that cover this upright plant, often still listed under *Kochia*, give burning bush a superficial resemblance to a bushy cypress. In late summer and fall, its pale green foliage turns a rich shade of red. An attractive plant to grow in individual pots as part of a formal design in a sunny spot, this plant grows up to 2ft (60cm) high.

To raise from seed, sow in warmth in early to mid-spring. Harden off before planting outdoors in late spring or early summer, using a soil-based mix.

REX BEGONIA

Begonia rex
EVERGREEN PERENNIAL ZONES 8–10
A range of highly ornamental perennials derived from *B. rex* are popular indoor plants, which can also be used outdoors in summer, either on their own or in combination with other plants.

Japanese maple *Acer palmatum* Dissectum Atropurpureum Group

Rex begonia *Begonia rex*

Although the hairy leaves are varied in shape and markings, many have patterns of red, bronze, or silver on shades of green (*above*). The pale pink flowers are less important than the decorative foliage.

Plant up in mid-spring, using a soil-based or soil-less potting mix, and move outdoors in late spring or early summer. Apply liquid fertilizer every two weeks.

BERGENIA
Bergenia
EVERGREEN PERENNIAL   ZONES 4–8
The bergenias are impressive foliage plants throughout the year and their sprays of pink or white flowers are an additional attraction in spring. Among the most appealing bergenias are those with foliage that turns rich shades of purple and red in winter. *B. cordifolia* 'Purpurea' has rounded leaves up to 30in (75cm) high that color richly as cold intensifies. The flowers in spring are magenta. *B. purpurascens* makes a clump of narrow leaves about 18in (45cm) high, which in winter change from dark green to deep plum-red with a vivid carmine underside. The pink flowers are borne on reddish stems. 'Abendglut' ('Evening Glow') is one of numerous hybrids that color well: its leaves form a low rosette, and in winter they are deep maroon with a brighter reverse. It grows to 12in (30cm) and has bright pink flowers in spring.
See also page **179.**

ORNAMENTAL CABBAGE
Brassica oleracea Capitata Group
ANNUAL
The most vivid of the ornamental cabbages are those in which the rosettes are wholly or partly red, or purple-red. Whether grown on their own or as a contrast to those with creamy variegation, they are among the most colorful foliage plants for winter container displays.
See also page **186**; *illustrations pages 95, 103.*

CANNA LILY
Canna
PERENNIAL   ZONES 7–10
Many hybrids of these handsome perennials have been raised, and in temperate regions they are grown mainly for their luxuriant foliage, which comprises paddlelike green or purple leaves (*below*). Where the climate is mild, they also carry showy flowers. Plants grow to 4ft (1.2m) high, or even taller. 'Roi Humbert' has bronze-red leaves and scarlet flowers, 'Wyoming' purple leaves and apricot-orange flowers. Like all cannas, they should be grown in a sunny, sheltered spot.

Start the rhizomes into growth in warmth during late winter or early spring, using a rich, soil-based potting mix to which leaf mold or other humus has been added. Transfer the growing plants into their final pots or tubs in mid-spring, but do not move these into the open until late spring. Water generously during the growing season and apply liquid fertilizer every two weeks, starting two to three weeks after moving plants outdoors. Lift plants before there is any risk of frost. During winter keep the rhizomes slightly moist and store them in frost-free conditions.
See illustrations pages 21, 111.

GRASS PALM
Cordyline australis Purpurea Group
EVERGREEN TREE   ZONES 8–10
The purple leaved forms of the grass palm add the interest of rich coloring to the jagged spiky shape of the plain-leaved form. Specimens used in containers are usually no more than 3–4ft (90–120cm) high, although these slow-growing plants can eventually develop into trees that produce large sprays of white flowers.
See also page **179–80**; *illustration page 111.*

HEUCHERA
Heuchera micrantha var. *diversifolia* 'Palace Purple'
EVERGREEN PERENNIAL   ZONES 4–8
This striking heuchera (*below*) is one of the most useful perennials for container planting in sun or shade. A clump of its deep purple or coppery leaves, broadly heart-shaped but boldly cut, makes an excellent background or contrast to more diffident plants. Specimens can have a height and spread of 18in (45cm) or more, and their sprays of minuscule

Canna lily *Canna*

Heuchera *Heuchera micrantha* var. *diversifolia* 'Palace Purple'

189

white flowers float above the leaves in early summer.

Plant in fall or early to mid-spring, using a soil-based or soil-less potting mix. Lift and divide the plants at least every other year and in between top-dress generously in spring.
See also page 186–87; illustrations pages 16, 106–107, 121.

Houttuynia *Houttuynia cordata* 'Chameleon'

HOUTTUYNIA
Houttuynia cordata 'Chameleon'
PERENNIAL ZONES 6–9
The variegation displayed in *H. c.* 'Chameleon' (*above*) is so vivid that this perennial is best planted on its own. The green, heart-shaped leaves are splashed with intense red, bronze, and yellow, making them far more eye-catching than the creamy flowers. Plants are 12in (30cm) high but spread to 18in (45cm) or more and look best spilling over the rim of a container placed in sun or partial shade.

Plant in early to mid-spring, using a soil-based potting mix. Keep plants well watered during the growing season and apply liquid fertilizer every two weeks, starting three or four weeks after planting. Repot annually in mid-spring.

SACRED BAMBOO
Nandina domestica
EVERGREEN SHRUB ZONES 7–9
This evergreen shrub – not a true bamboo – produces a clump of unbranched stems to a height of 4–6ft

(1.2–1.8m), well clothed with compound leaves. These are green in summer, tinged red in spring, but at their most beautiful in fall, when they turn shades of reddish purple. White flowers in mid-summer are sometimes followed by red fruit, which lasts into winter. The sacred bamboo must have a sunny spot and shelter from cold winds.

Plant in early to mid-spring, using a soil-based potting mix to which leaf mold or other humus has been added. Water generously during the growing season. Cut out old or weak growths after flowering, but repot only when the roots are congested. Top-dress annually in spring.

BLACK MONDO GRASS
Ophiopogon planiscapus 'Nigrescens'
EVERGREEN PERENNIAL ZONES 6–9
The black mondo grasss (*below*) is one of the most distinctive of all foliage plants and makes a striking contrast to snowdrops and to gray and gold foliage. Grassy tufts of arching leaves betray only a hint of green at the base of the clump, which is 8in (20cm) high and slowly spreads to 12in (30cm) or more. Short sprays of mauve flowers in summer are followed by black berries. Black mondo grass can be grown in either sun or partial shade.

Plant in fall or early to mid-spring, using a soil-based potting mix to which leaf mold or other humus has been added. Top-dress with fresh mix annually in spring.

Black mondo grass *Ophiopogon planiscapus* 'Nigrescens'

PELARGONIUM, GERANIUM
Pelargonium
EVERGREEN PERENNIAL ZONES 9–10
Markings in shades of red and bronze add distinction to the leaves of many pelargoniums, in particular the Zonals. 'Mrs Quilter' is a good example of those with bronze foliage; above its leaves stand heads of single pink flowers. More sensational is the creamy margined leaf of 'Dolly Varden', with its prominent red zone that merges with sage-green. The single flowers are red. Both these Zonals grow to a height of about 18in (45cm).

One of the most striking of the scented-leaved pelargoniums is 'Chocolate Peppermint'. Its large, three-lobed leaves have a conspicuous, red-brown mark down the center and release a powerful peppermint scent when bruised. Plants often exceed 20in (50cm) in height.
*See also pages 135, 147–48, **153–54**, 163, 170, 181–82, 184, 187, 194.*

NEW ZEALAND FLAX
Phormium tenax
EVERGREEN PERENNIAL ZONES 9–11
New Zealand flax is a stiffly upright plant with swordlike leaves, which is best grown in full sun. The largest of the purple-leaved cultivars can reach to more than 8ft (2.5m). More suitable for containers are several compact selections: the fan of reddish-purple leaves produced by 'Bronze Baby', for example, rarely exceeds 2ft (60cm) in height. 'Sundowner', about 3ft (90cm) high, has purple-pewter leaves with creamy margins. Both of these cultivars sometimes produce woody stems that carry dull red flowers.

Plant in spring using a soil-based potting mix. Top-dress or repot in fall.
See also page 185; illustrations pages 12, 121.

PIERIS
Pieris formosa var. *forrestii* 'Wakehurst'
EVERGREEN SHRUB ZONE 8
The genus *Pieris* provides a number of pleasing evergreen shrubs, most of which produce attractive, lily-of-the-valley flowers from mid- to late spring. The young growths of some are also spectacularly colored: one of the finest is *P. f.* var. *forrestii* 'Wakehurst', with its long-lasting, red foliage, which shows off the sprays of white flowers. In a container it is usually 6–8ft (1.8–2.5m)

high. Several more compact hybrids, including 'Forest Flame', have similar ornamental qualities. Because the young foliage of all of these shrubs is vulnerable to frost damage, give plants light overhead protection when there is any risk of frost.

Plant in mid-fall or early to mid-spring, using an acidic-soil mix to which leaf mold or other humus has been added. Keep well watered during spring and summer. Little pruning is needed, but faded flowers and any weak growths should be removed. Repot only if the roots are congested. Top-dress generously in spring.

SAGE

Salvia officinalis

EVERGREEN SUBSHRUB   ZONES 7–9

Sage is useful as an ornamental plant as well as being a valuable culinary herb. The purple sage (*S. o.* 'Purpurascens') is especially lovely, making a spreading bush up to 2ft (60cm) high, densely covered with grayish-purple leaves. *S. o.* 'Tricolor', which has leaves that are variegated purple, pink, and white, is less vigorous. All sages are best grown in a sunny, sheltered spot.
See also page 197.

SEDUM

Sedum spathulifolium 'Purpureum'

EVERGREEN PERENNIAL   ZONES 6–9

The yellow flowers that appear in late spring or early summer are but a short-lived attraction of this sedum (*below*);

Sedum *Sedum spathulifolium* 'Purpureum'

what sustains interest in this mat-forming plant are the tight rosettes of waxy purplish leaves. *S. s.* 'Purpureum' is normally under 4in (10cm) in height but can have a spread of 10in (25cm) or more. It often spills out of troughs, where it looks good planted with other sun-loving, alpine-garden plants.

Plant in mid-fall or early to mid-spring, using a gritty, soil-based mix.
See also page 195.

Houseleek *Sempervivum*

HOUSELEEK

Sempervivum

EVERGREEN SUCCULENT   ZONES 5–9

Houseleeks bear fleshy leaves arranged in neat rosettes, often with a beautiful waxen texture and in rich shades of mahogany, bronze, and red (*above*). They offset freely, and a single plant in a pot can create a tightly patterned colony of new plants over the whole surface. Houseleeks are also suitable for combining with small alpine-garden plants in sinks and trough gardens, and they need full sun.

Although the contrast of gray-green leaves and mahogany tips on the 3in (8cm) rosettes is attractive in the common houseleek (*S. tectorum*), many cultivars display even more striking colors: 'Commander Hay', for example, has rosettes 6in (15cm) or more across that are purple-red with green leaf tips. Most send up stems carrying sprays of starlike flowers in summer.

Plant between fall and mid-spring, using a gritty, soil-based potting mix. Repot every two to three years, or earlier if rosettes are congested, and top-dress with fresh mix in the intervening years.
See also page 195

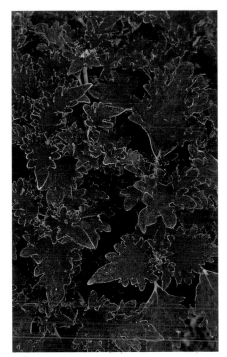

Coleus *Solenostemon*

COLEUS

Solenostemon

ANNUAL

The vivid foliage coloring of coleus (*above*) makes it a popular greenhouse plant, but it can also be used for summer planting outdoors. Mixed with other plants or on its own, it is best grown in a well-lit but lightly shaded spot, because fierce sunlight can cause scorching. The nettle-like leaves, sometimes elaborately cut, are patterned in an astonishing variety, with mixtures of green, red, bronze, purple, yellow, and white. Although coleus can be raised from overwintered cuttings, it is more frequently treated as a tender annual. Seed strains, including Wizard Mixed, give a mixture of compact, free-branching plants 12in (30cm) high. 'Scarlet Poncho' has glowing red leaves outlined in purple and pale yellow. This lax plant, 12in (30cm) in height and spread, is suitable for a hanging basket.

To raise from seed, sow in warmth during mid-winter in order to allow plants of good size to develop. The standard practice of pinching back growing tips to produce bushy plants is less important with compact selections. Repot as necessary before planting outdoors in late spring or early summer. Use either a soil-based or a soil-less potting mix and apply liquid fertilizer every 10 days. Remove flower spikes.
See illustration page 106.

GRAY, SILVER, AND BLUE FOLIAGE

Foliage in this color range is especially valuable in the container garden, where light colors help to ease the congestion of flowers crowded together for maximum effect. The silvers and grays, in particular, will calm potential color clashes and provide a sympathetic background to soft colors. Most foliage plants in gray, silver, or blue are best in full sun and many need free drainage.

WORMWOOD, SAGEBRUSH
Artemisia
EVERGREEN SHRUB/PERENNIAL
ZONES 5–8

The wormwoods include some of the loveliest plants with silvery foliage. One that adapts well to life in containers is the sprawling evergreen perennial *A. stelleriana* (Z3–8). This is an excellent edging plant in full sun, making a spreading clump up to 8in (20cm) high built up of beautifully cut, white-felted leaves (*below*). More suitable for a sunny trough of alpine-garden plants is the shrublet *A. schmidtiana* 'Nana'. It makes a low silvery dome, only 3in (8cm) high but up to 8in (20cm) wide, of soft, fernlike leaves.

Some of the taller aromatic wormwoods that are such valuable border plants in warm, sunny gardens are rather tender and in containers are best incorporated in summer plantings that thrive in full sun. Outstanding for its lacy and silvered foliage is the evergreen shrub *A. arborescens* (Z8–10), which grows to 3ft (90cm). This species is probably a parent of 'Powis Castle' (Z6–9), which makes a dense, silvery mound 2ft (60cm) high. The evergreen perennial *A. absinthium* 'Lambrook Silver' also has silver, much-divided foliage on plants up to 2ft (60cm) high.

Plant *A. stelleriana* and *A. schmidtiana* in early to mid-spring and well-grown specimens of the taller artemisias in mid- to late spring. Use a gritty, soil-based potting mix for all and top-dress with fresh mix in spring. Where the taller wormwoods are unlikely to survive outdoors in winter, overwinter rooted cuttings under glass.
See illustration page 119.

BRACHYGLOTTIS, SENECIO
Brachyglottis 'Sunshine'
EVERGREEN SHRUB   ZONES 8–10

Masses of yellow daisy flowers make *B.* 'Sunshine' (syn. *Senecio* 'Sunshine') a conspicuous shrub in early summer, but its enduring appeal lies in the gray-green foliage and the felted whiteness of the underside of leaves, stems, and the unopened flower buds (*below*). This sprawling shrub, which is 3–4ft (90–120cm) high but often spreads more

than 6ft (1.8m), needs a position in full sun and is particularly useful in coastal gardens.

Plant in fall or mid-spring, using a soil-based potting mix. Repot only when roots become congested, but top-dress with fresh mix annually in mid-spring. Removed faded flowers and any weak and straggly growths in mid-summer.

FALSE CYPRESS
Chamaecyparis
EVERGREEN CONIFER   ZONES 5–8

The Lawson false cypress (*C. lawsoniana*, Z5–7) has provided many dwarf or medium-sized cultivars in a wide range of foliage color, including gray-green and gray-blue. A cultivar that slowly forms a dense column up to 6ft (1.8m) high is 'Ellwoodii'. Its feathery sprays of juvenile foliage are gray-green in summer but turn a metallic blue color in winter.

The sawara false cypress (*C. pisifera*) also has many dwarf and slow-growing cultivars. 'Boulevard' has soft juvenile foliage that is steel-blue in summer but takes on a purplish tinge in winter. It makes a broad-based cone that slowly attains a height of 10ft (3m) or more.

Both of these conifers can be grown in full sun or light shade, the foliage of 'Boulevard' being brightest when it gets some shade.

Plant in early to mid-fall or mid-spring, using a soil-based potting mix. Repot only when roots become congested but top-dress annually with fresh mix in mid-spring.

RUSSIAN OLIVE
Elaeagnus angustifolia
DECIDUOUS SHRUB   ZONES 3–8

The Russian olive makes a spreading, loose shrub or small tree notable for the silveriness of its willowlike leaves and the honeyed fragrance of tiny flowers in late spring or early summer. The yellowish oval fruits that follow are edible. Its hybrid 'Quicksilver' is exceptional for the bleached gray of its foliage (*above right*).

In containers the Russian olive is best grown on a single stem with the head lightly shaped, and specimens maintained at an overall height of 6–8ft (1.8–2.5m). Position in full sun.

Wormwood *Artemisia stelleriana*

Brachyglottis *Brachyglottis* 'Sunshine'

Russian olive *Elaeagnus* 'Quicksilver'

Plant in fall or early to mid-spring, using a slightly gritty, soil-based potting mix. Insert a stake at planting and tie in. Trim plants in early to mid-summer, after flowering.

BLUE FESCUE
Festuca glauca
EVERGREEN PERENNIAL   ZONES 4–9
The blue fescue, a perennial grass, makes short tufts 8in (20cm) high of fine leaves that are gray to gray-blue. The flower spikelets in summer are purplish. This fescue, which needs a position in full sun, makes an attractive contrast in a trough of sprawling alpine-garden plants.

Plant in fall or early to mid-spring, using a gritty, soil-based potting mix. Divide large plants in fall.

CURRY PLANT
Helichrysum italicum
EVERGREEN SHRUB   ZONES 7–9
The powerfully aromatic foliage of several helichrysums have earned them the common name "curry plant." A large container of sun-loving plants could include *H. italicum*, which has needlelike silvery leaves and in summer clusters of yellow button flowers on stems that grow up to 2ft (60cm) high. *H. i.* subsp. *microphyllum*, a short, stiff plant under 8in (20cm) in height, is more suitable for a trough of alpine-garden plants.

Plant in early fall or mid- to late spring, using a gritty, soil-based potting mix. Cut back in mid- to late spring to promote dense new growth. Lift and replant in fresh potting mix every two to three years, and in other years apply a light topdressing of fresh mix in mid-spring.
See illustration page 100.

HELICHRYSUM
Helichrysum petiolare
EVERGREEN SHRUB
ZONES 8–10
H. petiolare (sometimes listed as *H. petiolatum*) is a tender shrubby perennial, but because it is fast growing, producing numerous trailing stems 2–3ft (60–90cm) long in a season, it is usually treated as an annual. Few foliage plants can touch this helichrysum as a moderator between strong colors, as an intensifier of pastel shades, and as a light-colored filler that works its way elegantly through other plants. It sometimes bears straw-colored flowers in summer which fit in with its subdued coloring.

Plant in late spring or early summer, using a soil-based or soil-less potting mix. Keep well watered and apply liquid fertilizer every two weeks, beginning two to three weeks after planting. Rooted cuttings can be overwintered under glass.
See also page 184; illustrations pages 12, 39, 97, 101, 104, 108, 113, 115, 116, 127.

HOSTA
Hosta
PERENNIAL   ZONES 3–9
The most distinguished of all the hostas have foliage in the gray to blue range, and the largest of these make outstandingly impressive container plants when well grown.

'Krossa Regal' is one of the largest hostas, the clumps of foliage sometimes exceeding 4ft (1.2m) and topped in late summer by spikes of mauve flowers. The glaucous leaves are long stemmed and pointed. 'Snowden' also has pointed leaves that make a large gray-green mound but its flowers are white with a tinge of lilac. *H. fortunei* var. *hyacinthina* is shorter but one of the best hostas in the gray-green range, the leaves having a distinctive fine glaucous rim. It makes a clump up to 30in (75cm) high and provides a good display of mauve flowers.

In the blue-gray range *H. sieboldiana* var. *elegans* holds its place as a plant of rare distinction. The huge rounded leaves, up to 30cm (1ft) long and more than that wide, are deeply veined and wrinkled, which adds depth to the glaucous coloring. There are mauve-white flowers over a clump that stands 30in (75cm) high. 'Halcyon' (*below*) is another good blue, showing its color best in shade. It grows to 18in (45cm) and has attractive mauve flowers.
See also pages 184, 187; illustrations pages 15, 18.

Hosta *Hosta* 'Halcyon'

JUNIPER

Juniperus

EVERGREEN CONIFER   ZONES 4–8

There are numerous dwarf forms of *J. communis* (Z3–7). One of the most popular is 'Compressa', which forms a narrow column up to 2ft (60cm) high of gray-green foliage with hints of blue. It is like a miniature version of the Irish juniper (*J. c.* 'Hibernica'), which is also suitable for containers but is a more uniform gray-blue and slowly attains a height of 10ft (3m).

Blue tints are found in many other junipers. 'Blaue Donau' ('Blue Danube') is a shrubby cultivar up to 6ft (1.8m) high of *J. sabina* (Z4–7). It has gray-blue, scalelike leaves on branches that can spread more than 8ft (2.5m). The range of blues is particularly remarkable in single seed juniper (*J. squamata*, Z5–7). 'Blue Star', for example, is a compact plant up to 20in (50cm) tall and 2ft (60cm) across that has foliage of an intense steel-blue. *See also page 181.*

HONEYBUSH

Melianthus major

EVERGREEN SHRUB   ZONES 8–10

Although the honeybush (*below*) is rather tender, it is worth taking the trouble to grow, because it is a foliage plant of great beauty. If necessary, it can be overwintered under glass or plunged in the garden. In the open garden established plants can reach 8ft (2.5m) or more, but in containers they do not usually exceed 4ft (1.2m). There may be maroon flower spikes in late summer, but they are much less important ornamentally than the large, gray-green leaves, which are deeply divided and notched with a jagged edge.

Plant in mid- to late spring, using a soil-based potting mix. Plants that have been cut down by frost will often shoot again from the base. In mid-spring remove dead and damaged foliage and add a topdressing of fresh potting mix. *See illustration page 13.*

PELARGONIUM, GERANIUM

Pelargonium

EVERGREEN PERENNIAL   ZONES 9–10

Several of the scented-leaved pelargoniums have attractive gray-green foliage that adds to their appeal, and makes them extremely useful in summer designs, where they will act as a foil to flowering plants with indifferent foliage. The jagged three-lobed leaves of 'Gray Lady Plymouth' are a subdued gray-green and when bruised smell of roses. This handsome scented-leaved pelargonium, which grows to about 18in (45cm), has small pink flowers with purple veining. The Fragrans Group covers a range of compact, scented-leaved pelargoniums with elegant gray-green foliage that is nutmeg scented. Their small flowers are white.

*See also pages 135, 147–48, **153–54**, 163, 170, 181–82, 187, 190.*

PLECOSTACHYS

Plecostachys serpyllifolia

ANNUAL/EVERGREEN PERENNIAL
ZONES 9–10

This silvery foliage plant, often listed as *Helichrysum microphyllum*, looks much like a small-leaved version of *H. petiolare* and is also usually grown as an annual. The lax stems, which are 24–30in (60–75cm) long and closely covered with tiny leaves, are seen to good effect trailing from summer plantings in hanging baskets.

Plant in late spring or early summer, using a soil-based or soil-less potting mix. Keep well watered and apply a liquid fertilizer every two weeks,

Honeybush *Melianthus major*

starting two to three weeks after planting. Overwinter rooted cuttings under glass.
See illustrations pages 10, 112.

SILVERMAT RAOULIA
Raoulia australis
EVERGREEN PERENNIAL   ZONES 8–9
While the tiny sulfur-yellow spring flowers of silvermat raoulia are easily overlooked, its gray-green leaves make a useful small ground-hugging mat that will fit neatly into the corner of a trough planted as a miniature alpine garden. This species, which needs a position in full sun, is under 1in (2.5cm) in height but can have a spread of 10in (25cm) or more.

Plant in mid-spring, using a gritty, soil-based potting mix.

WILLOW
Salix 'Boydii'
DECIDUOUS SHRUB   ZONES 4–8
The gnarled stems of this dwarf, slow-growing willow, in height and spread rarely exceeding 12in (30cm), help to give a trough of alpine-garden plants an established look. The catkins are not conspicuous but the rounded and prominently veined leaves are downy and silver-gray.

Plant in fall or early to mid-spring, using a gritty, soil-based potting mix. Top-dress with fresh mix in spring in alternate years.

LAVENDER COTTON
Santolina
EVERGREEN SHRUB   ZONES 8-9
Lavender cotton (*S. chamaecyparissus*, also listed as *S. incana*) makes a rounded bush with a height and spread of up to 2ft (60cm). It is densely clothed with soft feathery leaves, aromatic to the touch, which are silvery gray (*above right*). In mid-summer it is covered with yellow button flowers; in some color schemes it may be preferable to trim these off.

The dwarf form *S. c.* var. *nana*, with even whiter foliage, is only 6in (15cm) high. Another lavender cotton, *S. pinnata* subsp. *neapolitana*, has nearly white foliage that is delicately feathered and makes a loose bush up to 30in (75cm) high covered in mid-summer with lemon-yellow flowers. The dwarf lavender cotton can be used in window boxes or in trough containing sun-loving alpine garden plants. The taller

Lavender cotton *Santolina chamaecyparissus*

lavender cottons are best combined with other sun-loving plants in large pots or other containers.

Plant in fall or early to mid-spring, using a gritty, soil-based potting mix. Cut back hard in mid-spring to promote vigorous new growth and trim either before or immediately after flowering.

SEDUM
Sedum spathulifolium 'Cape Blanco'
EVERGREEN PERENNIAL   ZONES 5–9
This is similar in many respects to other forms of *S. spathulifolium*, a succulent evergreen that makes a mat of tight leaf rosettes, normally under 4in (10cm) in height and with a spread of 10in (25cm), topped in late spring or early summer by heads of yellow flowers. What distinguishes it is the silvery green of its waxy foliage.
See also page 191.

COBWEB HOUSELEEK
Sempervivum arachnoideum subsp. *tomentosum*
EVERGREEN SUCCULENT   ZONES 5–9
This houseleek makes rosettes of red-tipped, fleshy leaves that are covered by a curious criss-cross webbing of white hairs, which give the plant a silvered look (*right*). In summer stems 6in (15cm) high bear deep pink flowers. Plants often have a spread of more than 6in (15cm), with the parent rosette spawning a ring of smaller rosettes.
See also page 191.

SENECIO
Senecio
EVERGREEN SHRUB   ZONES 9–10
This popular component of summer bedding layouts, sometimes listed as *S. maritima* or *Cineraria maritima*, is also an adaptable foliage plant for container gardens. It is usually grown as a half-hardy annual, making a bushy plant about 12in (30cm) high in a season. There are several leaf forms, all felted and silvery gray, including the feathery 'Silver Dust', and 'White Diamond', with broader, less divided leaves. Another silvery senecio is the finely dissected *S. viravira* (also listed as *S. leucostachys*), an evergreen tender subshrub that can grow to more than 3ft (90cm) in a season.

To raise from seed, sow in warmth in late winter or early spring. Plant out in early summer. To achieve their most startling silvery whiteness, plants need full sun and a gritty, free-draining potting mix. Rooted cuttings can be overwintered under glass.
See illustrations pages 8, 23, 100.

LAMB'S EARS
Stachys byzantina
EVERGREEN PERENNIAL   ZONES 4–8
The woolly gray leaves that have inspired this plant's common name make an attractive feature at the edge of a large container planted with other sun-loving plants. The species is sometimes listed as *S. lanata* or as *S. olympica*. The felted stems can grow to 18in (45cm), the flowers in the woolly spikes being pinkish mauve. 'Silver Carpet' is a more compact, nonflowering cultivar.

Plant in fall or mid-spring, using a soil-based potting mix. Apply liquid fertilizer two or three times during the summer. Divide plants every two years.

Cobweb houseleek *Sempervivum arachnoideum* subsp. *tomentosum*

HERBS

Herbs are among the most worthwhile plants to grow in the container garden. Many culinary herbs are compact and so easily accommodated in a small space. The fresh sprigs and richly aromatic leaves they supply over a long season can make memorable meals of the simplest dishes. In addition, many have extremely attractive foliage.

CHIVES
Allium schoenoprasum
PERENNIAL   ZONES 3–9

Chives form grassy clumps up to 10in (25cm) high of hollow leaves that can be cut throughout summer to give a mild onion flavor to salads and other dishes. The rounded heads of starry pink flowers are decorative (*below*) but, if plants are being grown specifically for leaf cutting, remove the flowers as soon as they develop. Grow a single clump, consisting of a cluster of three or four chive plants, in a pot or as part of a mixture of moisture-loving herbs in a window box or trough. Chives thrive in sun or partial shade.

Plant from early to mid-spring, using a soil-based potting mix. Keep well watered and apply liquid fertilizer every three weeks, starting three to four weeks after planting. Plants die down in winter, but those taken under cover during winter will provide leaves for cutting in spring. Lift and divide established clumps every two years.

BORAGE
Borago officinalis
ANNUAL

The nodding blue starlike flowers make borage one of the prettiest herbs in flower. It quickly grows to 3ft (90cm) high, its hollow stems carrying rough hairy leaves. Because of their cucumber flavor, the young leaves – and also the sweet-tasting flowers – are sometimes added to fruit salads.

Borage is easily grown from seed in full sun in a soil-based or soil-less potting mix. Sow where it is to grow in mid-spring and, for a lasting supply of young leaves, continue sowing until mid-summer, thinning seedlings to 10in (25cm) apart.

BAY LAUREL, SWEET BAY
Laurus nobilis
EVERGREEN SHRUB ZONES 8–10

The leathery aromatic leaves of the bay laurel provide one of the indispensable flavorings of Mediterranean cooking, and the plant (*below*), grows well in a tub or large pot. It can reach 15ft (4.5m) or more, but in containers is traditionally grown as a standard with a clear stem of 3–6ft (90–180cm) or shaped as a cone or drum. These simple geometric shapes are useful for a formal arrangements of containers. The flowers are inconspicuous but on female plants they are followed by dark berries.

Plant from early to mid-spring, using a soil-based potting mix. Top-dress annually in mid-spring with fresh mix, and repot only when roots become congested. To create and maintain topiary shapes cut back in early and late summer. Use pruners to remove whole leaves.
See illustration page 13.

MINT
Mentha
PERENNIAL ZONES 5–9

Most mints are invasive in the open garden so there are good practical reasons for growing them in containers, where they can provide a supply of freshly piquant sprigs throughout the summer. Spearmint (*M. spicata*) has prominently veined, mid-green leaves on erect stems up to 2ft (60cm) high. Apple mint (*M. suaveolens*, also listed as *M. rotundifolia*) can grow to 3ft (90cm) and has hairy, pale green leaves, while its lovely cultivar *M. s.* 'Variegata' has irregular creamy markings to the leaves. Grow these mints in sun or light shade.

Plant in early to mid-spring, using either a soil-based or a soil-less potting mix. Keep well watered throughout the growing season and apply liquid fertilizer every two weeks, starting three to four weeks after planting. Divide and repot annually or every second year in spring. Top-dress with fresh potting mix in spring in alternate years. To provide fresh sprigs for cutting in early spring, keep potted plants under cover during winter.

SWEET BASIL
Ocimum basilicum
HALF-HARDY ANNUAL

The deep, clovelike flavor of sweet basil has earned this annual a high reputation as a culinary herb. Growing to about 2ft (60cm) high, it has large bright green leaves or, in the cultivar 'Purple Ruffles', shiny dark leaves that are fringed and crinkled. French or bush basil (*O. basilicum* var. *minimum*) is less strongly flavored, but its dwarf bushes, under 8in (20cm) high and packed with small, light green leaves, make pretty and useful pot plants. All basils need a warm, sheltered spot.

To raise from seed, sow in warmth in early spring. Harden off before

Chives *Allium schoenoprasum*

Bay laurel *Laurus nobilis*

planting outdoors in late spring or early summer, using a soil-based or soil-less potting mix. Allow the mix to become nearly dry between waterings. Apply liquid fertilizer every two weeks, starting three weeks after planting. Plants usually resprout after being cut back hard and will last into fall and winter if brought under cover. *See illustration page 102.*

MARJORAM

Origanum
PERENNIAL ZONES 4–8
Several marjorams are grown as culinary herbs. Wild marjoram (*O. vulgare*), which grows up to 18in (45cm) high, has mid-green leaves with a strong flavor. The golden-leaved cultivar *O. v.* 'Aureum' is more widely grown. Sweet marjoram (*O. majorana*, Z7–10) is a bushy plant growing to 2ft (60cm), with red stems carrying soft gray-green leaves and in summer mauve, pink, or white flowers. All these marjorams need a sunny, open spot.

Plant marjorams in mid-spring, using a soil-based potting mix. Apply liquid fertilizer every three weeks in summer, starting two to three weeks after planting. Trim plants to keep them compact and cut back hard in early to mid-spring. Top-dress with fresh potting mix in spring. To grow sweet marjoram as an annual, sow in warmth in early spring and plant outdoors after hardening off in late spring.

PARSLEY

Petroselinum crispum
ANNUAL/BIENNIAL
The attractive leaves of parsley are much used for flavoring and as a garnish, and the plant is easily grown in containers. There are two main types. Those with curled leaves make a dense mound of deeply divided and crested, bright green foliage (*above right*). Plain- or broad-leaved cultivars form clumps of much-divided flat leaves. Although less ornamental, they generally have a better flavor. The foliage of both types grows to about 18in (45cm). Remove flowers promptly so that the foliage remains useful.

To raise from seed, sow parsley in decomposable pots from early to mid-spring for summer supplies and from early to mid-summer for supplies to last from fall to the following spring. Transplant into a larger container in late

Parsley *Petroselinum crispum*

spring or late summer, using either a soil-based or a soil-less potting mix. Water regularly and apply liquid fertilizer every two weeks, starting two to three weeks after planting. In cold areas keep pots under cover in winter.

ROSEMARY

Rosmarinus officinalis
EVERGREEN SHRUB ZONES 8–9
The sweetly aromatic foliage of rosemary releases its scent when lightly touched, so it is a pleasing shrub to have in a sunny spot near a path or a garden seat. Plants can be upright or sprawling, the stems, up to 3ft (90cm) high, closely covered with narrow, deep green leaves that are felted and gray on the underside. Pale blue flowers are carried between late winter and mid-spring. The erect 'Miss Jessopp's Upright' is attractive in pots, while the laxer plants in the Prostratus Group (Z9) have arching or trailing stems that will hang over the edge of a container. Plant singly in early to mid-spring, using a soil-based potting mix. Top-dress annually with fresh mix in spring. Prune hard in mid-spring. In cold areas move under cover during winter.

RUE

Ruta graveolens 'Jackman's Blue'
EVERGREEN SUBSHRUB ZONES 5–9
Rue is a pungently aromatic bush with bitter-tasting leaves, and the cultivar most widely grown, 'Jackman's Blue', is generally cultivated for its ornamental foliage. It goes well with other herbs

that like sunny, well-drained conditions. Making a rounded bush with a height and spread of 2–3ft (60–90cm), it bears a dense cover of divided blue-green leaves and, in early to mid-summer, clusters of yellow-green flowers.

Plant from early to mid-spring, using a soil-based potting mix. Apply weak liquid fertilizer two or three times during the summer. Top-dress with fresh mix annually in spring. Cut back hard in mid-spring.

COMMON SAGE

Salvia officinalis
EVERGREEN SHRUB ZONES 6–9
The gray-green foliage of sage, forming a dense mound up to 2ft (60cm) high and as much across, provides a sympathetic accompaniment to other sun-loving herbs and many ornamentals. Its broad leaves are pungently aromatic and slightly rough to the touch. The purplish summer flowers must be removed to encourage leafy growth. The purple-leaved cultivars and also the compact 'Icterina' (Z7–9), with yellow-variegated, light green leaves, can all be used for culinary purposes in the same way as the common sage.

Plant in spring, using a soil-based potting mix. Apply liquid fertilizer four times in summer. Trim back and top-dress with fresh potting mix in mid-spring. Replace plants every three years. *See also page 191.*

THYME

Thymus
EVERGREEN SHRUB   ZONES 5–9
The deliciously aromatic foliage of the common thyme (*T. vulgaris*) has made it an indispensable culinary herb. It is a dwarf shrub up to 8in (20cm) high but spreading so that it makes a good edging plant. The wiry stems are densely clothed with narrow, dark green leaves, and in summer the plant is covered with short spikes of mauve flowers. Several other thymes with different flavors are available, including lemon thyme (*T. × citriodorus*), which grows to 12in (30cm). All thymes are suitable for planting with other sun-loving herbs and dwarf ornamentals or singly in pots.

Plant in fall or from early to mid-spring, using a soil-based potting mix. Top-dress with fresh mix in spring. Trim bushes in spring and summer and replace plants every three years. *See also page 185.*

FRUIT

A large number of fruit-bearing trees, vines, and perennials can be grown in containers. These are often highly ornamental as well as producing usable crops, even though yields are less than those provided by plants in the open garden. In selecting fruit-bearing plants for containers this factor and the level of management required must be taken into account. One of the advantages of growing fruit in containers – particularly relevant in cool-temperate regions – is that plants can be moved under cover during cold weather. Another is that the scale of container-grown plants makes them easily netted to prevent bird damage.

ORANGES AND LEMONS
Citrus
EVERGREEN SHRUB   ZONES 9–11
There is a long tradition in Europe of growing oranges and lemons (*below*) in containers. Plants are placed outdoors during the summer months and moved under glass in cold weather. Although some citrus fruits tolerate a light frost if it follows a period of steadily falling temperatures, a sharp drop in the temperature or a long spell of freezing

Lemon *Citrus limon*

weather is likely to prove fatal. The hardiest of the citrus fruits are tangerines and mandarins. Lemons are more tender, with the exception of the hybrid 'Meyer'.

All these citrus fruits grow up to 4ft (1.2m) high and have lustrous dark green leaves. The main season for the small clusters of creamy white, exquisitely fragrant flowers is spring, but there is often sporadic flowering at other times. Citrus trees are self-fertile so that in the right conditions a single tree will bear fruit. However, oranges and lemons are often grown simply for their ornamental value, with little expectation of fruit reaching maturity. For fruit to ripen, flowering must be followed by a period of six months or more when temperatures do not fall below 55°F (13°C), and higher temperatures are needed for their flavor to develop fully. The fruits ripen slowly, sometimes taking more than twelve months, so it is usual to see fruit and blossom on trees at the same time. When citrus trees are moved outdoors they should be placed in an open, sheltered spot.

Plants can be grown from pips, but for reliable fruiting buy grafted specimens of named cultivars. Plant in a frost-free environment in late winter or early spring, using a soil-based potting mix. Citrus trees dislike root disturbance, yet may need to be repotted annually in winter until they have reached the required size, after which they should be top-dressed in mid-spring, using fresh mix. Water regularly in summer, but in winter keep the potting mix just moist. Apply liquid fertilizer every two weeks from late spring to late summer. Prune young trees in early spring to encourage them to develop a balanced, compact shape.

FIG
Ficus carica
DECIDUOUS TREE   ZONES 7–10
In subtropical and warm temperate regions figs, which have deep green, attractively lobed leaves, can produce two or three crops annually. In a cool-temperate climate only two crops are carried in a year, although only one usually ripens. In areas with severe winters pot-grown specimens can be

moved under cover with the onset of cold weather.

Figs are well suited to growing in containers, the restriction of their roots encouraging plants to produce fruit rather than foliage. A single plant does not need to be cross-fertilized in order to bear fruit. Bushes can be restricted to a height of about 3ft (90cm) or plants can be grown as short standards with a clear stem to a height of 3–4ft (90–120cm). Cultivars such as 'Brown Turkey', 'Brunswick', and 'White Marseilles' – with red, yellow, and almost transparent flesh, respectively – are grown on their own roots.

Plant singly in mid- to late fall or early spring, using a soil-based potting mix, in a container about 12in (30cm) wide and deep. There is no need to repot each year; just remove 2–3in (5–8cm) of old mix and top-dress with fresh in mid-spring. Water regularly throughout spring and summer and apply liquid fertilizer every two weeks from late spring to late summer.

STRAWBERRY
Fragaria
PERENNIAL   ZONES 3–9
The strawberry, the most widely grown of all the soft fruits, gives quick returns and does well in containers (*above right*). Special pots and tubs for strawberries are also available: terracotta pots with holes in the sides, and wooden barrels with 2in (5cm) wide holes bored in the sides at regular intervals about 10in (25cm) apart are the most common.

There are three main types of strawberry: the ordinary, luscious, large-fruited strawberries, which crop only once, in early summer; the perpetual (sometimes known as remontant) strawberries, which are similar but crop in a succession of irregular flushes throughout summer and into fall; and the alpine strawberries, which bear small, dry fruit prolifically, also in flushes throughout summer. All types can be grown in containers, but the yields from perpetual strawberries are poor in the second year and they are not much grown in this way. All strawberries are prone to virus diseases and certified virus-free stock should always be obtained.

Plant strawberries in mid- to late

Strawberry *Fragaria vesca*

summer, using a soil-based potting mix to which humus such as well-rotted garden compost has been added. Containers with holes in the sides should be planted up at the same time as they are filled with potting mix. Strawberries will crop the year after they are planted. Plants need regular watering during the growing season, although excess moisture in spring will encourage foliage at the expense of fruit. Avoid wetting the fruit and water early in the day, because lingering dampness encourages the development of gray mold (*Botrytis*). With summer-fruiting strawberries, rotate the container once the fruit appears so that it ripens evenly. Apply weak liquid fertilizer every two weeks in summer, starting when flowers appear. Apply a balanced general fertilizer in the spring of subsequent years. Remove any runners. Discard plants after two or three seasons of cropping and use fresh potting mix for another planting. *See illustration page 61.*

APPLE

Malus domestica

DECIDUOUS TREE   ZONES 3–10

The apple (*right*) is the most widely grown fruit in temperate gardens, the number of cultivars, including dessert and cooking kinds, running into many hundreds. Apples can make large trees but they are rarely grown on their own roots and the rootstock on which a cultivar is grafted will determine the eventual size. The availability of dwarfing rootstocks such as M.27

makes container-growing of apples feasible – these dwarf bushes having a stem height of a mere 18–24in (45–60cm). Place container-grown apple trees in an open, sheltered spot where frost does not linger. In frost-prone areas choose late-flowering cultivars.

Cross-pollination is necessary to get a good set of fruit, so a single apple tree is unlikely to crop well. Buy trees from an established nursery so that you can get advice on the flowering period and compatibility of different cultivars.

Buy two- or three-year-old trees that already have lateral branches; the formative pruning has been started and they will begin to bear fruit in a year or two. Soak the roots of bare-rooted trees thoroughly before planting. Plant between fall and early spring, using a soil-based potting mix. Keep well watered during the growing season and apply liquid fertilizer high in potassium every two weeks until the fruits begin to ripen. On young trees allow only two or three fruits to develop. Prune in the dormant season, initially to consolidate the open-centered framework of permanent branches. Subsequent pruning is mainly confined to cutting back laterals, which will encourage the development of fruiting buds. Repot every second year and in other years top-dress with fresh potting mix.

PEACH, NECTARINE

Prunus persica

DECIDUOUS TREE ZONES 6–9

The peach, which has fruit with a soft downy skin, and the nectarine, a harder-but smooth-skinned sport of the peach, are widely grown in warm-temperate regions. Although quite hardy, in cool temperate areas peaches and nectarines often require protection in early spring so that the pink blossom avoids being damaged by frost. They also need a

Apple *Malus domestica* 'Ribston Pippin'

warm, sheltered spot for fruit to ripen. Provided the growing conditions are suitable, single trees will bear fruit.

Genetically compact peaches are available as short standards, usually 3–4ft (90–120cm) high, which are suitable for containers. They make a dense head about 2ft (60cm) across that does not need pruning, and they start fruiting when still young trees.

Plant trees in mid- to late fall, using a soil-based potting mix. Trees grown in containers about 18in (45cm) or more deep will not need repotting for several years, provided the top 2–3in (5–8cm) of potting mix is replaced with fresh mix every spring. Water regularly in the growing season and apply weak liquid fertilizer every three to four weeks from late spring to late summer.

GRAPE

Vitis

DECIDUOUS VINE ZONES 5–9

The grape vine (*V. vinifera*) has a record of cultivation extending far back into antiquity and is today one of the most widely planted of all fruits. Its many cultivars can be container grown as vigorous ornamental vines, but they must be pruned regularly to ensure good crops of fruit in late summer or fall. In parts of the United States the bunch grapes, of which the fox grape (*V. labrusca*) is the main parent, can also be grown in containers.

There are numerous variations on the pruning of grapes, but all are based on the need for a permanent framework and the controlled production of fresh lateral shoots, on which the flowers and fruit are carried. One of the most convenient ways to grow a vine grape in a container is as a standard, with a main stem 3–5ft (90–150cm) high and a head of short spurs from which fresh laterals grow each year. A pot-grown plant can be placed in a sunny, sheltered spot in the garden and, if necessary, moved under cover in winter.

To grow a grape vine as a standard, plant a one-year-old vine in fall or early winter, using a soil-based potting mix. Cut back to a strong bud at a height of about 6in (15cm) and in the following summer train the vine up a stake, pinching the laterals back to one leaf. Top-dress with fresh potting mix in late winter. Keep well watered in the growing season and apply liquid fertilizer every two weeks

VEGETABLES

A wide range of vegetables can be grown successfully in pots, window boxes, and growing bags. The selection here includes crops such as zucchini and some salad vegetables that are easy to grow and give a good yield even in the small space of a container. There are also some more demanding vegetables, such as sweet peppers, that are decorative as well as useful.

SWISS CHARD

Beta vulgaris Cicla Group
BIENNIAL

This member of the beet family, bred for its leaves, is a versatile crop with a long season. Its bold foliage also makes it attractive in the container garden. Plants grow to about 18in (45cm) and have white stems that are wavy at the edge. Even more eye-catching is the red-stemmed ruby chard, which has stems and ribs of scarlet and reddish-purple leaves.

Sow in mid-spring to harvest in summer and in areas with mild winters in mid- to late summer to harvest in winter and spring. Use a soil-based potting mix. Water well and apply weak liquid fertilizer every two weeks once plants are 5–6in (13–15cm) high. *See illustration page 94.*

SWEET PEPPER

Capsicum
ANNUAL

The glossy and colorful fruits of sweet peppers (*C. annuum* Grossum Group), which can be used in a wide range of cooked and salad dishes, are showy as they ripen, and they make attractive pot plants (*above right*). They grow to a height of 2–3ft (60–90cm). Thriving in heat, in areas with cool summers they are often grown as greenhouse plants, but they can be planted outdoors in sunny sheltered spots. It is often best to plant them in their final container under glass and to move them outdoors only when temperatures rise.

Chili peppers (*C. annuum* Longum Group and *C. frutescens),* like sweet peppers, can have fruit that at maturity is green, red, or yellow. The most familiar are bright red chilis, which have an explosive flavor and are sometimes curiously tapered and twisted. These plants, which grow

Sweet pepper *Capsicum annuum* Grossum Group

18–24in (45–60cm) high, need warmer conditions than sweet peppers but can be grown in the same way.

Sow seed in warmth during mid-spring. Thin and pot up, using a soil-based or soil-less potting mix, until plants are in containers 8–10in (20–25cm) deep. Harden off before moving containers outdoors in early summer. Keep well watered and move into light shade in very warm weather. Apply a liquid fertilizer high in potassium (such as a tomato fertilizer) every two weeks once fruits begin to form.

ZUCCHINI

Cucurbita pepo
HALF-HARDY ANNUAL

When harvested in their immature state, summer squashes are known as zucchini. Bush cultivars, bred to be picked at an early stage, are good container plants for sunny sheltered spots, growing 2ft (60cm) high and with a spread of 3ft (90cm). They quickly produce heavy crops, best harvested when they are 4–6in (10–15cm) long. The large yellow flowers can be eaten either raw in salads or fried in batter.

Provided zucchini are harvested regularly, plants will crop over many weeks. As well as cylindrical zuccchini with deep green skins there are also round forms and skin color includes

yellow and shades of gray and green.

Sow in warmth in mid-spring and plant out after hardening off in late spring, using a soil-based or soil-less potting mix. Once there is little risk of frost, seed can be sown directly in a tub outdoors between mid- and late spring. Sow two seeds in the center and, if two seedlings germinate, remove the weaker. Keep the potting mix moist at all times and apply liquid fertilizer every 10 days from early summer.

ROCKET, ARUGULA

Eruca sativa
HARDY ANNUAL

The nutty and peppery flavors of arugula make it a delicious salad ingredient. It can be sown thickly and cut at the seedling stage, then allowed to regrow – a process that can be repeated three or four times. Leaves can also be picked from fast-growing plants spaced about 6in (15cm) apart or interplanted among other crops in tubs and window boxes.

Make successional sowings in either soil-based or soil-less potting mix, in sun or light shade, from mid- to late spring and again from mid- to late summer. Keep well watered and apply weak liquid fertilizer every two weeks, starting two to three weeks after sowing.

LETTUCE

Lactuca sativa
HARDY/HALF-HARDY ANNUAL

The types of lettuce that form a heart include the Romaine, mainly large and upright with crisp leaves ('Little Gem' is a well-flavored, small, Romaine lettuce) and flat "cabbage-head" lettuces, including soft-textured butterheads and crispheads of the 'Iceberg' type. Leaf lettuces do not form a heart, and there is regrowth after individual leaves are picked or the head cut.

For containers the most suitable are small cultivars of the Romaine and cabbage-head types such as 'Tom Thumb' and various leaf lettuces, of which there are several with attractive foliage. The oak-leaved kinds have deeply cut leaves, often bronzed, and the 'Lollo' lettuces, red and green, have frizzy, tightly curled leaves. A mixture, often available as packeted seed, provides a range of leaves.

Sow indoors in mid-spring and, after hardening off, transplant into outdoor planters from late spring through to mid- or late summer, using soil-based or soil-less potting mix. Water regularly to ensure that plants grow quickly, and apply liquid fertilizer every two weeks.

TOMATO
Lycopersicon esculentum
HALF-HARDY ANNUAL

Tomatoes (*below*) can be grown successfully outdoors in containers, even in a cool-temperate climate, but they need a warm sheltered spot. There is a large range to choose from, varying in size and form from the "currant" tomatoes, with strings of tiny fruit, to the giant, fleshy American beefsteak and 'Marmande' tomatoes. Besides red, there are also cultivars with fruit that is yellow, orange, pink, striped orange and red, and white. Tall-growing tomatoes can be more than 6ft (1.8m) high and must be trained to supports. Bush tomatoes, with a height and spread of about 18in (45cm), are generally hardier and less trouble to grow.

To raise tomatoes from seed, sow in warmth during early or mid-spring. After hardening off, move seedlings outdoors and transplant them into their final containers, which need to be at least 8in (20cm) deep, in late spring or early summer. Use soil-based or soil-less potting mix and insert a stake or

Tomato *Lycopersicon esculentum*

provide other support for tall-growing cultivars. Water regularly and apply tomato fertilizer every 10 days once the fruit begins to swell. Tie in tall-growing cultivars and pinch back side shoots as they develop. Remove the growing tip at three leaves beyond the topmost truss two to three weeks after mid-summer. At the onset of cold weather pick any unripened fruit and ripen indoors.

Navy bean *Phaseolus vulgaris* 'Royalty'

BEAN
Phaseolus
ANNUAL

This elegant twining or bush perennial is not hardy and is almost invariably grown as an annual. In summer it carries pretty sprays of flowers, usually red but also pink and white. Its ornamental qualities, combined with the good crops of succulent green pods from mid-summer to fall, make it a good choice for containers. Two main species are grown for eating. The climbing forms of the scarlet runner (*P. coccineus*) are best planted in a large tub with a wigwam of stakes up to about 6ft (1.8m) high as support. Position the stakes before sowing. Scarlet runners can also be kept low by pinching out the growing point at an early stage then regularly stopping laterals to maintain compact bushy plants. In addition to the vining cultivars, there are true dwarf scarlet runners, which grow to about 18in (45cm). The green or navy bean (*P. vulgaris, above*) has many cultivars, mostly bush forms but some

climbing. The bush kinds grow 12–16in (30–40cm) high and, although self-supporting, will be weighed down by heavy crops unless stiffened by a few twiggy sticks.

Sow seed of scarlet runners under glass in mid-spring for planting out in early summer, or sow directly outdoors in the container in late spring, spacing the seeds about 9in (23cm) apart. Green beans are best sown where they are to grow, and thinned to 2–3in (5–8cm) apart when the first true leaves appear. For both species, use a soil-based potting mix to which humus such as well-rotted garden compost has been added. Place the container in a sunny, sheltered position.

Mist flowers and foliage regularly with a fine water spray, and apply a weak liquid fertilizer every two weeks, starting when the first flowers are produced, but avoid excessive use of fertilizers, which will encourage foliage at the expense of flowers and beans. Harvest beans while they are still young and tender.

EGGPLANT, AUBERGINE
Solanum melongena
TENDER ANNUAL

Eggplants thrive in a Mediterranean-type climate, and this is reflected in the many delicious southern European dishes in which they are an important ingredient. In cool-temperate areas they are often raised under glass but can do well outdoors provided they are grown in a sunny, sheltered spot. The bushy plants are usually 2–3ft (60–90cm) high and are easily grown in containers, as are a few more compact cultivars. Fruits start ripening in mid-summer, the typical eggplant having a lustrous, deep purple skin, although some cultivars have white skins. Most have fruits that are 8–10in (20–25cm) long and about 3in (8cm) in diameter.

Sow seed in mid- to late winter in warmth. Pinch back the growing tip of young plants so that two leading shoots develop, and remove all side shoots. Harden off in late spring and plant in containers outdoors in early summer, using soil-based or soil-less potting mix. Keep well watered and apply liquid fertilizer (a brandname tomato fertilizer is ideal) every two weeks, starting once fruits begin to form. Allow four to six fruits per plant and let them ripen before harvesting them.

BERRYING PLANTS AND GRASSES

All the plants listed here help to extend the interest of the container garden beyond the conventional flowering display. Berrying shrubs are particularly useful in providing touches of color during fall and winter. Although a number do well in shade, the best crops are usually produced when the shrubs are grown in a reasonably open spot and, in the case of those that bear male and female flowers on different plants, when there is a male plant close by, either in the container or in the open garden. Grasses often provide a long-lasting display, the flowers and later the seed heads adding appealing texture rather than vivid color.

JAPANESE AUCUBA
Aucuba japonica
EVERGREEN SHRUB   ZONES 7–10
The plain-leaved and variegated Japanese aucubas are handsome and useful evergreens that tolerate a wide range of conditions. In containers they grow to about 6ft (1.8m). Their berrying capacity is often overlooked, partly because the sexes are on different plants, females berrying only when there is a male nearby. The small clusters of bright scarlet berries, which develop in fall, attain their richest color in spring. For good crops plants need to be grown in a reasonably sunny spot.

The variegated 'Crotonifolia' is female, as is 'Longifolia', with long glossy green leaves.
See also page 183.

GREATER QUAKING GRASS
Briza maxima
ANNUAL
In late spring and summer this tufted grass bears clusters of heart-shaped, purplish-green spikelets on slender arching stems. They are beautiful when still and move gracefully in the breeze.

Sow seed where plants are to grow from early to mid-spring, using a soil-based potting mix. Thin seedlings to 4–6in (10–15cm) apart.

COTONEASTER
Cotoneaster
DECIDUOUS/EVERGREEN SHRUBS
ZONES 5–7
The cotoneasters include some berrying shrubs that are widely grown in the open garden. One of the most compact, and a useful addition to a trough of alpine-garden plants – as much for the tight growth that molds it over the edge of a container as for its berries – is the evergreen *Cotoneaster congestus* (Z7–8). Forming a mat or hummock up to 10in (25cm) high but with a spread that can exceed 2ft (60cm), its stiff, closely packed branches are covered in small dark green leaves. Small pink flowers in early summer are followed by red berries.

Even more distinctive in habit is the deciduous *C. horizontalis* (*below*). The main stems, each with a fishbone pattern of smaller branches, form a fan 2ft (60cm) and about 4ft (1.2m) across. The branches are tightly clothed in neat, dark green leaves and in early summer there are numerous small pink flowers. This shrub is attractive in all seasons but especially in fall, when the leaves turn red and a thick crop of berries hugs the branches. Birds eat the berries, but often leave them on the shrub until well into winter. *C. horizontalis*, which is best grown on its own or with other shrubs in a very large container, tolerates shade but berries most freely when grown in an open spot.

Plant cotoneasters in fall or from early to mid-spring, using a soil-based potting mix. Top-dress with fresh mix annually in spring and repot every three to four years.

Cotoneaster *Cotoneaster horizontalis*

WINTERGREEN
Gaultheria
EVERGREEN SHRUB   ZONES 7–9
The wintergreens are among the best of the compact berrying shrubs, and their small white flowers in early summer are also an asset. Male and female flowers are usually borne on different plants. For a good display of berries, female cultivars are best planted as a group with a male plant in a large container. Female cultivars of *G. mucronata* provide a good color range, from the startling 'White Pearl', through shades of pink in 'Pink Pearl' and 'Rosea', to the stronger reds of 'Cherry Ripe' and the rich 'Mulberry Wine'. These all have a height and spread of 2–3 ft (60–90cm) in sun, and slightly more in shade. A compact male wintergreen, forming a dense hummock 12in (30cm) high and with a spread of 2ft (60cm), is 'Thymifolia'. Its presence will encourage the production of fruit. Rather similar to the berrying cultivars of *G. mucronata* is *G. × wisleyensis* 'Wisley Pearl', which has mat dark green leaves and bears purplish-maroon berries in fall. The berries of all the wintergreens are extremely long-lasting.

Plant in fall or from early to mid-spring, using a potting mix based on acidic soil. Top-dress with fresh mix annually in spring, and repot only if the roots become congested. Cut back lightly in spring to keep plants neat and compact.

SQUIRREL-TAIL BARLEY, SQUIRREL-TAIL GRASS
Hordeum jubatum
ANNUAL
This relative of barley is an exceptionally pretty, graceful grass. In early to mid-summer flower spikes up to 2ft (60cm) high arch over the short tuft of blades (*opposite left*). The feathery heads open green or purplish and later turn a light brown, the reason for the plant's common names.

Sow in pots during late summer or early fall and overwinter under glass but without heat. Plant in containers in mid-spring, using a soil-based potting mix. Alternatively, sow from early to mid-spring in the container where the plants are to grow and thin the seedlings as necessary.

HARE'S-TAIL GRASS

Lagurus ovatusz
ANNUAL

This charming grass has soft fluffy heads that bob lightly in any breeze. These heads, produced throughout summer, are at first greenish-cream, sometimes tinged purplish-pink, and turn light brown as they age. They are carried on stems up to 20in (50cm) high above clumps of hairy, gray-green foliage that is soft to the touch. Hare's-tail grass is attractive combined with other easy annuals

Sow in pots during late summer or early fall and overwinter under glass but without heat. Plant in containers in mid-spring, using a soil-based potting mix. Alternatively sow where plants are to grow from early to mid-spring and thin the seedlings as necessary.

FOUNTAIN GRASS

Pennisetum villosum
ANNUAL/PERENNIAL   ZONES 8–10

Although a true perennial in mild climates, fountain grass (sometimes listed as *P. longistylum*) is best treated as an annual when grown in a planter. It makes a nondescript clump during summer, but comes into its own in fall, when numerous arching stems carry bristly 4in (10cm) spikes that are a soft creamy pink. This late surprise is a delightful bonus in a mixed planting.

Sow seed in warmth in early spring. Harden seedlings before planting out in a sunny, sheltered spot in late spring, using a soil-based potting mix.

ROSE

Rosa 'Fru Dagmar Hastrup'
DECIDUOUS SHRUB   ZONES 3–8

Several roses that produce ornamental hips are too large to be conveniently accommodated in containers. However, 'Fru Dagmar Hastrup' (*right*) is relatively compact, with a height of 3ft (90cm) and a spread of up to 4ft (1.2m). Its single, fragrant, pale pink flowers, borne intermittently throughout summer, are followed by magnificent, tomatolike hips, which are often well colored before the flowering season is over and remain ornamental for several weeks. They are used to make jam.
See also pages 136, 142, 148, 154, 163, 170.

SKIMMIA

Skimmia japonica
EVERGREEN SHRUB   ZONES 7–9

With the evergreen, shade-tolerant skimmias the male and female flowers are borne on separate plants, female plants carrying large crops of conspicuous, long-lasting berries provided there is a male plant close by. The dwarf *S. j.* subsp. *reevesiana*, 18–30in (45–75cm) high with a spread of 3ft (90cm), has white spring flowers followed by crimson fruits which persist through the winter.

A good male that will ensure a set of fruit is the free-flowering 'Rubella', which is usually less than 4ft (1.2m) in height and spread. Its buds are an attractive red-brown in winter; the petals open white, but with a pink

tinge derived from the red stalks.

Plant in fall or mid-spring, using an acidic-soil mix. Top-dress annually in spring with fresh mix; repot only if the roots become congested.
See illustrations pages 122, 123.

Rose *Rosa* 'Fru Dagmar Hastrup'

WINTER CHERRY

Solanum capsicastrum
EVERGREEN   ZONES 8–10

The winter cherry (*below, right*), a tender subshrub, is usually grown as an indoor pot plant. Where the weather is mild it can be used outdoors in window boxes and other containers. The copious round scarlet fruits, ½in (1cm) or more across, are set against dark green leaves on a bush 12–18in (30–45cm) high.

Buy well-shaped plants carrying plenty of fruit in late fall or early winter. Plant outdoors, in full sun, in either soil-based or soil-less potting mix. Pinch back the growing tips of young plants to encourage copious bushy growth.

EUROPEAN GUELDER ROSE

Viburnum opulus 'Compactum'
DECIDUOUS SHRUB   ZONES 4–8

Translucent red berries in fall, heads of white flowers in spring, and maplelike leaves that color well in fall, all help to make the European guelder rose a very pleasing shrub. Although the species itself grows to more than 12ft (3.7m), the cultivar 'Compactum', which is free-flowering and bears heavy crops of berries, is usually less than 6ft (1.8m) in height, and a useful plant for containers. The best crops are produced when two or three plants are grown close together in a sunny spot.

Plant in fall or from early to mid-spring, using a soil-based potting mix. Prune only to remove dead, damaged, and weak growth.

Squirrel-tail grass *Hordeum jubatum*

Winter cherry *Solanum capsicastrum*

USEFUL PLANTS FOR CONTAINERS

These lists are intended as another way to look at plants for containers, supplementing the organization according to flower and foliage color and season in the plant directory (*see pages 126–203*). The page number following the plant name refers to the main entry in the directory.

FLOWERING SHRUBS
The following list of flowering shrubs does not include ground-hugging dwarfs. Plants with E after the name are evergreen, those with E/D are of genera that include evergreen and deciduous species and hybrids.
Anisodontea E 158
Brugmansia E 146
Camellia E 156
Choisya E 131
Fuchsia 168
Gaultheria E 202
Hebe E 168–69
Hydrangea 133
Lavandula E 169
Myrtus E 135
Nerium E 163
Pieris E 129
Rhododendron E/D 156–57
Rosa 154
Rosmarinus E 197
Skimmia E 203
Viburnum 203
Yucca E 136

SHRUBS GROWN MAINLY FOR THEIR FOLIAGE
Some of the following shrubs, which do not include ground-hugging dwarfs, have interesting flowers, but their chief ornamental value lies in their foliage. Plants with E after the name are evergreen, those with E/D are of genera that include evergreen and deciduous species and hybrids.
Acer 178
Aucuba E 183
Buxus E 179
Chamaecyparis E 179
Cordyline E 179–80
Elaeagnus E/D 192–93
Euonymus E/D 183
Fatshedera E 180
Fatsia E 180
Ilex E 187
Juniperus E 181
Laurus nobilis E 196
Nandina E 190
Pinus E 182

Prunus lusitanica E 182
Salvia officinalis E 170
Thuja E 182

LONG-FLOWERING PLANTS
The following are capable of flowering over a long period, in some cases even for several months. Regular dead-heading will help prolong the season.
Ageratum 173
Argyranthemum 130–31
Begonia × tuberhybrida 151–52
Bellis 156
Brachyscome 173–74
Browallia 174
Brugmansia 146
Calendula 146
Calluna 159
Cuphea 146
Diascia 160
Dimorphotheca 132
Erica 137
Felicia 174–75
Fuchsia 168
Heliotropium 169
Hemerocallis 'Stella de Oro' 141
Impatiens 161–62
Nerium 163
Osteospermum 135
Pelargonium 153–54
Petunia 176
Rosa (some) 154
Salvia (many) 170
Scaevola 176
Tagetes 148
Tropaeolum majus 149
Verbena 171
Viola 143–44

ORNAMENTALS WITH SCENTED FLOWERS
All of the following are scented but the strength varies and appreciation differs from individual to individual.
Brachyscome 173–74
Choisya 131
Crocus (most) *138*
Dianthus 160
Elaeagnus 192–93
Erysimum 138
Heliotropium 169
Hyacinthus 172
Iris 144
Jasminum 133
Lathyrus 162
Lavandula 169
Lilium (many) 134
Lobularia 135
Lonicera 153

Narcissus (most) 138–39
Nicotiana 135
Primula auricula 139
Reseda 136
Rosa (many) 154
Skimmia 203
Tropaeolum majus 149
Wisteria 177

ORNAMENTALS WITH AROMATIC FOLIAGE
In addition to the following plants, most herbs (*see pages 196-97*) have strongly aromatic leaves.
Artemisia 192
Chamaecyparis 179
Choisya 131
Helichrysum italicum 193
Lavandula 169
Myrtus 135
Nepeta 176
Pelargonium (Scented-leaved exceptionally aromatic) 153–54
Pinus 182
Salvia (many) *170*
Santolina 195
Thuja 182
Thymus *197*

VINES
This list of climbing plants could also include several vegetables, of which runner beans are the most ornamental.
Bougainvillea 152
Clematis 131–32
Cobaea 167–68
Jasminum 133
Ipomoea 175
Lapageria 162
Lathyrus 162
Lonicera 153
Rhodochiton 170
Rosa (some) 154
Tropaeolum (some) 149
Wisteria 177

TRAILING PLANTS
Those listed with an asterisk* are grown mainly for their flowers, those without mainly for their value as foliage plants. All are particularly attractive in hanging baskets. Most of the plants listed as vines (*see above*) can also be grown without supports and allowed to trail from tall containers.
Begonia × tuberhybrida (some)* 151–52
Bidens＊ 140
Convolvulus sabatius＊ 174
Diascia (some)＊ 160

Fuchsia (some)* 168
Glechoma 186
Hedera 180
Helichrysum petiolare 193
Lamium 187
Lobelia (some)* 175–76
Lotus 147
Lysimachia 185
Pelargonium (Ivy-leaved)* 153–54
Petunia (many)* 176
Plecostachys 194–95
*Scaevola** 176
Verbena (some)* 171

DWARF BULBS

In addition to the many tall or medium bulbs there are a number of small-sized bulbs that do extremely well in containers. Check the directory for the flowering season.

Chionodoxa 172
Crocus 138
Cyclamen 165
Fritillaria 166
Galanthus 137
Iris 144
Muscari 172
Narcissus (some) 138
Scilla 173
Tulipa (some) 150–51

ALPINE-GARDEN PLANTS

The following low-growing plants are suitable for growing in containers, and look attractive combined with dwarf bulbs. Dress the surface of containers with small stones.

Aethionema 158
Anacyclus 130
Anthemis 130
Aquilegia (some) 167
Armeria 151
Artemisia schmidtiana 'Nana' 192
Aubrieta 166
Aurinia 138
Campanula 174
Cotoneaster congestus 202
Dianthus 160
Euphorbia myrsinites 138
Geranium (some) 161
Helianthemum 141
Lavandula (some) 169
Phlox subulata 129
Primula auricula 139
Pulsatilla 166
Raoulia 195
Salix 'Boydii' 195
Saxifraga 140
Sedum spathulifolium 191
Sempervivum 191

PLANTS FOR SMALL POOLS

Many aquatics and marginals are very vigorous but the following genera include plants suitable for small pools.

Eichhornia 174
Nymphaea (some) 142
Juncus 181
Typha 182

SHADE-TOLERANT PLANTS

All of the following plants are shade tolerant to some extent and those marked with an asterisk* are especially shade-tolerant.

Acer 178
*Adiantum** 178
Ajuga 188
Alchemilla 178
*Asplenium** 179
Astilbe 158–59
*Athyrium** 179
*Aucuba** 183
Begonia × *tuberhybrida* 151–52
*Bergenia** 179
*Buxus** 179
Camellia 156
*Cyclamen** 165
*Dryopteris** 180
Fatshedera 180
Fatsia 180
Fuchsia 168
Glechoma 186
Hakenochloa 184
*Hedera** 180–81
Heuchera 189–90
*Hosta** 184
Houttuynia 190
Hydrangea 133
Impatiens 161–62
Lobelia 175–76
*Matteuccia** 181
Mimulus 147
Myosotis 173
Nicotiana 135
Osmunda 181
*Polystichum** 182
Rhododendron 156–57
Skimmia 203
Viola 143–44

SURVIVORS

Even plants that show remarkable tolerance of drought in the open garden may succumb in containers when not watered regularly, since their restricted root run places them at a disadvantage. The following, however, will often survive short periods of neglect.

Aethionema 158
Agapanthus 173

Anacyclus 130
Anthemis 130
Arctotis 145
Argyranthemum 130–31
Artemisia 192
Aucuba 183
Aurinia 138
Bergenia 179
Bidens 140
Brachyglottis 192
Bougainvillea 152
Calendula 146
Convolvulus sabatius 174
Cyclamen 165
Dianthus 160
Dimorphotheca 132
Elaeagnus 192–93
Euphorbia 138
Felicia 174–75
Ficus 198
Hedera 180–81
Helianthemum 141
Helichrysum 193
Heliotropium 169
Iberis 133
Lavandula 169
Lobularia 135
Melianthus 194
Lotus 147
Nepeta 176
Nerium 163
Osteospermum 135
Pinus 182
Pelargonium 153–54
Rosmarinus 197
Ruta 197
Salvia 170
Santolina 195
Scaevola 176
Sedum 191
Sempervivum 191
Senecio 195
Stachys 195
Thymus 197
Yucca 136

ORNAMENTALS EASILY RAISED FROM SEED

In addition to these plants, several vegetables, including beans and peas, are easy to grow from seed.

Calendula 146
Clarkia 159
Cosmos 132
Helianthus 141
Iberis 133
Lavatera 162
Lathyrus 162
Lobularia 135
Reseda 136
Tropaeolum 149

ACKNOWLEDGMENTS

AUTHOR'S ACKNOWLEDGMENTS

My warmest thanks to everyone who has contributed to the making of this book, especially to the editorial, design and picture research teams at Frances Lincoln: Jo Christian, Louise Tucker, Anne Fraser and their colleagues; and also to Tony Lord, John Elsley, Carole McGlyn, Joanna Chisholm, Alison Freegard, Penelope Miller and Helen Baz.

PHOTOGRAPHIC ACKNOWLEDGMENTS

d = designer, *t* = top, c = center
b = below, *l* = left, *r* = right,

Deni Bown 128*t*, 131*l*, 146*b*, 147*tl*, 149*r*, 161*t*, 166*t*, 167*l*, 169*bl*, 171*b*, 176, 181, 182*r*, 187*r*, 189*br*, 195*t*, 196*l*

Karen Bussolini 19*b*, 43*tr*, 45*bl*, 81*b*, 149*l*

Neil Campbell-Sharp 1 and 9*r* (Barters Farm, Chapmanslade, Westbury, Wilts.), 17*l* (Kilmokea, Ireland), 23*b* (John Sales), 118, 174*r* (Old Rectory, Berkshire), 179*t* (Butterstream, Ireland)

John Fielding 8*r*, 9*l*, 25*r*, 45*tl*, 75*tc*, 124, 125, 127, 130*b*, 135*l*, 138*l*, 139, 141*t*, 143*tl*, 144*tr*, 144*b*, 147*tr*, 148, 150*t*, 151, 155*l*, 156, 157*b*, 159*t*, 162*t*, 163*bl*, 163*br*, 165*br*, 166*bl*, 166*br*, 168, 169*br*, 170, 175*t*, 177*l*, 184*r*, 186*l*, 189*t*, 192*l*, 193*t*, 195*b*, 197, 199, 200, 201, 203*br*

Garden Picture Library/Brigitte Thomas 39*t*, Jon Bouchier 43*tl*, Lynne Brotchie 46, John Glover 91, Marijke Heuff 113

Jerry Harpur 2 (Ann Alexander-Sinclair), 10*l* (Manor House, Noordhoek, S.A.), 14*l* (Sean Egerton), 20*l* and 22 (*d*: Tessa Hobbs), 24 (Stellenberg, S.A.), 41*tr* (Bourton House, Gloucestershire), 50*b* (*d*: Penelope Hobhouse), 58, 75*tr* (*d*: Tessa Hobbs), 76, 94 (*d*: Dan Pearson), 112 (G. Keim and P. Wooster, USA), 119 (Helen Coucher), 165*bl* (G. Keim and P. Wooster, USA), 190*t* (Sheila Chapman), 198

Marijke Heuff 4 (Mr and Mrs Lauxrermann, Holland), 14*r* (Florentine van Eeghen, Holland), 23*t* (*d*: Els Proost, Holland), 39*br* (Nursery: Overhagen, Holland), 40*b* (Sissinghurst, Kent), 61 (Mr G. van den Brink, Holland), 105 (Tintinhull, Somerset)

Roger Hillier © FLL, 38, 41*b*, 42, 47, 51*bl*, 52, 53, 54, 55*b*, 56, 57, 59, 60, 63–65, 66*t*, 67–69, 71, 73, 74*l* and *c*, 75*tl*, 81*t*, 82*tl*, 83*tl* and *bl*, 90, 92, 165*l*

Holt Studios International 79 all by Nigel Cattlin except second row, far left by Duncan Smith

Anne Hyde 15, 45*br*

Michèle Lamontagne 48, 75*bl*, 97, 135*r*, 172, 173*t*, 178*l*, 188*b*

Andrew Lawson 10*r* (Whichford Pottery, Warwickshire), 11 (Chilcombe House, Dorset), 12 (Bourton House, Gloucestershire), 16*r* © FLL, 20*r* (*d*: Rupert Golby), 21 (*d*: Sue Dickinson), 27 (Pots and Pithoi, West Sussex), 40*t* (Connie Franks, Oxfordshire), 41*tl* (*d*: Rupert Golby), 43*b*, 49*br* and 66*b* (*d*: Rupert Golby), 70 (*d*: David Hicks), 74*r* (Gothic House, Oxfordshire), 87 (The National Trust, Powis Castle, Wales), 88 (*d*: Rupert Golby), 102, 108 (Gothic House, Oxfordshire), 109 (*d*: Pamela Schwerdt and Sibylle Kreutzberger), 111 (*d*: Sue Dickinson), 114 (The National Trust, Powis Castle, Wales), 122 and 123 (Gothic House, Oxfordshire), 128*bl*, 128*br*, 129, 130*t*, 131*r*, 132, 133, 134 (Gothic House, Oxfordshire), 136*l*, 137*t*, 137*b*, 138*r*, 140, 141*b*, 142, 143*b*, 144*tl*, 146*t*, 147*b*, 150*b*, 153, 154 (*d*: Rupert Golby), 155*r*, 159*b*, 160, 164*b*, 169*t*, 171*t* (*d*: Lucy Gent), 178*r*, 179*b*, 180*tl* (*d*: Thomasina Tarling), 180*b*, 184*l*, 185, 186*r*, 187*l*, 188*l*, 189*bl*, 191, 192*r*, 193*b*, 194 (*d*: Rupert Golby), 196*r*, 202, 203*t* and *bl*

Tony Lord 93, 116

S. & O. Mathews 161*b*

Clive Nichols 7 (*d*: Anthony Noel), 8*l* (The Old School House, Essex), 16*l* (*d*: Dan Pearson), 18*c* FLL (*d*: Sue Gernaey), 19*t* (*d*: Anthony Noel), 25*l* (Bourton House, Gloucestershire), 39*bl* (*d*: Jill Billington), 45*tr*, 62, 72 (Chenies Manor, Buckinghamshire), 96 (*d*: David Joyce), 101 (Bourton House, Gloucestershire), 103 (*d*: Dan Pearson), 104, 106–7 and 110 (*d*: David Joyce), 115 (Bourton House, Gloucestershire), 145 (Kukenhof Gardens, Holland), 175*b* (Mr and Mrs Coote, Oxford), 183 (*d*: Flowers Galore, London), 190*b*

Photos Horticultural Picture Library 143*tr*, 157*t*, 163*t*, 173*b*, 180*tr*, 182*l*

Tim Ridley © FLL 28 to 37, 44, 49*t*, *c*, *bl*, 50*t*, 51*t* and *br*, 77, 80, 81*c*, 82*tr* and *b*, 83*tr*, *c* and *br*, 84, 85, 100

Stephen Robson 98–9

David Schilling 55*t*

The Harry Smith Horticultural Photographic Collection 75*br*

Graham Strong 89, 120, 121

Darryl Sweetland 136*r*, 152

Juliette Wade 17*r*, 158, 164*t*, 177*r*

Steve Wooster 13 and 95 (*d*: Anthony Noel)

PUBLISHERS' ACKNOWLEDGMENTS

Frances Lincoln Limited wish to thank the following companies and individuals for their contribution to this book.

For the loan of tools and equipment for photography
Camden Garden Centre, 2 Barker Drive, St Pancras Way, London NW1 0JW
City Irrigation Limited, Bencewell Granary, Oakley Road, Bromley Common, Kent BR2 8HG
Traditional Garden Supply Company Limited, Unit 12, Hewitts Industrial Estate, Elmbridge Road, Cranleigh, Surrey GU6 8LW

For providing locations for photography and kindly allowing us to photograph their containers
Clifton Garden Centre, 5a Clifton Villas, Little Venice, London W9 2PH
Pots and Pithoi, The Barns, East Street (B2110), Turners Hill, West Sussex RH10 4QQ

Our special thanks to Robin and Rosie Lloyd of Pots and Pithoi for their advice and for planting pots for photography; to Tessa Hobbs for help and advice; to Sean Egerton and Helen Coucher, who planted containers especially for the book; and to Pam Mitchell of Flowers Galore, 21 Glazebrook Road, London N16 0HU, who planted and tended containers and provided help with photography. Many thanks also to Coleen O'Shea, for her editorial advice and support.

Planting plans by Sandra Pond and Will Giles

Project Editor Jo Christian
Art Editor Louise Tucker
Picture Editor Anne Fraser
Editor Carole McGlyn
Editorial Assistants James Bennett
                      Zoe Bowers
                      Bridget Rendell
Assistant Designer Margherita Gianni
Page checker Patti Taylor
Production Kim van Woerkom

Horticultural Consultants Tony Lord
                           John Elsley

Editorial Director Erica Hunningher
Art Director Caroline Hillier
Production Director Nicky Bowden

USEFULNESS ZONES

The Usefulness Zones given for each plant in the section on Plants for Containers represent the range of zones, according to the USDA system, in which the plant may be successfully grown in North America. The lower figure gives the coldest zone in which the plant will be hardy without winter protection, the higher shows the limit of its tolerance of hot summer weather. The map on the endpapers shows the range of zones in North America. The chart indicates the average annual minimum temperature of each zone.

It must be remembered that zoning data can only be a rough guide. Plant hardiness depends on a great many factors, and within any one zone particular regions may be endowed with more or less favorable conditions, just as on a smaller scale in any one garden plants can be positioned in individual situations that will suit their needs to a greater or lesser extent.